$15^{\underline{00}}$

10/2C

YOU'RE NO GOOD TO ME DEAD

R E S T R I C T E D

GENERAL HEADQUARTERS
                                     SOUTHWEST PACIFIC AREA
AG 210.453(20 Nov.43)

                                                    APO 500
                                                    20 November 1943

SUBJECT: Orders.

To   : O and EM concerned.

          Following-named O and EM WP on or about 21 Nov. 43 fr APO 500
to points outside continental limits of Australia for purpose carrying
out instructions of C-in-C upon completion will return to proper sta:

                    Techn 3rd gr Robert E Stahl 33236898

          Travel by mil if available, otherwise commercial aircraft (par
3b, AR 55-120, 26 Apr 43), AA priority, USAT, belligerent vessel or aircraft, Govt motor T and rail atzd. EWM.

          In lieu of subs flat per diem $6.00 atzd O and monetary alws in
lieu of rat and/or qrs atzd EM in accordance with SecII, Ex O 9386, WD
Bull 29, 21 Oct 43, while traveling within the cintinental limits of
Australia only. TCNT. TDN. 1-5600 P 432-02 A 212/40425.

          By command of General MacARTHUR:

                                        /s/ B. M. Fitch
                                        B. M. Fitch
                                        Colonel, A.G.D.,
                                        Adjutant General.

DISTRIBUTION:
    PRS (1)
CO Hq Co USAFFE (1)
CG USAFFE(1)
FO USASOS SWPA (1)

FO Base Sec 3 (6)
O and EM concerned (5each)
AG Records

                    R E S T R I C T E D

YOU'RE NO GOOD TO ME DEAD

Behind Japanese Lines in the Philippines

BOB STAHL

Naval Institute Press
Annapolis, Maryland

Library of Congress Cataloging-in-Publication Data
Stahl, Bob, 1920–
   You're no good to me dead : behind Japanese lines in the
Philippines / Bob Stahl.
      p.   cm. — (Naval Institute special warfare series)
   Includes bibliographical references and index.
   ISBN 1–55750–793–7 (alk. paper)
   1. Stahl, Bob, 1920– . 2. Allied Forces. South West Pacific
Area. Allied Intelligence Bureau—History. 3. World War,
1939–1945—Military intelligence—United States. 4. World War,
1939–1945—Military intelligence—Philippines. 5. World War,
1939–1945—Personal narratives, American. 6. Intelligence officers—
United States—Biography. I. Title. II. Series.
D810.S8S737   1995
940.54'8673'092—dc20
   [B]   95–11424

Printed in the United States of America on acid-free paper ∞
02 01 00 99 98 97 96 95   9 8 7 6 5 4 3 2
First printing

Frontispiece: Orders assigning the author to "points outside continental limits of Australia."

TO HOLLY

Contents

Preface

One of the best-kept secrets of World War II is the story of the activities of the Allied Intelligence Bureau (AIB). In the Southwest Pacific Area, the AIB, an operating agency of theater G-2, was the counterpart of the Office of Strategic Services (OSS) in the other theaters. It carried out clandestine activities behind enemy lines from the Solomons to Singapore, from Port Moresby to Manila, reporting Japanese shipping movements, aerial activities, weather information, and military intelligence. An inter-Allied agency, the AIB was composed of Australian, British, Dutch, and American intelligence units, each operating in the geographical areas that had been under their country's jurisdiction before the Japanese invasion. By penetrating Japanese-held islands far in advance of the many military campaigns, AIB agents gathering intelligence information paved the way for the Allied victory over Japan.

The Philippine Regional Section (PRS) was the AIB's operating arm in the American sector. Under the PRS, the First Reconnaissance Battalion (Special), an amalgamation of the 5217th Reconnaissance Battalion (Provisional) and the 978th Signal Service Company, furnished these intelligence-gathering services throughout the Philippine archipelago.

A two-volume unit history of the battalion and the signal service company was written in 1945, when the need for the units' activities ceased to exist and they were disbanded. However, the document was immediately classified "Secret," not to be downgraded to "Unclassified" until July 1953. By that time it was of little interest, for America became engaged in the Korean conflict. The report languished unnoticed in a few military libraries and in the National Archives in Washington, D.C.

In 1985, Alfredo H. Despy, who had been a member of the First Reconnaissance Battalion, sent a copy of the history to the U.S. Army Intelligence and Security Command (INSCOM). From the INSCOM history office, on 22 May 1985, Despy received a letter thanking him for sending "certain information on the history of U.S. Army intelligence operations in World War II *which was not previously available to us*" (emphasis added). The letter went on to note that "the 1st Reconnaissance Battalion and 978th Signal Service Company were the first and only Army units to undertake such a specialized mission during the course of the Second World War. While similar functions were carried on in other theaters, they were executed by the Office of Strategic Services, not the U.S. Army." To this day, the story of these activities remains one of World War II's best-kept secrets.

You're No Good to Me Dead takes its name from the admonition given this brash, young enlisted man and my comrades by Gen. Douglas A. MacArthur immediately prior to our departure from his headquarters in Brisbane, Australia. Our primary mission was to gather intelligence information and send it to Australia. Since we were to avoid physical contact and armed combat with the Japanese, this is not a blood-and-thunder tale of combat with the enemy. It is, rather, an account of the experiences of a young man who suddenly finds himself in the role of a spy in a totally alien environment, living a life of anxiety, boredom, frustration, loneliness, some pleasure, occasional excitement—and constant danger.

Originally, this story was a sketchy collection of anecdotes of my personal experiences, written soon after I returned from the war. I envisioned its future as a dust-collecting notebook of some sixty typewritten pages that might be of interest to one of my descendants should he or she delve into family history in future years. Forty years later I came across the notebook, blew off the dust, and decided to enlarge on its information.

One's memory of experiences past is oftentimes adversely affected by infrequent recall—from time to time the mental picture changes to reflect what might have been rather than what actually was. For me this was not a problem, since I had three controls: my previously written notes; a copy of the First Reconnaissance Battalion unit history; and, most important, a complete log of all the messages, except for ship and aircraft sightings, that passed through station S3L, my main radio station, neatly lettered in pencil in two elementary school composition notebooks and on some loose pages torn from a third notebook. These were paraphrased versions of the actual messages, for making exact copies would have been a violation of cryptographic security requirements. (Having at hand a coded message and an exact copy of its plain text is a cryptanalyst's delight!) These three collections quickly stabilized my thinking if I began to drift from the facts.

Unfortunately, I did not record descriptions of the towns, the terrain, and the people. For these I had to rely on my fifty-year-old memory. If discrepancies are discovered by others who were in the same areas at the time, I apologize for my faulty recall. The errors make no difference in the accuracy of the story as a whole.

For information about the events of World War II that influenced or were influenced by my activities, I referred to news media publications of the period. When I doubted the authenticity of these sources, I turned to a historian friend who has made an in-depth study of the activities of the war in the Pacific, and particularly of the activities of the Philippine guerrillas. This led to his reading my notes and to his urging me to write my story for publication. I am most deeply indebted to Douglas E. Clanin, an editor at the Indiana Historical Society, for without his prodding this book would not exist.

My thanks go to David L. Edelman, a former technical editor, a writer, and a classmate at Lehigh University in the immediate postwar era, who not only pressed me to write but also critiqued the product; and to the members of the American Guerrillas of Mindanao, with whom I have met at biennial reunions for many years, sessions that afforded me the opportunity to refresh my memory by reminiscing about the wartime days. These men graciously admitted me to membership in their organization even though I was on "their island" for less than a month.

And most of all, I thank my wife, who put up with days and days of my moodiness when the words wouldn't come out right. Thank you, Ruth.

Introduction

You're No Good to Me Dead is the hitherto untold story of the wartime experiences of Lt. Robert E. Stahl. His role as an intelligence agent in the Philippines with the U.S. Army 978th Signal Service Company, First Reconnaissance Battalion (Special), Philippine Regional Section, G-2/Allied Intelligence Bureau, is both extraordinary and unique. Stahl spent the fifteen months between November 1943 and February 1945 in a strange and alien environment, behind enemy lines, enduring incredible hardships and dangers far removed from those of conventional military service. Yet he and his comrades, most of whom were Filipinos specially recruited for such duties, made contributions to the war effort and witnessed historical events that had an enormous impact on the military operations leading to the liberation of the Philippines and the ultimate Allied victory in the Pacific.

Stahl's memoirs provide a bird's-eye view of service in a specially created U.S. Army unit that was attached to the combined Allied Intelligence Bureau (AIB). The AIB was a hybrid organization that has largely been forgotten or overlooked by historians writing about the Pacific War. The only major published work on the agency, entitled *Allied Intelligence Bureau: Our Secret Weapon in the War Against Japan,* was written by its American deputy controller, Lt. Col. Allison W. Ind, in 1958. No further works on the bureau have yet emerged in the fifty years since World War II. But the

AIB's significance was far greater than one would surmise from the limited existing literature. Simply put, the AIB did much to lay the groundwork for Allied victories throughout the Southwest Pacific, especially in New Guinea and the Philippines. In many situations and locales prior to 1944, it was the only unit capable of providing accurate intelligence on enemy air, sea, and land movements and of carrying out the other special and unconventional warfare activities needed by Allied forces.[1]

The AIB was created in 1942 during the darkest days of the war, well before Stahl's arrival in the Philippines. In the six months following the attack on Pearl Harbor, the Japanese conquered most of Southeast Asia and the South and Central Pacific Ocean areas. In the Philippines, in the forefront of the Japanese advance, American and Filipino forces under Gen. Douglas MacArthur retreated to the Bataan Peninsula and Corregidor Island by early January 1942. Despite being outnumbered and short of supplies, they managed to hold out until early May before surrendering. Elsewhere, small bands of Americans and Filipinos scattered into the hills and jungles of the vast archipelago to continue their armed resistance to the Japanese.[2]

While American and Filipino armies were besieged in the Philippines, British Commonwealth forces were suffering monumental defeats at Hong Kong and Singapore and were being driven from Malaya and Sarawak. By May 1942 the British Empire in Asia was lost, and beleaguered Allied units manned hastily thrown together defenses in Assam and northern Burma in expectation of a Japanese assault on British India itself. In the East Indies, Dutch military units gallantly, but futilely, attempted to defend the vast Indonesian archipelago against overwhelming enemy forces that landed at several locations from Borneo, to Sumatra, to the Celebes and Java, in March 1942. Sweeping aside all resistance, the Japanese established complete control over the Dutch colony by late May. Farther to the southeast, Australians clung to Port Moresby, well aware that this small portion of Papua was the last Allied toehold north of the Australian continent.[3]

The ferocious Japanese onslaught had not only caught the Allies ill prepared and off guard but had completely destroyed intelligence-gathering networks and lines of communication, while stranding thousands of Allied soldiers and civilians behind enemy lines. As shattered armies poured into Australia, General MacArthur arrived from the Philippines to find the hastily organized ABDACOM (Australian-British-Dutch-American Command) in confusion and disarray. Perhaps no problem was more salient than the complete dearth of news and information from the territories recently lost to Japan. The Allies were operating in a virtual intelligence vacuum, MacArthur discovered, and were relying on articles and maps from *National Geographic* and photographs gleaned from tourists and missionaries evacuated from recently overrun areas. Sporadic and haphazard radio contacts with American and Filipino holdouts in the Philippines continued to reach Australia, though with diminishing frequency, following the surrender of Corregidor, but these transmissions ended altogether in August 1942, effectively denying MacArthur's command of all knowledge of enemy strengths and activities to the north. Just as the Americans were blinded to events in and around the Philippines, the British, Dutch, and Australians similarly lost contact with their prewar colonies.[4]

In mid-April 1942, MacArthur began to build an intelligence organization. Fortunately, there was then gathering in Australia a vast collection of Allied personnel, many of whom possessed the talents, specialized language skills, and cultural and geographic knowledge so desperately needed. A myriad of Dutch, British, and Australian intelligence groups were already in operation when the Southwest Pacific Area (SWPA) was formed under MacArthur's command on 18 April 1942, yet each was organizing its own schools and training bases, gathering its own intelligence, establishing supply depots and mapping infiltration routes, and devising operational plans largely focused on their prewar colonial holdings. Such varying and dispersed groups, all operating independently yet duplicating each other's efforts, seemed to MacArthur and his assistant chief of staff for intelligence (G-2), Col. Charles A. Willoughby, to be a recipe for disaster.

MacArthur also refused to have American forces, or any Allied force, committed to operations in marginal areas that would divert strength away from the war-winning strategy he was devising. His planned counterattack would move north through New Guinea to the Philippines, while a separate northward advance from the South Pacific through the Solomon Islands by U.S. naval and marine forces under Adm. William Halsey, and a westward advance through the Central Pacific by Adm. Chester W. Nimitz, occurred simultaneously. Allowing the various intelligence agencies to continue operating in the current manner virtually assured diversions from this master plan. The Allies thus needed unity of command in SWPA and an umbrella agency to coordinate their activities, preferably a bureau under the tight control of MacArthur's General Headquarters (GHQ).

The solution was the combined AIB, officially established on 6 July 1942 in a directive issued by Col. Van S. Merle-Smith, the executive officer of the Intelligence Section (G-2), GHQ/SWPA.[5] The new AIB absorbed all intelligence agencies then in Australia and was itself incorporated into the theater command structure under the control of GHQ/G-2. As originally configured, the AIB performed many tasks in addition to intelligence gathering, and the bureau ultimately organized guerrilla groups, trained and infiltrated sabotage and special operations teams, evacuated Allied airmen trapped behind the lines, and conducted propaganda campaigns. Because of the diversity of these missions, the AIB was divided into four alphabetical sections: Section A (Special Operations–Australia), Section B (Secret Intelligence Service), Section C (Combined Field Intelligence Service), and Section D (Military Propaganda).[6]

Section C of the AIB was further subdivided into geographic areas, in recognition of the individual national interests in SWPA. Thus the Netherlands East Indies became an area of Dutch attention, the Philippines were reserved for American and Filipino activities, and Papua, New Guinea, the Solomons, Bismarcks, and Admiralties, collectively known as the Northeast Area, were reserved for Australian operations. Each geographic subsection coordinated planning, transport, and supply needs with the larger AIB sections. Other outside agencies under nominal GHQ control, such as the Netherlands Forces Intelligence Services, the Netherlands East Indies Government Information Service, the Allied Translator and Interpreter Section, the Allied Geographic Section, and the Central Bureau, a combined cryptographic office, supported AIB operations.[7]

The AIB was often called "MacArthur's OSS." Although it did perform missions in SWPA that were similar to those carried out worldwide by the OSS (Office of Strategic Services), the AIB was a diffuse, combined Allied agency, employing military and civilian personnel from at least four nations, most not subject to American authority. The OSS, a much larger agency, employed over 9,800 people, primarily American military and civilian personnel. A forerunner of the Central Intelligence Agency, the OSS operated with a budget, physical infrastructure, logistics base, and a degree of analytical and intellectual sophistication that dwarfed the capabilities of the much smaller and localized AIB. Through the efforts of its director, Maj. Gen. William J. Donovan, the OSS initially enjoyed a high degree of autonomy in the military theaters abroad and was responsible only to the U.S. Joint Chiefs of Staff (JCS). As an organization it was therefore theoretically above and beyond the command and control of even those at the highest levels of the War and Navy Departments, including theater commanders like MacArthur, Nimitz, and Halsey.[8]

Yet, MacArthur's staff was quick to claim that the AIB was indeed the OSS in SWPA. The reason for this is that MacArthur did not want the highly independent OSS, or General Donovan, threatening, or interfering with, his control of intelligence gathering, special operations, and psychological warfare in the Southwest Pacific. MacArthur therefore used the existence of the AIB, a bureau whose own multinational and fragmented command structure was not entirely to his liking, to convince the JCS and the War Department to keep the OSS out of SWPA. Willoughby would later claim that MacArthur could not wait for the OSS to send personnel to Australia, where intelligence was needed immediately in April 1942, yet the Office of the Coordinator of Information (COI), the OSS predecessor agency created by President Roosevelt in July 1941, had already placed agents in Europe, Africa, and Asia by the time of Pearl Harbor. COI had even provided anti-Japanese propaganda to MacArthur, through its Foreign Information Service, while he was still on Corregidor in early 1942. But despite attempts by Donovan to create a SWPA niche for the OSS in 1942, 1943, and 1944, all of his efforts were rebuffed.[9]

By October 1942, the AIB, MacArthur's smaller, yet more satisfactory OSS substitute, was already fully operational throughout SWPA, including the Philippine subsection of Section C, AIB/G-2, commanded by AIB Deputy Controller Allison Ind. The subsection's mission was to establish an intelligence network in the Philippines, create a chain of communications, set up escape routes for downed pilots and prisoners of war, and develop an organization for covert and propaganda warfare. The subsection established radio contact with guerrilla bands in Cebu, Mindanao, Luzon, Panay, and Negros in November 1942 via the Philippine Message Center at MacArthur's Brisbane GHQ, and it dispatched the first penetration team to Negros under Maj. Jesus A. Villamor, a Filipino, on 27 December 1942. The Villamor team was followed by five other AIB teams dispatched to Panay, Negros, Mindanao, and the Sulu Archipelago by the end of July 1943.[10]

As the American buildup in SWPA gathered speed and strength, and as operations in New Guinea and the Solomons continued, inter-Allied differences began to surface within the AIB. Conducting combined operations in areas previously controlled by several powers, each with contradictory interests and postwar aims, was proving tremendously difficult. The United

States did not want to promote Allied imperial designs or be associated with them but was nonetheless compelled to cooperate with those nations whose aid was necessary to defeat the Japanese. Thus, while the AIB contained Americans and supported MacArthur's operations, the United States, and GHQ, did not recognize any political interests in the Dutch East Indies or in Melanesia and preferred to have direct control over all activities that stood to even remotely affect American military operations.[11]

Increasingly, GHQ treated Philippine activities as an exclusive U.S. Army concern while concomitantly withdrawing support from the AIB, perceiving its operations to be irretrievably connected with the imperial interests of the Allies and involving units and personnel not directly under U.S. Army control. In addition, by March 1943, GHQ was able to begin a regular system of supply for guerrilla groups using cargo submarines capable of carrying about one hundred tons of supplies per trip to the Philippines without AIB assistance. Colonel Willoughby and the AIB controller, Australian Col. C. G. Roberts, thus decided that the AIB required some fine-tuning.[12]

In May 1943 GHQ announced that it was renaming the Philippine subsection of the AIB the Philippine Regional Section (PRS) and placing it under the control of Col. Courtney Whitney of MacArthur's G-2 staff. The AIB alphabetical sections were replaced with sections allotted to specific nations and regions, similar to the older geographic subsections that had existed under Section C, AIB. The new PRS would maintain contact with guerrilla units and intelligence teams already in the Philippines, which would still report to the AIB, but GHQ was now free to create additional teams under U.S. Army and American leadership. It had been decided that the task of creating bases in Mindoro, Samar, and Luzon and closing the gaps in the networks in southern Luzon was best left to specially trained U.S. Army personnel operating under GHQ supervision rather than through the AIB. Comprised entirely of U.S. Army soldiers controlled by Whitney, the new PRS teams would be drawn from the 978th Signal Service Company, a unit scheduled for activation in July 1943. Team members would be highly trained specialists capable of building, operating, and maintaining radio stations, identifying enemy aircraft and warships, forecasting weather conditions, using sophisticated technical equipment, and devising cryptographic systems. Most important, the PRS teams would not be directly connected to the AIB.[13]

Whitney took command of the PRS on 24 May 1943. The section

immediately assumed nearly autonomous status within the theater, as Whitney reported directly to the chief of staff, GHQ, through MacArthur's assistant chief of staff for intelligence. From June 1943 until June 1944, the PRS, although officially a part of the AIB and nominally under its control, was actually a semi-independent staff section of GHQ that took over many AIB training and communications facilities for its use while handling most administrative and supply matters through the GHQ staff. Under Whitney's command, the PRS would insert sixteen U.S. Army teams into the Philippines by the time of the invasion of Leyte on 20 October 1944.[14]

The immediate impact of the creation of the PRS was that most of the AIB teams in the Philippines were increasingly ignored by GHQ, or were not fully exploited. Within weeks Whitney further consolidated PRS control over intelligence activities in the Philippines by announcing that guerrillas would be responsible for providing intelligence from areas south of twelve degrees north latitude, an area of decreasing U.S. Army concern, while the newly inserted PRS teams would provide intelligence north of this line, in areas already targeted for U.S. Army invasions. These shifting command structures and responsibilities, the steps leading to the creation of the PRS, and the inter-Allied political rivalries and tensions were unknown to Stahl during the war, but they nonetheless had a significant impact on his service, especially after the U.S. Army landings at Leyte and Luzon in late 1944 and early 1945.[15]

It was soon after the founding of the PRS that Stahl arrived in Australia. He had been inducted into the U.S. Army Signal Corps in the summer of 1942 and sent to Fort Monmouth, New Jersey, for cryptographic training before undergoing further instruction with the OSS. In April 1943, just before GHQ announced its plans to create the PRS, he was shipped to Australia for assignment to AIB headquarters. For the next seven months Stahl monitored infrequent radio transmissions coming from the Philippines. Stirred to intense anger by reports of Japanese brutality, he volunteered for Maj. Charles M. Smith's penetration team, which was going to establish a base on Samar and the Bondoc Peninsula of southern Luzon.

Trained as a radio operator and cryptographer, Stahl had to prepare for additional duties in the Philippines, as well as a lifestyle that would turn out to be anything but typical. In late November 1943, accompanied by two Americans and nine Filipinos, he boarded the USS *Narwhal* for the fifteen-hundred-mile trip to the enemy-occupied Philippines. Landing first on Mindanao for a rendezvous with American guerrilla leader

Wendell W. Fertig, Smith's team soon reached Samar, where they established a radio station overlooking the San Bernardino Strait, made contact with local guerrilla groups, and began to provide vitally needed military intelligence to MacArthur's forces advancing through New Guinea. In late May 1944, Stahl took his own team and traveled to Bondoc Peninsula in Luzon, where he established a new intelligence network. According to SWPA reports, he transmitted his first message from Luzon on 31 May 1944. Between that time and January 1945, he broadcast a further 109 messages.[16]

Through it all, Stahl survived an incredible number of hazards. The Japanese stationed on Samar and Luzon were a constant and ever-present threat, both to Stahl and to those Filipinos who knew of his whereabouts. Frequent enemy sweeps of Stahl's zone of operations, in search of arms caches, guerrillas, and intelligence agents, prompted him to change locations often. Maintaining security and avoiding capture often became his top priorities, especially after he discovered that the first PRS team inserted into Mindoro, under Maj. Lawrence Phillips, was wiped out in February 1944, while another, part of Stahl's own network, was discovered and destroyed in Masbate in May 1944. The knowledge of his certain fate if captured could never have been far from his mind, as the Japanese were well known for their barbarous treatment of prisoners in general and of intelligence agents in particular. Many grim stories regarding the loss of Dutch AIB agents in the East Indies, who were often tortured for days before being beheaded, were circulating around the AIB before Stahl landed in the Philippines.[17]

Threats to Stahl's life were not just confined to the Japanese. As he recounts, many Filipinos knew of his location, and while the vast majority were loyal and clearly anti-Japanese, Stahl, like all guerrillas and intelligence agents, had a price on his head that could easily induce betrayal. Surprisingly, however, one of the greatest threats to his continued well-being came not from the Japanese but from the numerous Filipino guerrilla bands. Although ostensibly anti-Japanese, several of these units more closely resembled bandits than cohesive military forces. Always short of food and often burdened with malfunctioning or inadequate equipment, Stahl lived in crude and remote camps in the disease-infested jungles. Simple creature comforts such as clothing, decent shelter, and, most of all, food—items taken for granted by many American soldiers—were unobtainable luxuries for Stahl, located fifteen hundred miles behind enemy lines.

While Stahl carried out his duties and maintained friendly relations with the local guerrillas during 1944, the U.S. Army cleared New Guinea and prepared for the liberation of the Philippines. Unbeknownst to Stahl, however, the American victories prompted significant changes within GHQ, the AIB, and the PRS. No longer in need of constant Allied troop and material support or the services of the multinational AIB, GHQ/SWPA officially announced on 2 June 1944 that the PRS/G-2 was being abolished and that its duties were being split between the newly created Philippines Special Section of G-3 (Operations), and Philippines Special Section, G-4 (Supply), both under Whitney and the GHQ/SWPA staff. Now all intelligence and guerrilla activities in the Philippines came exclusively under GHQ/U.S. Army control, permanently ending the GHQ/G-2/AIB relationship.[18]

Thus by August 1944 the intelligence network that included Stahl and eighty-two other stations in the Philippines came completely under the jurisdiction of GHQ and the U.S. Army, even though Stahl was never told the technical details or personal ramifications of the command change. In the months before American forces invaded Leyte in October 1944, Stahl came into contact with many new U.S. Army intelligence-gathering and weather teams that were inserted by GHQ near his base in Luzon entirely without his knowledge or any headquarters notification.

Once the PRS was abolished, the AIB largely withdrew from the Philippines and had little connection with activities there after October 1944, even though it maintained a small liaison office at GHQ. After the Leyte and Luzon invasions, the agents and guerrillas inserted by the AIB and the PRS were absorbed into the Philippine Special Sections of GHQ as soon as they made contact with advancing U.S. Army units, their missions now considered complete. Thus, in December 1944, Smith's network was turned over to U.S. Sixth Army control, while Stahl continued to operate from Luzon until his evacuation from behind enemy lines in February 1945.[19]

Robert Stahl's riveting, informative, and frequently humorous reminiscences are invaluable. They are the first and only detailed memoirs from an American soldier's perspective that vividly describe the difficult daily existence of clandestine agents and the average Filipino living under the Japanese occupation, as well as the color and complexity of wartime peasant society and culture. His narrative makes plain that the relationships between Americans and Filipinos, between guerrilla units and their allies, and between MacArthur's headquarters and agents in the field were not always cooperative or efficient, and, in fact, were usually tenuous and ad hoc, contrary to the popular image of the immediate postwar years. What emerges from Stahl's powerful and meticulously reconstructed account is an accurate portrayal of the tremendous dangers such duty behind the lines entailed, as well as a confirmation of the value of the intelligence provided at great personal risk by this small minority of Americans and Filipinos. Unlike the heavily publicized exploits of guerrilla units in the Philippines, the activities of those U.S. Army soldiers, including Stahl, who volunteered to leave the safety of MacArthur's headquarters in Australia to gather intelligence in enemy territory, until now was known only to a few.[20]

—Dr. Clayton D. Laurie,
Center of Military History, U.S. Army

NOTES

1. Allison W. Ind, *Allied Intelligence Bureau: Our Secret Weapon in the War Against Japan* (New York: David McKay, 1958).

2. For the Philippines, see Louis Morton, *The Fall of the Philippines* (Washington, D.C.: U.S. Army Center of Military History, 1993); and D. Clayton James, *The Years of MacArthur, 1941–1945* (Boston: Houghton Mifflin, 1975), Part 1, Chapters 1–3.

3. For the first six months, see Ronald Spector, *Eagle Against the Sun: The American War with Japan* (New York: Random House, 1984).

4. *Operations of the Allied Intelligence Bureau, GHQ, SWPA,* Charles A. Willoughby, comp. (Tokyo: GHQ, Far East Command, 1948), 4:1; for ABDACOM, see Spector, *Eagle Against the Sun,* 127–34, 330; and Louis Morton, *Strategy and Command: The First Two Years* (Washington, D.C.: U.S. Army Center of Military History, 1962), 166–80.

5. *Operations of the AIB,* 4:7, and Appendix 2.

6. *Operations of the AIB,* 4:7, and Plate 3; also Ind, *AIB,* 10–12.

7. *Operations of the AIB,* 4:7–15, and Plate 3; Ind, *AIB,* 7–8.

8. OSS Manpower Report, 30 April 1944, Box: 101, Entry: 99, Record Group 266, National Archives and Records Administration (NARA), Washington, D.C.; for the OSS and attempts to get into SWPA, see Kermit Roosevelt, *War Report of the OSS,* 2 vols. (New York: Stewart, 1976); Anthony Cave-Brown, *The Secret War Report of the OSS* (New York: Berkeley Medallion Books, 1976); R. Harris Smith, *OSS: The Secret History of America's First Central Intelligence Agency* (Berkeley: University of California Press), 250–51; Bradley F. Smith, *The Shadow Warriors: The OSS and the Origins of the CIA* (New York: Basic Books, 1983), 195–96, 254, 310; Anthony Cave-Brown, *Wild Bill Donovan: The Last Hero* (New York: Times Books, 1982), 515, 517, 780; and Richard Dunlop, *Donovan: America's Master Spy* (New York: Rand McNally, 1982), 185, 402–13, 437.

9. Willoughby's argument is covered in Charles A. Willoughby and John Chamberlain, *MacArthur, 1941–1945* (New York: McGraw-Hill), 144; and Ind, *AIB,* 10. See "Basic Military Plan for Psychological Warfare in Southwest Pacific Theater," PG/26, 9 June 1943, later designated JPS (Joint Planning Staff) 212/D and JPS 214/D.

It was rejected by the JCS on 8 July 1943. See also File: Chronology, July–Dec. 1945, Box: 3, and File: Japan, Box: 6; Memo, Donovan to JCS, 12 June 1943; Memo, MacArthur to JCS, 18 Jan. 1943; Memo, MacArthur to JCS, 22 June 1943; Memo, MacArthur to JCS, 30 July 1943; all in File: Chronology, Apr.–June 1943, Box: 3; Interview, Lilly with Col. J. Woodhall Greene, 16 Oct. 1951, File: SWPA, Box: 13; Memo to Adm. King for C/S Sig, re: OSS in SWPA, 29 Sept. 1944, File: PWB/SWPA, Box: 9, all in Entry: Edward P. Lilly Papers, Record Group 218, NARA; see also Memo, E. A. W. re: History of Relations of OWI with GHQ, 5 May 1943, File: OWI Propaganda to NEI, Entry: 283K, Box: 10, Record Group 331. *Operations of the AIB,* 4:42, n. 11.

10. *Intelligence Activities in the Philippines During the Japanese Occupation,* Charles A. Willoughby, comp., vol. 2 (Tokyo: GHQ, Far East Command, 1948), Plate 4; also *Operations of the AIB,* vol. 4, Plate 12; Ind, *AIB,* 115–45; and Jesus A. Villamor, *They Never Surrendered: A True Story of Resistance in World War II* (Quezon City: Vera-Reyes, 1982). The six AIB teams were led by Maj. Jesus A. Villamor, Maj. Jordan A. Hamner, Lt. Col. Charles M. Smith and Comdr. Charles A. Parsons, Maj. Emidgio Cruz, Lt. T. Crespo, and Lt. Ireneo Ames.

11. For the American-Allied difficulties, see William R. Louis, *Imperialism at Bay: The United States and the Decolonization of the British Empire, 1941–1945* (New York: Oxford University Press, 1978); and Christopher Thorne, *Allies of a Kind: The United States, Britain, and the War Against Japan, 1941–1945* (New York: Oxford University Press, 1978); see also Letter, John Davies to Lt. Col. Paul Pennoyer, 24 Apr. 1944, re: American Psychological Warfare in CBI, File: CBI, Box: 2; also File: "A Brief on American Psychological Warfare," Box: 18, p. 14; and Annex "A," sub: Information on OSS and OWI, USAF/GHQ/CBI, 20 Sept. 1944, File: CBI; and File: Chapter 3, Section 3, Box: 16, all in Entry: Lilly Papers, Record Group 218, NARA.

12. *Operations of the AIB,* 4:35–42, and Plate 9.

13. *Operations of the AIB,* 4:39–42, n. 9, n. 11, also 4:68–71, 78–80; *Intelligence Activities,* 2:32–34; George Raynor Thompson and Dixie R. Harris, *The Signal Corps: The Outcome* (Washington, D.C.: United States Army Center of Military History, 1991), 273; and Ind, *AIB,* 174.

14. *Operations of the AIB,* 4:57–58, 68, 91–92, and Plate 19; also *Intelligence Activities,* 2:34, and Plate 4. PRS teams were led by Lt. Comdr. "Chick" Parsons, Maj. Lawrence H. Phillips, Lt. Col. Charles M. Smith (including Stahl), Capt. Robert V. Ball, WO Lucien V. Campeau, 1st Sgt. Amando S. Corpus and Sgt. Carlos S. Placido, M.Sgt. Richie D. Dacquel, Lt. Comdr. George G. Rowe, Capt. Bartolomeo C. Cabangbang, Capt. Enrique L. Torres, Lt. J. V. Valera, 1st Lt. E. T. Pompea, Maj. George Miller, and Maj. J. D. Vanderpool, and Lt. Col. Eutiquio B. Cabais.

15. *Operations of the AIB,* 4:68–71, 78–80; Thompson and Harris, *Signal Corps,* 273; and *Intelligence Activities,* 2:30–31, 34–35, and Appendixes 11, 13, 15, and 16. The arrangements to send Signal Corps personnel (including Stahl) to Australia were made by Ind prior to the creation of the PRS.

16. For Smith and Stahl's activities, see *Intelligence Activities,* 2:39–51, 86–87, 90–91, 98–99; Plates 5, 9, 10, 12, 15.

17. For Dutch agents in the NEI, see *Operations of the AIB,* vol. 4; for the Phillips party and its fate, see *Intelligence Activities,* 2:36–39, Plate 6.

18. Ibid., 4:84, 91–92.

19. Ibid., 4:92; Thompson and Harris, *Signal Corps,* 273.

20. Among accounts of guerrilla operations in the Philippines are Russell W. Volckmann, *We Remained: Three Years Behind Enemy Lines in the Philippines* (New York: W. W. Norton, 1954); Philip Harkins, *Blackburn's Headhunters* (New York: W. W. Norton, 1955); Edward P. Ramsey and Stephen J. Rivele, *Lieutenant Ramsey's War* (New York: Knightsbridge, 1990); Jesus A. Villamor, *They Never Surrendered: A True Story of Resistance in World War II* (Quezon City: Vera-Reyes, 1982); John Keats, *They Fought Alone* (Philadelphia: Lippincott, 1963); Ira Wolfert, *American Guerrilla in the Philippines* (New York: Simon and Schuster, 1945); Travis Ingham, *Rendezvous by Submarine* (Garden City, N.Y.: Doubleday, 1945); Elliott Thorpe, *East Wind, Rain* (Boston: Gambit, 1969); and *The Guerrilla Resistance Movement in the Philippines: 1941–1945,* Charles A. Willoughby, comp. (New York: Vantage Press, 1972).

YOU'RE NO GOOD TO ME DEAD

Prologue

Moving quietly at less than two knots, the American submarine slipped through the narrow passage of Surigao Strait on the northeast coast of Mindanao Island. Easing gently into Butuan Bay, where the forces of Imperial Japan occupied all the surrounding land, the old submarine was in a war for which it had not been designed. The knocking and clanking of her old hull and fittings heightened the tensions of the men aboard. The modern submarines of late 1943 were much smaller and swifter, like mako sharks in comparison to this plodding old walrus from the days of World War I.

But this was a special mission that could not be handled by the sleek undersea killers of the U.S. Navy that terrorized Japanese shipping throughout the Pacific Ocean and the seas of the Orient in World War II. Nearly twice the size of the modern boats, the old *Narwhal* was able to carry the hundred tons of cargo and the twelve U.S. Army passengers that comprised the reason for this invasion of enemy waters.

Arriving early in the afternoon of 2 December, the *Narwhal* had ample time to inspect the surface of the bay and examine the beaches. The submarine's captain wanted no surprises during the execution of his boat's mission. For hours he maneuvered around the bay at periscope depth, looking for some telltale sign that the Japanese were waiting to ambush him and wreck the mission. At last, the skipper slapped up the handles of the periscope and ordered it down.

"It's almost sundown," he said. "Bring her up, and we'll move closer to the shore. The place is dead ahead, and the recognition signs are rigged up proper."

Compressed air surged into the ballast tanks, and the old vessel began to rise. I wiped the curtain of sweat from my forehead and gripped the Thompson submachine gun. Now, I would meet the enemy in our occupied Philippine Islands.

For almost two years, my life had been leading to this moment—ever since that day of horror and death at the end of 1941.

It was a usual Sunday morning for most Americans until the Japanese bombs awoke us from our dream of neutrality. From those hours of terror and tragedy, a date was burned into the minds of all of us: Sunday, 7 December 1941; Pearl Harbor Day. This day saw a major portion of the U.S. Navy die under the blazing sun of the Japanese Imperial Navy. World War II had engulfed the United States of America.

The outrage of America's citizens flamed instantly, and so great was that burning that the events of subsequent days rumbled past us almost unheeded as we reeled in shock. Soon President Franklin Delano Roosevelt would call it a "dastardly attack" and in his call to Congress for a declaration of war label this "a date which will live in infamy!"

Across the international date line it was 8 December. Here, too, the Japanese Imperial Air Force attacked the Philippine Islands without warning. Beginning at dawn, wave after wave of bombers struck at U.S. and Philippine military installations, primarily on the island of Luzon. They met with little resistance, for the Americans and the Filipinos were unwarned, unprepared, and completely off guard. Squadrons of fighter aircraft followed the bombers, strafing the areas to disrupt any attempts to mass a defense.

At Clark Field, on Luzon, the major U.S. Army Air Corps base in the Philippines, the aircraft were aligned in neat rows along the taxiways— the commanding general insisted on orderliness, and they were set up like toys on a playroom floor. Later it was said that they were so aligned "to protect against sabotage." The Japanese planes destroyed them like a clumsy-footed father would wreck a child's toys. A few planes survived the bombing and strafing to become airborne, but those that weren't shot down in the ensuing fray had difficulty finding enough undamaged runway to land on when they returned. America's Southwest Pacific air arm was virtually destroyed in one day.

The few remaining aircraft and some of the Air Corps personnel were quickly moved to other, more southerly, airfields, primarily Del Monte Airfield, on Mindanao. The remaining airmen were issued rifles and, with no training, became infantrymen. What followed was an intensive land, sea, and air assault on the American and Filipino forces throughout the archipelago. Without air support, the ill-equipped and poorly trained defenders were overwhelmed. The results would have been the same even with air support, for they were completely out-manned in numbers and outclassed in armament and military skills. The defenders collapsed in disarray.

In March 1942, President Roosevelt ordered Gen. Douglas A. MacArthur to Australia, there to regroup the Allied military forces. To Gen. Jonathan M. "Skinny" Wainwright fell the task of assuming MacArthur's command and leading a valiant but hopeless fight against the invaders. Bataan was lost. Then Corregidor. Then the rest of the islands. Two months later, General Wainwright suffered the ultimate indignity of surrendering the Philippines to the Japanese. Along with most of his troops, he became a prisoner of war, not to be released until 1945.

Much of the blame for the rapid demise of the Allied defensive effort must be laid at the feet of those holding commissioned officer rank. When the order to surrender was issued, late in May 1942, many of the soldiers on Mindanao never received the order. Of those who did, some could not get information from their superiors on where or how to surrender. Some could not even *find* their superior officers! In short, there was a complete collapse of command and communications. As a result, most of the Filipino soldiers discarded their uniforms and faded into the civilian population, while many of the Americans moved off into the jungles in small groups to await MacArthur's counteroffensive, certain to occur in a short while—"six months at the most," they told each other.

It was a long wait.

The Japanese Imperial Army sealed its conquest by demonstrating its capacity for inhumanity. The Western world did not learn of the unbelievable atrocities inflicted on the captured American and Filipino troops for another year, when the first group of American POWs escaped from the Davao Penal Colony on Mindanao and the story unfolded. Written first-person accounts by former POWs are numerous, and all attest to one fact: not since the Middle Ages had a conqueror treated the conquered with such inhumane cruelty.

The Japanese treatment of the civilians was no different. They looked upon the Filipinos with disdain and loathing and sought to control the natives through fear, a serious psychological error. Although it could be argued that the United States exploited the Philippines for half a century, the relationship between the two peoples was always friendly, and the Filipinos were always allowed their dignity. Not so with the Japanese. It was not surprising that most natives remained loyal to the Americans.

Despite its obvious failure, the Japanese continued the policy of fear. Wives and daughters were raped and killed; sweethearts and sisters were kidnapped and forced to travel with the Japanese troops to supply entertainment and sexual gratification for the Sons of Heaven.

The Filipino men and boys seethed at the harsh treatment. Some openly resisted. Many were killed. They were "too Americanized" and "against the Greater East Asia Co-Prosperity Sphere," said the Japanese. They were taken to nearby fields and forced to dig pits into which they tumbled as they were slaughtered, there to be covered over with the soil of the land they loved.

The townspeople were forced to witness these executions. The Japanese spokesmen said the executions were held publicly to show the Filipinos that the Japanese were interested only in "helping" the Philippines become a "strong and independent nation." Just whom did they think they were deluding—the Filipinos or themselves?

Yet more men resisted, and the executions became more cruel. They were bayonetted, decapitated, burned alive, hanged—even boiled alive in large metal drums, the fires stoked by their neighbors, who, prodded to the task by Japanese bayonets, cooked their fellow countrymen until they screamed and screamed, mercifully soon to pass into unconsciousness—and to die.

Seeing that open resistance was useless, the Filipinos took a new approach—passive resistance. They worked for the Japanese, certainly, but slowly—ever so slowly. The Japanese forced them to work harder, prodding them with sticks, then with whips, and soon with their favorite instrument, the bayonet.

Men took their families and sneaked away at night. Others followed, knowing that if they stayed they would be punished when the first desertions were discovered. Into the hills they went, where they could conceal themselves in the dense, green jungles and stay alive—if they could survive the ever-present menaces of disease and hostile natives. As Christians, they were not welcome in the lands controlled by the

Moslem tribes, the Moros, who believed that killing a Christian afforded direct access to heaven. Nor did the Igorot or other semicivilized tribes take kindly to interlopers.

Finding a fairly level spot in a jungle, the refugees would clear a field and plant rice, corn, and *camotes,* degenerated sweet potatoes, for food. Soon brothers, sisters, and friends would move into the same area. When the Japanese came looking for them, the fugitives would move farther into the jungles. They learned that by teaming together they could move faster and more safely; at the new location, four or five men working together could clear a field and build shelters quickly. Community effort became the rule.

As more and more families "buckwheated" (a name for this relocation that derived from the way Filipinos pronounced the English word "evacuate"), the Japanese patrols reached deeper and deeper into the jungles, seeking them out until the pursued were cornered in the deepest and most formidable lands, where a move in any direction would be a move toward the enemy. But a cornered animal is a vicious animal. The people knew that certain, cruel death awaited them if they were captured, and took to the offensive with their *bolos,* machete-like, sharp-edged knives used for all types of work by the Filipinos. Bolos had been used to kill animals for food. Now they were used to kill humans.

They ambushed Japanese patrols along the trails, besting the well-armed enemy with their primitive tools and boundless courage. They set deadly traps fashioned with the unique ingenuity of one pursued— a barbed stick, sometimes tipped with poison, rigged by bending a small tree to the ground in such a way that when an unwary enemy stepped on a loose log on the trail the trap was sprung and the barbed stick propelled by the bent tree silently hit its mark, sending to his ancestors another Son of Nippon, one who nevermore would toss a baby into the air and catch the infant on the tip of his bayonet, who never again would rape, maim, and kill.

Tales of the ambushes and the silent death traps reached the Japanese garrisons. Now it was the enemy soldiers' turn to experience fear. Their patrols no longer penetrated the deeper jungles. This success inspired the natives. "We have driven the Hapons from the jungles," they cried, "and we will drive them from our towns!"

The urge for revenge surged through the blood of the mistreated men. They formed small fighting bands, selected leaders, practiced ambush tactics, *planned* their attacks on the patrols—the beginnings of the guerrilla armies. They sought out the Japanese patrols, killed the enemy, and carried away their weapons to the jungle camps, to be used against the former owners in the next ambush.

Their numbers grew with men from the towns who had suffered all the humiliation they could stand from their Japanese "benefactors." A town's doctor, summoned to care for a wounded guerrilla, would hurry to be of help. He knew full well the dangers, but he responded. Then, fearing Japanese retaliation, he and his family would "buckwheat" to escape execution.

And their numbers continued to grow. Men who were "cooperating" with the Japanese in the towns would serve as spies, telling the guerrillas where the next Japanese patrol was going and how many soldiers would be in it. They would stash food in secret places for retrieval by the guerrillas. Ammunition would be spirited away from the Japanese supplies and sent to the guerrillas, to be used against the enemy in the weapons already captured.

And still their numbers grew. Men from the larger cities, and from neighboring islands, who were on the Japanese lists of pro-Americans, ran to the guerrillas. Soon there were many unarmed men in the hills, men able and willing to share the work and the fighting, but for whom there was no work, and no arms with which to fight. They were deadwood with whom the rations of the fighting men had to be shared, and food supplies were pitifully short without that extra burden.

The critical arms shortage led to bringing tribes of semicivilized natives into the camps to teach the new members the use of another deadly and silent weapon—the bow and arrow. Soon there were squads of archers to help with the ambushes. The urgent need for weapons produced another idea—the *baltik*. Shotguns had been used for game hunting prior to the war. Now they were available, but there was no ammunition for them. To convert them to warring weapons, wooden plugs were fashioned to fit the chamber of the shotgun. A hole was drilled lengthwise through the plug to accommodate a rifle cartridge. When fired, the small slug would literally rattle as it flew down the oversized barrel and out at its target. Like the zip gun used by American inner-city youth in years yet unborn, this homemade modification could not be used at long range. Nor was the baltik accurate, for without a rifle's bore to send it point first on a direct course, the slug, *if* it hit its target, often hit broadside, with very effective results. Crude as it was, the baltik had killing power, and that was what mattered.

And so the guerrilla bands grew into a mighty fighting force, inspired by one aim: a peaceful existence in their beloved Philippine Islands.

My War Begins

PART 1

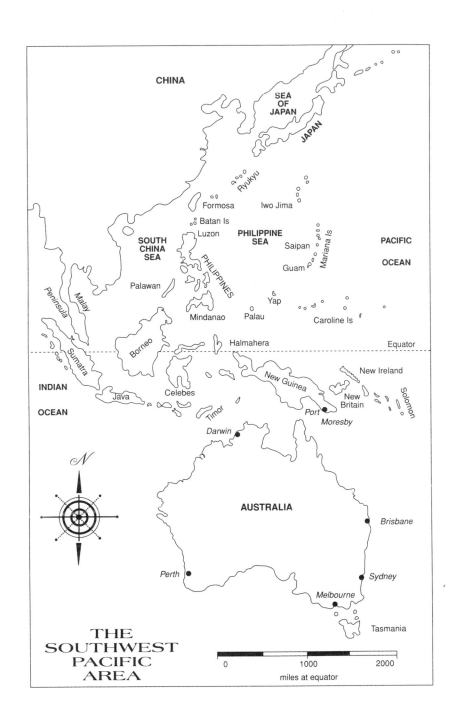

CHINA

SEA
OF
JAPAN

JAPAN

Ryukyu

Formosa

Iwo Jima

Batan Is

Luzon

PHILIPPINE
SEA

Saipan

Mariana Is

PACIFIC

OCEAN

SOUTH
CHINA
SEA

Guam

PHILIPPINES

Palawan

Yap

Mindanao

Palau

Caroline Is

Malay
Peninsula

Sumatra

Borneo

Halmahera

Equator

New Guinea

New Ireland

New
Britain

Solomon

INDIAN

OCEAN

Java

Celebes

Timor

Port
Moresby

Darwin

N

AUSTRALIA

Brisbane

Perth

Sydney

Melbourne

Tasmania

THE
SOUTHWEST
PACIFIC
AREA

0   1000   2000

miles at equator

To Brisbane

CHAPTER 1

Never in my weirdest nightmares in early 1942 did I find myself in the Army, let alone in Brisbane, Australia.

Sunday, 7 December 1941, was a sunny day, and the usual group of guys just past teen age collected in front of our favorite ice-cream parlor in Shamokin, Pennsylvania. Most of us were still dressed in suits and ties, for we were on our way home from church. This was our Sunday ritual. Here we would lay our plans for the rest of the day. Which fellows had dates? Who had cars or could borrow the family auto to go fifteen miles down the road to cruise the streets of Sunbury? Who had money for gas? Major decisions had to be made to assure a good social life. I was one who owned a car, if you could call a 1934 Plymouth sedan that burned more oil than gasoline a car. I also had no money, for I had a low-paying job as a clerk in an automobile tire store. My car payments ate up most of my salary. Using my car today would require a joint venture with someone with cash in his pocket.

As I pulled into one of the available parking spaces along the sidewalk, I was listening to a news broadcast on the radio: "The Japanese have bombed Pearl Harbor, and are expected to attack American positions in the Philippine Islands," intoned the announcer. My mind ran through my limited knowledge of geography, searching for places with those names. "Heavy damage has been inflicted on the Navy's Pacific Fleet."

All the war news we had been hearing concerned the events taking place in Europe, and I was reasonably up to date on the contest between the Allies and the Nazis. I had not been paying much attention to the diplomatic negotiations taking place between the United States and Japan, though. Suddenly, halfway around the world, another confrontation with a new enemy was beginning.

I was not alone in having sketchy knowledge of the Pacific area. To me and to most others living in the anthracite region of Pennsylvania, the Pacific was a vast unknown. Understandably so. The citizens of our town and countryside were of European descent. Anglo-Saxons—some of whom claimed ancestry to the Revolution, some even to the *Mayflower*—owned the factories, mines, and stores. My ancestors had come from Germany and worked in the construction trades or as farmers. Many others were recent arrivals from Ireland, Wales, Scotland, and middle Europe, mostly coal miners who had sought and found in the United States a better life for themselves and their children. In this adopted land they were rewarded for their hard labor, and they prospered. They were not wealthy, but they could live comfortably and with a sense of dignity. In fact, they were living in luxury compared with their relatives and friends who had remained in the old country. While they maintained strong ties to their ancestral lands in the British Isles, Poland, Yugoslavia, Latvia, Russia, Italy, or elsewhere, they took great pride in their American citizenship. They were not Polish Americans, Irish Americans, or Italian Americans, but simply *Americans*. Yet, with their strong ties to the homelands, their mental images of the world consisted of only America and Europe. Asia and the Pacific were almost nonexistent, except that people knew Japan existed because of the shoddy goods imported from there.

This mentality reached into the curricula of our public schools. In addition to the three Rs, we studied American and European history, but not much world history. The languages taught were English, Latin, French, and Spanish, but not German, for the bitterness against the Germans had continued since World War I. Russian and Slavic children learned those native tongues in schools operated by denominational churches and, of course, at home, for the native tongues prevailed in the homes of most of the families from non-English-speaking countries. On the matter of languages in my home, confusion reigned. My mother, and my grandmother who lived with us, were bilingual and spoke Pennsylvania Dutch, as were many of our neighbors. Dad was not. Out of deference to him, Mother spoke only English when he was around, and she never encouraged the rest of the family to speak "Dutch." Thus, we were not a bilingual family. Interestingly enough, although we Pennsylvania Dutchmen were of German descent, we were accepted because of our deep ancestral roots in America.

Geography and social studies covered the same American and European territories, with an occasional hint that several other continents existed. While we learned which countries were rich in certain raw materials and which grew certain food staples, we never learned that half the people of the world ate rice three meals a day. Those people lived in the never-never lands of Asia and the Pacific Islands.

Nor did knowledge of geography come about from travel. Although our ancestors had emigrated from Europe to America, that was a once-in-a-lifetime happening. Travel was the luxury of the rich. Anyone who made a pleasure trip to Europe or returned to the old country to visit relatives was looked upon in awe for having amassed the wealth to do so. Even traveling cross-country was a rarity and placed those who did so only a small status step below those who had gone abroad. My parents had taken our family—four boys, two girls, and Grandma—on some trips from time to time, never more than five hundred miles from our hometown, yet we were listed among those who traveled a lot. So, it seemed quite natural that I had difficulty determining where the Hawaiian and Philippine Islands were located.

Before I had turned off the engine, several fellows jumped into my car, eager to hear the news broadcast. They, too, were unsure of what countries—what continents—lie west of California. We decided to go to my home, pick up a high school geography text, and get our bearings straight.

As we listened, the impact of the news slowly took effect on all of us. Soon we were not the usual boisterous, effervescent group laying plans for the day's and night's activities. In fact, dates, cars, gasoline, spending money, and all the other normally important items suddenly were forgotten. It didn't take us long to realize we were in for a great change in our lives.

Most of the gang tried to enlist immediately after the hostilities began. We recognized that military service was, for us, inevitable. Being drafted was a minefield of uncertainty, and we realized that life in the military would be more bearable if we joined the service of our choice.

With my best friend, Kim Savidge, I tried to enlist in the U.S. Army Air Corps. He was accepted. I was rejected. My vision was too bad, they said. I took this rejection badly. I wanted to be one of the guys in uniform—one of the gang. Contributing to the war effort by working in a defense plant would not be much of a show of courage. But I seemed to have no choice.

I immediately enrolled in a night school course to learn a trade. My only job since graduating from high school three years previously, selling automobile tires, had not afforded me experience highly useful in the war-production industry. I was halfway through a course in machined-parts inspection when my number came up in the draft. I reasoned that reporting to the draft board would be a mere formality, for the Air Corps had already rejected me. I forgot that the Infantry didn't require 20/20 vision.

Dr. Sidney Kalloway Sr., a local physician (and Northumberland County Coroner) who served as the medical examiner for the draft board and who was the father of another of my friends, labeled me as fit for service. He had already certified his son's health so that he could become a U.S. Navy pilot.

"Your eyes are fine," he said. "The Army will keep you fitted with glasses."

I was inducted into the U.S. Army in the summer of 1942. Soon after, Lt. Sidney Kalloway Jr., USNR, was shot down and lost at sea.

That August I had the first train ride of my life, to the U.S. Army Reception Center at New Cumberland, Pennsylvania, courtesy of Uncle Sam. Half the town's population milled around the train platform in a scene being duplicated in many towns throughout the United States: Parents, relatives, friends, and girlfriends vied for the last-minute attention of the young men going off to war. Roman Catholic nuns passed out St. Christopher medals to all who would take them. Not to be out-done, the local Baptist minister handed out New Testaments, while members of the American Legion and the Veterans of Foreign Wars, most of whom were attired in the parts of their World War I uniforms that still more or less fit, provided each draftee with a sewing kit.

Finally the conductor sounded his "All aboard," the recruits boarded, and the train steamed off. There were teary eyes both inside and outside the train, for many were certain that they would never see each other again. And, unfortunately, some were right.

The train took a most circuitous route to cover the seventy miles to New Cumberland. The unofficial home guard was making sure that no saboteurs disrupted the civilian war effort, so the train's path was kept a top military secret. Get there we did, however, albeit many hours later.

At New Cumberland, with the rest of the recruits, I spent several days in lines for clothing, physical exams, shots, orientation movies, and lectures, and passed many boring hours waiting for some corporal or sergeant (probably picked and promoted out of the group of recruits that had passed through this routine the week before) to line us up again. It got to be a habit to join the end of any line I saw, hoping I had stumbled on a chow line.

Gradually, the recruits were shipped out in small groups to various basic training centers. I was disappointed when I wasn't part of a group going to Randolph Field and the Air Corps, happy when I didn't go along with the group to Fort Benning and the Infantry.

By the end of the first week I was the only one left in my barracks except for the noncom who was the barracks orderly. On Saturday afternoon I stripped off my clothes, dropped them on my cot, and headed for the shower. On my return I couldn't find my cap. I headed for the orderly's room to complain about someone stealing it. There he sat, calmly sewing piping on a brand-new overseas cap that looked suspiciously like mine, while he told me that if I had lost mine I'd have to go to the quartermaster and purchase a new one. I had learned my first lesson in self-preservation in the Army! I promptly sat down and labeled, with indelible ink, all my gear with the regulation last initial and last four digits of my serial number. For the rest of the weekend I walked around the camp out of uniform, for I had only been issued one cap. On Monday I bought a new one—the cost to be deducted from my first pay.

That day I also became a part of a new bunch of recruits. The first time I protested that "I had that shot before," I was escorted to the mess hall to scrub pots and pans. From then on I followed the crowd, figuring that a double dose of the shots was not lethal, and certainly preferable to KP. By the end of the second week I was finally given an assignment—to the Signal Corps at Fort Monmouth, New Jersey.

My second train ride took me to Camp Edison in Seagirt, New Jersey, the Basic Training Center for the Signal Corps. Being a service unit rather than a combat unit, Signal Corps basic training was not the rigorous, twelve-week ordeal that combat soldiers were given. It was the most basic of basic trainings—two weeks of broad-brush exposure to the skills all soldiers should have. It was almost as though they didn't expect us to ever see any action. We did have some close-order drill, firing range practice, and other associated garbage, but nothing to prepare us for combat. The most difficult part was a fifteen-mile hike with full field pack that included an overnight bivouac to get to Fort Monmouth when basic training was completed.

Life at Fort Monmouth was great! We were students in the

Cryptographic School—the elite of the Signal Corps. We marched to school in the morning, marched back to the barracks in late afternoon, and the rest of our time was our own, with unlimited passes to town. Such things as guard duty and KP did not exist.

It was too good to last, and last it didn't, for the Cryptographic School was moved en masse to Vint Hill Farms Station in Warrenton, Virginia, just as the winter of 1942 was approaching. We arrived just in time to help convert a cattle farm into a military base. It was mud, mud, mud, and more mud. The soil was so unstable that the road from the main gate to the woods where our barracks compound was located was corduroyed. New logs were added periodically as those in place disappeared into the mire.

And it was cold! Building contractors had erected one-story prefab barracks units, six or so surrounding a similar building with showers, washbowls, and toilets. Each of the enlisted men's barracks housed about forty men. A short distance away was a similar building that held the company's orderly room, bachelor officers' quarters, and the officers' latrine. The buildings were uninsulated and were very inadequately heated with potbellied stoves. It wasn't unusual to find the plumbing frozen on a bitterly cold morning.

A half mile away, accessible via another corduroy road, stood a few more prefab buildings that housed the Cryptographic School. Unfortunately, we saw the interior of the school buildings rarely during the first few months after our arrival, for Vint Hill Farms was also to be the War Department's Radio Intercept Station, and the first priority was to get the intercept station in operation. Here a large complement of radio operators would soon be copying, around the clock, volumes of coded messages being sent between the major radio stations of foreign governments, both friend and foe, amassing reams and reams of messages for cryptanalysts to study in their search for the keys to the messages' contents.

A feeble attempt at camouflage was being made here. The intercept station, with its operators, was to be located in a couple of barnlike buildings. Leading away from the barns was what was supposed to look like, from the air, a cattle runway, but which would really be a runway for the lead-in wires from the reception antennae to the radios. In the pastures were the antennae—sixteen of them. Each consisted of four telegraph poles set in a diamond configuration with a wire suspended from top of pole to top of pole, the long axis of the diamonds oriented so as to box the compass. Thus, when a weak signal was heard, the operator would be able to switch to an antenna of different orientation in hopes of getting better reception. Instead of going to crypt school, we were assigned the priority job of digging holes for the poles that would support all of these antennae and the lead-in wires. We had no powered augers to drill these holes in the frozen ground, so we used human-powered posthole shovels.

By mid-January our physical labors were completed, and we were able to get down to our purpose—cryptanalysis studies. Our instructors at the school were recent college graduates—professorial types—many of whom would later hold high positions in business, industry, and government. One was Lt. McGeorge Bundy, a Harvard graduate who after the war held many prestigious positions in education and government and served as president of the Ford Foundation. Another was his equally well known brother, Lt. William Bundy, who followed his military career serving the government in positions with the CIA and the Department of Defense. With several other brains, they tried to develop in us the ability to solve complex crossword puzzles. We also were given crash courses in foreign languages. I was exposed to Japanese, but it didn't take.

My favorite instructor in crypt school was S.Sgt. George Bailey. George was also an enlisted man, and we became drinking buddies. On most any evening we could be found in the noncommissioned officer (NCO) club drinking 3.2 beer. We both applied for appointments as warrant officers and were turned down. Then we both applied for Officer Candidate School (OCS) and were accepted.

When our names appeared on the bulletin board list of accepted OCS candidates, we decided to go into Warrenton to celebrate. And celebrate we did! We came back to camp well looped and went to the NCO club for still another drink. There we grew louder and drunker, and no one could miss our vocal derision of the officers who ran the school. On the very next day we found that our names had been scratched from the OCS list, and one day later we were on an overseas assignment list. Next stop, Brisbane, Australia. Both Bailey and I eventually got direct commissions: he for being a member of a team that cracked a Japanese cipher system and I for my role in the Philippine guerrillas.

In Brisbane I was to be a code clerk, technician, fourth grade, Signal Corps, U.S. Army, assigned to the headquarters of the Allied Intelligence Bureau (AIB). I was one of a group of eight enlisted men who, with four commissioned officers, were being rushed to Australia from Vint Hill Farms in April 1943. We were all trained to some degree in cryptography and cryptanalysis.

Preparation for overseas assignment began in early March. Orders were cut for a seven-day delay en route to go home and say good-bye to the folks, and then to report to Arlington Hall, a top-secret military intelligence operation outside of Washington, D.C. There, in a few weeks, the Office of Strategic Services (OSS) gave us a crash course in espionage operations. Their efforts, aimed at turning us into secret agents overnight, were not very successful. The training might have served us well had we been going to infiltrate Paris, but it would be rather useless in the jungles of the Pacific Islands. However, I had been in the service for almost a year and had learned that an enlisted man did as he was told, no questions asked. Each of us, individually, was put through the hare and hounds routine in the streets of Baltimore, Maryland, some forty miles north of the nation's capital. This exercise consisted of being given a four-hour head start before being pursued by "the enemy," then trying to keep from being apprehended for the next twenty-four hours. What a joke! It didn't take long for me to be caught in one of the strip-joint bars on Baltimore's famous Block.

We soon entrained from Washington, D.C., to Hamilton Air Base, just north of San Francisco, where we were rushed through the overseas physical and shots routine. We then enplaned for Australia. With 1st Lt. Charles B. Ferguson in charge, our group consisted of 2nd Lts. Kenneth F. Bry, Edward H. Hale, and Clinton B. McFarland; T.Sgts. George K. Bailey and Walter G. Clark; T3gs. Marion W. Bugh; T4gs. Seymour Ginsberg and myself; and T5gs. George F. Gregory, Norman J. Lipman, and Irving H. Robinson.

California to Hawaii was a first-class flight. Our little group occupied a C-47 cargo plane, the military version of the DC-3, which was used by civilian airlines of the United States and other countries. The crew included a steward serving drinks and snacks. *This is real living,* I told myself.

The flight from Hickam Field in Honolulu to Australia was quite different. Apparently we were bumped from our commodious accommodations by higher-ranking brass, who had in turn been bumped by Eleanor Roosevelt, who was en route to Australia on a morale-boosting excursion. So, from Hickam Field to Canton Island, to Suva in the Fijis, to New Caledonia, and on to Brisbane, we rode the same kind of plane, but without its bucket seats. Instead, we made ourselves as comfortable as possible in the cargo area, sprawled on top of the mailbags, as our pilots and navigators sought out those wee dots of land in the vast Pacific Ocean. I've often wondered how in the world they found those little atolls, like Canton Island—about three square miles of coral in the middle of a million square miles of sea. I've also been afraid to ask.

That I was a part of a group of very resourceful individuals became evident during this trip. We were not great military men, to be sure, but certainly survivors and opportunists. For example, Norman Lipman, a short, rotund Chicagoan, was obviously of use to the Army because of his brain and not his brawn, for he could speak, read, and write twelve languages, including Hebrew and Greek (but not Japanese). He arranged some mailbags into a semblance of a card table, produced a deck of cards, and cleaned the clocks of all of us in a poker game that lasted for three days.

Our lives in Brisbane were about the same as civilian life would be in any midsized American city, although all of Australia seemed to be twenty years behind America in development. Perhaps much of this contrast came about from their suffering the privations of war close to home. There were also noticeable little things that had nothing to do with the war. For example, my future father-in-law sent me a large can of pretzels from his hometown of Reading, Pennsylvania. My Australian friends were amazed when they saw and ate these tasty morsels, for pretzels were unknown in their country.

The city was overrun with uniformed Americans who manned the various offices of MacArthur's General Headquarters (GHQ), drove the Army's vehicles, and did all the other tasks that needed to be done. All the offices were open around the clock seven days a week, and we worked rotating eight-hour shifts. After all, there *was* a war going on.

Trolley cars clanged along the streets, and our uniforms afforded us a free ride. Those Australians who owned automobiles sported charcoal burners mounted beside the engine bonnet. These created an aerated gas that served as fuel for the engines, for gasoline was in extremely short supply.

We were domiciled in a vacated fire station. The ground floor, where the fire engines had been housed, was now a mess hall. Because our days did not begin and end with the rising and setting of the sun but were determined by our work schedules, we could get breakfast, lunch, or dinner at any time of the day or night, without question—all cooked to order. On the second floor (which Australians call the first floor) was the dormitory. Here were row upon row of army cots, each with a footlocker neatly positioned to its side under a rack on which uniforms were hung. This was home, and no undue noise was permitted day or night, again because of our work schedules.

Whenever we were not on the swing shift, we would head for the local pub just before 5:00 P.M., unless we were on the wrong side of pay-day. The pub would open at that time, but the daily ration of beer would not last long, and we stood three deep at the bar and quaffed as fast as possible to get our share. When the beer tap ran dry, we would drink rum from the small keg hanging behind the bar, a brass cup dangling under its spigot to catch the drips.

Payday came on the last day of the month. We would line up outside the orderly room, and when our turn came we would enter, salute the pay officer, sign the pay roster, and collect our cash. Immediately outside the exit from the orderly room, the supply sergeant had a regulation-sized craps table set up. This was his concession—the profits to be shared with the company commander. Next to the table was a bottled-goods stand, which rarely had anything other than Gilbey's gin for sale. The scotch and whiskey went to the officers clubs.

We were treated well by the Australian citizens, who invited us to their homes for tea and/or supper. It didn't take me long to learn that tea was the main evening meal, while supper was a snack later in the evening. Occasionally we were invited to "boil the billy," that is, to join in a picnic in a nearby park, where the tea would be steeped in a billycan over an open fire. Usually we would travel in a charcoal-fueled automobile. And, of course, we were always invited to join them at a Sunday church service.

We were not received as well by the Australian soldiers. We Yanks were paid much better than they were, which translated into more available female companionship. The girls liked the things that the American soldiers could afford, and they made no bones about taking advantage of this wealth. Sometimes this led to confrontations that became severe enough that "American martial law" would be declared, and the Aussies were restricted to quarters. This did nothing to improve international relations.

The Australian Red Cross operated canteens where we could while away time with coffee, doughnuts, and dancing. In addition, they operated a rest and recreation area at Coolangatta, a seashore resort not far from Brisbane. There we could get reasonably priced meals and a bed and spend days off duty lazing about in the surf. Also, the place had some very comely hostesses with whom most of us dreamed of getting lucky, while few did.

Pleasant as life was, we had a job to do. It interfered with our pleasure, but it took priority. We worked in Heindorf House, a multistoried office building in downtown Brisbane. It was one of several buildings housing MacArthur's GHQ, with several floors devoted to the AIB. One floor was occupied by the AIB's Philippine Regional Section (PRS), our sector of the operations. Our code room on this floor held about a half-dozen desks and chairs and several filing cabinets. In one corner was a teletype machine,

The author in 1943.

which afforded us communication with some mysterious location where a radio station transmitted and received our messages.

Guards in the lobby prevented visitors' access to the building unless they were cleared to enter. In addition, outside our office door sat, around the clock, guards who would let no one but our personnel into our area. Security was so tight that sometimes, if a new guard was on duty, we couldn't get in until we were properly identified by someone already in the office. Even people who worked in other offices of the AIB could not enter our sanctuary. If one of us was there alone, he could not leave until another of our crew came in, for the room could never be left empty of our personnel at any time. Our operation was the acme of top secret.

We worked in duty groups of one officer present as a boss and two or three enlisted men as his crew. The guerrilla movement was just beginning, and radio traffic was sporadic. This made the job very boring, with nothing to do but read books, work crossword puzzles, or sleep. One of the lieutenants took to reading the dictionary. I think he was up to the D's when I left to go to the Philippines.

The war in the Pacific was now somewhat more than a year old. During that time several radio stations claiming to belong to guerrilla units had successfully established contact with MacArthur's GHQ in Australia. Some claimed to have salvaged radios left behind by the Army during the surrender. Others said they had confiscated some of the Philippine Postal Service's radiotelegraphy equipment. Their authenticity was suspect, and the cipher systems they used varied from poor to nonexistent.

We had been brought in with a twofold purpose. First, we were to establish the authenticity of the guerrilla stations. Were they for real, or were they some sort of Japanese ruse? Second, if they were verified, we were to establish secret cryptographic systems to maintain message security. Establishing authenticity would have been difficult but for Yankee ingenuity. Our guerrilla correspondents had identified themselves by name, rank, and serial number. With this information we were able to have Secret Service agents in the States visit their families, from whom they obtained personal information only the callers would know and which we could use to question those men who were sending messages from the Philippines.

Possessing this information, we would send a very military-sounding message with a personal ending, such as "MARY, MARK, AND SUZIE SEND THEIR LOVE, AND HOPE YOU WILL BE HOME SOON." Now we had to depend on him, and his ingenuity. We purposely left out the name of someone else of equal importance in his life. If the reply was "TELL THEM I LOVE THEM TOO," we considered that he might be in trouble, and probably a prisoner of the Japanese, for we had not included, for example, his son Adam in our transmission to him. If his message was "TELL THEM, AND ADAM, THAT I LOVE THEM TOO," we felt relatively sure he was authentic. This was a touch-and-go way of establishing creditability, but it was the best we could do under the circumstances.

Establishing a secure code system was more difficult. Few of the guerrilla radio operators knew much about cryptography. Some had pocket-size encoding devices that the Army had used for years in the field to yield a substitution cipher. Anyone with a yen for newspaper crossword puzzles and cryptograms could break these codes in minutes. In a few cases we were able to set up more complex codes using the same sort of personal information we used to authenticate the stations, but our results in this respect were very unsatisfactory.

In only one way can top-secret code systems be established without fear of their being compromised: they must be exchanged between the stations by physically handing them over in a face-to-face meeting. This becomes a rather difficult feat when the two parties are separated by fifteen hundred miles of ocean controlled by the enemy and when one of the parties is located deep in the jungles of enemy-held territory. This meant that someone from our unit had to penetrate the Japanese lines to establish the cipher systems. None of us wanted this assignment. Sure, we tried to demonstrate our bravado by boasting to each other about wanting to be the first of our group to go into the Philippines, but each of us secretly hoped that someone else would be chosen. Life in Brisbane was calm, peaceful, and, except for the inconvenience of working an occasional night shift, the best way to fight a war. Why do anything else?

Then we encountered several Americans who had been POWs. They were from a group of ten men who had escaped from the Davao Penal Colony on Mindanao, formerly a prison farm for felons but now holding a mixture of soldiers and civilians under the Japanese. They had made their way to Australia via the guerrillas and a U.S. submarine. Their stories of the unbelievable atrocities being committed by the Japanese against American and Filipino prisoners got to me. Suddenly the work I was involved in seemed infinitely more important. I volunteered to carry secret cipher systems into the Philippines, then become a guerrilla and a coastwatcher, where I hoped to be even more useful.

To Mindanao

CHAPTER 2

At this stage of the proceedings, I met one of three Americans who had firsthand knowledge and experience of the Philippines, Maj. Charles M. Smith. He had been a mining engineer in the Philippines and was trapped there when America surrendered the archipelago to the Japanese. He had sent his family, wife Kathryn and their two young sons, to their former home in Texas when war became imminent. Charlie stayed on, for he was near the end of a three-year employment contract that included a sizable bonus if completed. He had gambled and lost, for war came before his contract completion date. He did not collect the bonus—and wound up committed to a life with a very unpredictable future.

After several months in the jungles of Mindanao, he and fellow mining engineers Jordan Hamner and Charles "Chick" Smith, with two Filipinos as crew, sailed to Australia in a *cumpit,* a twenty-one-foot sailboat with an eight-foot beam, which they modified by adding weight to the keel, a deck, and a small Japanese diesel engine. The engine would be used only in emergencies, for they could carry precious little fuel. They made their thirty-day journey on an ocean filled with Japanese naval vessels, past islands occupied by Japanese troops, and made landfall at the northern coastal town of Darwin on 4 January 1943. From time to time, other Americans tried to make this journey. Most died in the attempt.

Before leaving Mindanao, the trio had promised still another mining engineer, Wendell Fertig, the leader of a budding guerrilla band, that they would attempt to get General MacArthur to send supplies from Australia to the guerrillas. Smith and Fertig had met MacArthur socially in Manila from time to time before the war started, so Smith did not feel he would be approaching a stranger in making this request.

U.S. Navy submarines had carried Dutch, Australian, and English coastwatchers into several of the Pacific islands to report Japanese shipping movements to Naval Operations and to report military intelligence to the AIB. Even as the Smiths and Hamner were sailing south, a submarine was plying its way northward below the surface of the same ocean, carrying a landing party to the Philippines. These intelligence-gathering teams were dropped off by operational submarines on the way to bigger things—combat with the Japanese Navy—much like a truck driver carries a hitchhiker to the next town.

No attempt had been made, however, to carry major cargo loads of supplies to the growing guerrilla units. The operational submarines had no extra space for cargo. Carrying a few extra men and their personal gear made for crowded quarters until they were left at their destination. A larger vessel assigned to supply duty alone was needed. The USS *Narwhal*, a submarine of World War I vintage and almost twice the size of this war's operational subs, was pressed into this service. How the supply lines were established and the missions conducted has been described elsewhere.

The Navy was rightfully concerned about the security of a vessel being stationary for hours on the surface of enemy-controlled waters while being unloaded. They insisted that an Army officer with vast knowledge of the Philippines and Filipinos be responsible for the security of such an undertaking. Smith obviously had the requisite knowledge, but he was not of the military. He also had a promise to keep to guerrilla leader Fertig. So, instead of remaining a civilian and returning to his family in El Paso, Smith accepted an Army commission as captain in the Corps of Engineers. Jordan Hamner, not to be outdone by his friend, also accepted a captaincy and later led a penetration party into Tawitawi and Borneo. "Chick" Smith, somewhat older than his two companions, opted to return to the United States as a civilian.

At the same time, one of the most bizarre escapes of the war was taking place. In 1921, Charles "Chick" Parsons had gone to the Philippines, a member of the crew of a merchant ship. There he left the ship to join an uncle who lived in Manila. Having stenographic training (not an unusual skill for a male at that time), Parsons served a stint as secretary to Governor-General Leonard Wood, a position that led him to and through the doors of the homes and clubs of the American and Filipino elite. Three or four years later he joined the Luzon Stevedoring Company, eventually rising to the top of its executive echelon. He settled in Manila and married a Filipina, with whom he had three children.

Chick had a love of the seas and a deep interest in naval activities. This led him to join the U.S. Naval Reserve in 1932. He was called to active duty in December 1941 and served a very short term with the Intelligence Office in Manila.

The social life of the capital city included many affairs of state, attended by dignitaries of countries from around the world. At one time Panama did not have a permanent consul assigned there, and Parsons was appointed honorary consul, to represent Panama whenever necessary. When the Japanese overran the Philippines, Parsons claimed Panamanian citizenship and the right of repatriation for him and his family to Panama. After much negotiation, including intercessions by representatives of other countries that had maintained neutrality, he and his family were flown to Hong Kong, and from there repatriated to Panama on the *Gripsholm*. Had the Japanese known that this repatriate was Comdr. Charles A. Parsons, USNR, it would never have happened.

So, about the time the Smiths, Hamner, and two Filipinos were about to make landfall at Darwin in January 1943, Chick and Katsy Parsons were dancing the night away at a New Year's Eve celebration in Washington, D.C. Chick would soon be joining his old friends in Australia and then returning to the Philippines in different guise. He would become the coordinator of GHQ's supply lines to the guerrillas. He would shuttle between Australia and the Philippines by submarine many times and become GHQ's one reliable envoy to all guerrilla groups. Parsons would parachute into Leyte a week before the Allied landing in October 1944 and, with the cooperation of the local guerrilla units, secretly evacuate all the civilians from the vicinity of Tacloban, away from the devastating naval bombardment, without the Japanese realizing it. This was probably his finest hour.

Now the Navy had one of its own to join with Charlie Smith in making a major submarine supply run to the Philippines a secure venture. Despite this fact, and even in the pressing urgency of war, agreement on operational plans between the services took considerable time. So, while awaiting this agreement, Captain Smith and Commander Parsons penetrated Mindanao by operational submarine late in February 1943. Parsons worked out security details for the *Narwhal's* upcoming landing on Mindanao with Col. Wendell Fertig, while Smith established a radio station overlooking the harbor at Davao. With few interruptions, this station continued to send out extremely valuable reports of Japanese shipping movements and other intelligence information until the war's end. Smith and Parsons returned to Australia soon after the station was in operation.

With agreement still pending, Smith was sent to the United States to locate materiel suitable for clandestine missions in the jungles. Armed with almost dictatorial power, he selected radios and supporting gear for priority shipment to Brisbane. He then returned to Australia—and waited.

In November 1943 he was *Major* Smith and was organizing another invasion party to go to the Philippines to establish additional radio stations and an espionage network, this time on Samar Island and southern Luzon. In addition, he, with Parsons, would be responsible for the security of the *Narwhal,* carrying arms, ammunition, and other supplies to the guerrillas on Mindanao, where his party would go ashore.

I first met Smith in early November at Heindorf House, the location of our code room and the headquarters of the AIB. He was a forty-year-old Texan of medium build, height, and weight, with not an ounce of fat. If you had to find an Army officer who didn't look the part, Charlie was your man. He had not been a cadet at West Point, nor had he been exposed to a ninety-day-wonder OCS course in the Army, so spit and polish was not his bag. His uniform was not tailor made of expensive fabric. He wore the suntans of an enlisted man which he purchased from the quartermaster, never pressed, and his insignia of rank was always askew on his collar. His face was weather-beaten and lined, his eyes displayed a subtle twinkle, and he rarely trimmed his greying blond mustache. Bald on top and fringed around, he appeared to have a self-inflicted haircut. He demonstrated a disdain for military protocol. That I liked. He had shown his combat and survival skills on his previous missions. I liked that, too. If I was going to get into this mess, I wanted to serve with him, or someone like him.

When I asked if I could go with him on this mission, he stared at me and said, "Man, are you crazy?"

"I don't think so," I replied. "I've read the messages that come from the islands, and know what's going on. I have a pretty good idea of what must be done and what to expect. I think I could do it. At least, I'd like to try."

He asked me what I knew about communications. I told him of my civilian experience with amateur radios and my Army training in cryptography and cryptanalysis. I also spoke of the urgent need to set up secure cipher systems throughout the islands. He decided I might be useful and added me to his group.

I sometimes wish Smith had asked me if I liked rice. My resounding "No!" would have ended my participation.

Selection and training of the men who would carry out the operations of the PRS was, like most military undertakings that were not refined by years and years of repetition, rather clumsily handled.

Originally, Col. Allison Ind was in charge of the PRS. Between December 1942 and July 1943, under his direction, several penetration teams made up of Americans and Filipinos were organized and dispatched to the islands. They were escapees or evacuees from the Philippines, and had undergone training in schools established by the Australian Army to prepare coastwatchers to be sent to islands immediately north of the Australian mainland. These schools offered training in intelligence gathering, commando skills, amphibious operations, radio operation, ship and aircraft recognition, weather observation, and other skills essential to combat intelligence work. However, similar training on a much larger and more concentrated scale would be needed in order to blanket the Philippines with intelligence networks.

Col. Courtney Whitney, who succeeded Colonel Ind as chief of the PRS, went to California in the spring of 1943 to select a group of volunteers from the First and Second Filipino Infantry Regiments to be the nucleus of the unit's operatives. As these men arrived in Australia, they were temporarily assigned to the Australian schools until a new camp was established. Camp Tabragalba, located near Beaudesert, Queensland, known only as Camp X, was kept under heavy secrecy and security wraps. The camp and the 5217th Reconnaissance Battalion (Provisional) became realities on 8 October 1943.

The camp's training program thoroughly covered the skills needed by agents entering enemy-held territory; survival, weaponry, hand-to-hand combat, and communications, to name only a few. I was not able to participate in any of these activities, except for a few days of Morse code practice to polish my hand and ear, and one night's exposure to handling a rubber boat to go ashore. The rest of the skills I would have to learn through on-the-job training from Major Smith.

Capt. James L. "Doc" Evans Jr., M.D., was also a missioner, as we were labeled. Although Captain Evans was a doctor, his professional skills were not his reason for being in Smith's party. Doc was an exceptionally good radio operator. He had been a radio ham for more than fifteen years before entering the service, and he was also an excellent radio technician. He, too, did not receive any training at Camp X.

We spent two weeks gathering together the equipment we would need for the first six months of our stay in the Philippines. We hoped that this would be the length of our mission. Our gear consisted mainly of radio and ordnance equipment and a minimal amount of clothing. We took only a few cases of GI food rations, for we planned to live largely off the land. We included several cases of whiskey, some wheat flour, and several cases of sacramental wine. The whiskey was for us; the flour and wine were for the Roman Catholic priests and their parishioners, our extremely faithful allies.

Everything that had to be cushioned for shipment was wrapped in newspapers telling of the Allied victories in the islands south of the Philippines. The packing materials would be carefully removed, then circulated for public relations purposes. Lastly, we had lots of cigarettes, matches, pencils, and chocolate bars, all packaged in wrappers emblazoned "I Shall Return!—MacArthur."

Although Evans would not be on a healing mission, he did select a supply of medicines to be taken aboard. These included aspirin, sulfanilamide powder and sulfathiazole tablets (miracle drugs in 1943), morphine for the painfully wounded, atabrine to prevent malaria and quinine to treat it, adhesive tape but no bandages (they could be rolled of cloth in the islands), and a host of other drugs, supplies, and medical instruments. These would be shared with Fertig.

Oh, yes. We also carried thousands of Philippine pesos—real money newly printed in Washington, D.C., minted with engraving plates taken from the Philippine treasury when the islands fell—loosely packed with water and sand in sealed, five-gallon metal containers. The water-and-sand mixture was intended to age the money, since Filipinos would be hard pressed to explain to the Japanese where they got crisp, new paper money. Aging the currency this way was a brilliant idea—until it came time to dry it so that it could be spent. If we had sunlight we would spread it on the ground and hope it wouldn't blow away while it dried. During the rainy season, which seemed to be all the time, we sat beside fires waving wads of currency over the heat to drive out the moisture. We also had counterfeit Japanese invasion currency (called APA in the islands), American made, to spend freely to inflate the Japanese currency.

All in all, our party's gear weighed about ten tons. In addition, the submarine carried ninety tons of arms, ammunition, and medicine destined for Colonel Fertig on Mindanao. Moving this mass of supplies in a clandestine mission—including a landing by submarine, hauling it through jungles, clambering up mountains, and avoiding discovery by Japanese patrols—was either brave or foolhardy. I had trouble selecting the proper adjective. I wanted to do something significant in the war, and I wanted it to be physical as well as mental activity. At that point (I was aged a full twenty-three years), I recognized that the mission might prove fatal to me, but that didn't seem too likely just then. I could just as easily be hit by a truck on the streets of Brisbane. The mission would certainly be an adventure and a bit out of the ordinary for a guy from Pennsylvania. When I tried to envision myself toothlessly telling my grandchildren about the exciting times in the code room in Brisbane, the picture was blurry. Of course, relating tales of soggy heat in the insect-ridden jungles seemed a bit on the weird side, too. As a result, I gave up such thoughts and focused on the job immediately at hand.

We flew from Brisbane to Darwin, Australia, on 24 November 1943. Our invasion team consisted of we three Americans and nine Filipino soldiers who had been educated in America, infantrymen-turned-agents who had been schooled at Camp X.

The one hundred tons of cargo had been loaded on the *Narwhal* at a dock in Brisbane, save for our personal gear, which we toted in barracks bags. The cargo had to be packed in containers small enough to fit through the sub's hatch openings and narrow interior passageways. Barrels for 37-millimeter antiaircraft guns didn't fit inside, so they were stowed in two aft torpedo tubes accessible from the deck. The submarine departed Brisbane for Darwin several days before we enplaned to meet it.

I was a basket case on the flight to Darwin. As soon as we were off the ground, I barfed my breakfast. I continued with dry heaves on each of the remaining three legs of our journey. I would like to say I was airsick, but I was just plain scared.

On 26 November 1943 we boarded the *Narwhal* at Darwin, bound for Butuan Bay and the Agusan River on the north coast of Mindanao. There we would rendezvous with the Mindanao guerrilla forces on 2 December. The submarine trip was an interesting new experience. Most of the time we traveled on the surface, making about twelve knots. On several occasions, either for practice or because of an unidentified plane or surface craft, we would crash-dive. Underwater we traveled at about two knots. The popping, crackling, knocking noises inside a submerged submarine can give a landlubber an entirely different perspective on submariners. Reassurances that the boat was not about to come apart at the seams could not quite overcome my concerns during crash dives. Some people cannot quite get accustomed to traveling underwater. I was not particularly bothered by the dives, except for the bad vibes transmitted to me by one electrician's mate who was paranoid about depth bombing. I liked the guy as a conversationalist, but he made me uneasy with his fears.

Otherwise, the trip was uneventful except for one occasion when an enemy plane was not sighted until it was almost directly above our vessel. Doc Evans was on sun lookout, a euphemism for getting some fresh air on deck, when the dive alarm sounded. He was the first man through the hatch but wasn't fast enough going down the ladder. The next man stepped all over him. He was a sorry sight with a black eye and facial cuts as a result.

"How do you like that?" he complained. "I earn the Purple Heart before I meet the enemy!"

The Not-So-Secret Landing

CHAPTER 3

We were to have a top-secret rendezvous with the guerrillas under the command of Colonel Fertig. Through the Surigao Strait, we entered Butuan Bay on the northeast coast of Mindanao early in the afternoon of 2 December. We circled at periscope depth for several hours. Lt. Comdr. Frank D. Latta, the sub's captain, checked the bay for problem craft, then located the prearranged security signals on the beach—a white sheet suspended between two coconut trees with smoking fires one hundred yards to the left and right.

Just before dusk, the *Narwhal* surfaced and moved to a spot less than a half mile from shore. Doc Evans and I, both newcomers to the islands and to guerrilla warfare, did not know what to expect. We were prepared for anything, half expecting to engage in a hand-to-hand battle with a Japanese boarding party upon surfacing. When we climbed through the hatch to the deck, Evans wore a side arm, while I packed a submachine gun. Commander Latta was already on deck, and when he saw us with arms he bellowed, "Put those damned guns away! Do you want to hurt someone!"

I looked around, and, instead of seeing Japanese naval vessels approaching us, I saw a most beautiful sunset. Dusk moves in and out very rapidly in the tropics. All the spectacular colors of a leisurely northern sunset flash by in rapid succession. I watched the sun disappear over the mountain jungles to the west, and then my eyes dropped down to the

30

beach in front of us. There stood fully two hundred natives, cheering and shouting greetings to us, while a small band played "Anchors Aweigh." So much for the secret rendezvous! All that was missing were some Madison Avenue advertising men.

Two diesel-powered launches towing a large lighter moved out of the Agusan River and made fast to the submarine. The sub's four hatches were opened, and Filipino laborers swarmed around them like flies. The submariners raised the cargo up through the hatches, and the laborers carried it to the lighter. While the unloading operations were going on, the natives traded bolos, bananas, coconuts, and even Japanese cigarettes for the American cigarettes the sailors possessed. With all this activity, I had one disturbing thought.

"Where are the Japanese?" I asked an American guerrilla who was on the deck with us.

"See those lights over there?" he replied, pointing to a spot on the shoreline roughly ten miles to the west. "That's Nasipit, where one garrison is, and the other is over there." He pointed to another cluster of lights about the same distance to the east, which I later learned was the town of Cabadbaran.

"My God!" I said. "Why aren't they trying to stop us?"

"They're as scared of us as we are of them," he answered. "We whipped their asses lots of times, and they leave us alone."

In the hills behind Nasipit there was another large light. It seemed to be flashing, like the lights on a Christmas tree. I pointed to it and asked, "Are there Japs there, too?"

"Nah. Them's fireflies. Them bugs swarm on one tree and sometimes there's enough of 'em to light up the sky," he said.

In the next fifteen months I saw lots of brilliantly lighted trees—firefly sex orgies.

The *Narwhal* did not return to Australia empty. Replacing our invasion team on board were Chick Parsons, on the return leg of one of his many trips between Australia and the Philippines, and seven evacuees—a mixture of military and civilian personnel, including one woman and an eight-year-old girl. Replacing a small portion of our cargo was about a ton of bananas, the only gift the guerrillas had available to thank the crew for their services.

Major Smith, Captain Evans, and I boarded a third launch, Colonel Fertig's command vessel, to move up the Agusan. In typical officer-to-enlisted-man fashion, Fertig acknowledged Smith's introduction of me—then ignored me completely. He had a small goatee, which he stroked like a kitten as he talked. The colonel was thin, but I could tell that normally he was a big man on whom the poor diet of the last two years had taken its toll. He was a middle-aged man with kindly eyes that, I discovered later, hid a very stern manner. This manner was responsible for his success in dealing with the Filipinos and building a genuine fighting organization. It also made him less than popular with the American guerrillas he commanded. Many hated him but held their feelings in check. They realized that survival was their first aim, and cooperation among the Americans was the key to that end.

From Fertig's launch we said good-bye to the submarine and its crew and then sailed up the Agusan River.

On 4 December 1943, Capt. Charles B. Ferguson, chief of the code room in the Heindorf House in Brisbane, carried a message to Col. Courtney Whitney, chief of the PRS. It was from Fertig, and read as follows:

> CARGO UNLOADED IN THREE HOURS AND SUCCESSFULLY MOVED UP THE AGUSAN BY DAWN, 3 DECEMBER. VESSEL CLEARED AT 2230 H. CP [Parsons] OUT AND CMS [Smith] IN. QUANTITY APPRECIATED AND HELP IMMENSELY.

The message carried Whitney's endorsement when it went to General MacArthur as follows:

> Message confirms previous information in re operation but adds that supplies were moved up AGUSAN by dawn 3 December. I understand that in the river movement a 100-ton lighter is employed with launches to tow. By completion of the movement in the manner indicated the area of the BUTU-AN BAY was cleared of all supplies by dawn of the night during which delivery was effected. This discloses satisfactory organization and preparation.

The feasibility of supplying the guerrillas via submarine was now established.

Undoubtedly, the brass in Brisbane were comforted to know that they could supply the troops in the bush, but the job was only half done as far as we were concerned. We did not plan to operate at Butuan Bay with the Japanese looking over our shoulders. Still to come was the minor chore of moving one hundred tons of supplies up the Agusan River for several miles—a task simply stated but not easily accomplished. For starters, the lighter with its supplies was not clear of the Butuan Bay area, as Fertig's message to GHQ had said. Poor navigation had put the launch towing the lighter high and dry on a sandbar. Our supplies were barely out of the bay at the mouth of the Agusan River.

By midnight on the night of our landing we were in the town of Butuan, the gateway to the Agusan River. Throughout the war this town was the scene of much guerrilla activity. Whoever held Butuan controlled the river valley. From its source in a vast jungle swamp, the Agusan winds its way northward through a wide, flat plain for twenty-five miles before it reaches the bay. Rice fields abound in the valley, making it one of the most productive farming areas on Mindanao.

Control of this important food source seesawed between the guerrillas and the Japanese. At one time, a guerrilla unit under the leadership of Col. Ernest E. McClish and Maj. Clyde C. Childress was occupying Butuan and was under a stiff siege by Japanese troops. The guerrillas ran short of ammunition—as did the Japanese. A truce was declared, with each side occupying half the town. There was one store located in the middle of the town, and it was patronized by both sides at the same time.

McClish soon realized that the Japanese had what he didn't have—a source of supply. It would be only a matter of time until the Japanese would receive a shipment of ammunition and the guerrillas would be overwhelmed. With a last-ditch show of strength, the guerrillas attacked the Japanese, who had holed up in a concrete-block schoolhouse with a corrugated-steel roof. For nine days the guerrillas tried to drive them out of this building. McClish and his men had no artillery or other heavy weapons, and their small-arms fire was ineffective against this concrete bunker. The standoff ended when the Japanese called in aircraft to bomb the guerrilla positions. The guerrillas retreated to the surrounding jungles.

Apparently, the Japanese felt they could not maintain their advantage, and they moved out soon after. The guerrillas had controlled the town, and the valley, ever since. We stopped at Butuan only long enough to ensure that the guard company stationed there had the munitions needed to hold the river when our hundred tons of supplies moved in.

From Butuan we went to Amparo, a *barrio,* or small village, several miles upriver. It was now four o'clock in the morning. Colonel Fertig and Major Smith went into one of the houses near the river while Major

Childress and Capt. Paul Marshall took Doc Evans and me to a house about two hundred yards away. The rest of our party had stayed on the lighter. I was ready for some sleep.

In semidarkness broken only by the eerie light of a native coconut oil lamp, Evans unrolled his jungle hammock, a GI contraption with a canvas bottom, a waterproof top, mosquito netting on the four sides, and a zippered flap on one side to provide an entrance to this protection from the elements and the bugs. He tried to suspend it between two of the house's supporting posts, but it was a losing battle. I was asleep before he gave up, for I had spread my hammock on the floor like a mattress. He soon did the same. Less than an hour later I awoke. The bamboo floor had wrinkled my back like a washboard, and the mosquitoes were driving me crazy. I got up and went outside to await the dawn. Soon Evans joined me, while Childress and Marshall, being used to this life, slept on. Evans and I, too, would soon become accustomed to bamboo houses and mosquitoes.

With the coming of daylight I was able to examine our luxurious quarters. The hut was built against a small hill, supported about six feet off the ground by stout posts. A bamboo ladder served as the front steps. The roof was made of *buri* palm leaves—large, fan-shaped leaves that served the purpose of shingles very well—on bamboo rafters. The exterior walls were of matting formed by splitting bamboo poles into half-inch strips and weaving them into a flat panel. The flooring, too, was made of bamboo, this time split into half-round strips and laid side by

The submarine *Narwhal,* which transported men and materials to the guerrillas and carried evacuees to Australia. *(U.S. Naval Institute collection)*

side on a framework of bamboo poles. All this was fastened together with *rattan,* a strong but flexible vine that worked like thick twine. The cost of nails, even if they were available, would be prohibitive, so homes were made of the available jungle materials.

There was no furniture except for a kitchen stove and a long, low table. The stove was a three-foot-square bamboo box supported about two feet off the floor and filled with six inches of dirt. Here a fire could be built to heat clay cooking pots of food suspended on rattan vines dangling from a ceiling rafter. Fifteen feet long and twelve feet wide, this one-room house, I learned from Marshall, was considered ample space for a family of ten, plus in-laws, by Philippine standards. It provided the only housing they needed—a place to get out of the rain.

As the sub was being unloaded the day before, I had noticed young boys shadowing the Americans wherever they went. Whenever an American wanted a small task done, he would call one of these boys to do it. In the morning I found out why. Instead of our having to repack our gear, two boys, seeing that we were awake, came into the house and reassembled our packs. Then they carried them to the launch and guarded them while we went to a nearby house for breakfast. I asked Clyde Childress about this, for I wasn't exactly enthused about risking having my gear stolen.

"These kids really love the Americanos, and want to be around us all the time," said Clyde. "They are our interpreters, translators, guides, lackeys—and seem to be able to smell danger coming. They're good to have around. And don't worry. Your things are safe."

Major Childress, a graduate of a military school in the States, had been a U.S. Army officer on temporary duty as a battalion commander in the Philippine Army prior to the war. Unsurrendered, he roamed the mountains and jungles of Mindanao for almost a year before joining Colonel McClish in forming the 110th Division of the Mindanao Guerrilla, a unit that, by December 1944, had a strength of more than three hundred officers and five thousand enlisted men.

Captain Marshall was one of the ten men who were the first escapees from Davao Penal Colony to reach the safety afforded by the guerrillas. Several of this group of escapees were the men I had met in Australia—who caused me to volunteer for this mission. A private first class at the time, Paul and two other enlisted men decided to stay with the guerrillas rather than be returned by submarine to Australia. By January 1945 he had been commissioned and promoted to lieutenant colonel. At that time, McClish and Childress were evacuated to Australia, and Marshall took command of the 110th Division. This division was instrumental in the mopping up operations when the Allies returned to Mindanao.

Breakfast was an experience. It was prepared by a Filipina, the first woman I saw in the islands. She was beautiful! *If all the women here are like her, I must have died and gone to heaven,* I told myself.

They weren't.

Small, with waist-length black, wavy hair, she had the complexion and skin color American girls—and men, too—try to imitate every summer by sitting in the hot sun hour upon hour. She was slender and shapely, and anyone observing me would have said I was ogling her, and would have been right. She spoke very good English and was obviously a good cook. What she lacked was a variety of ingredients.

For breakfast, she presented what looked like Cream of Wheat covered with milk and sweetened with brown sugar, a side dish of fried potatoes, and coffee. But how different it all tasted. What we really had was soft-boiled rice, or *lugao*, coconut milk, unrefined native brown sugar, or *calami*, fried *camotes*, and rice coffee. This delightful beverage was made with roasted and ground rice, and it tasted worse than GI coffee, if that's possible. Although the meal looked good and I was plenty hungry, I couldn't eat it. I wondered how much weight I would lose before I got used to eating native food.

After breakfast we continued our launch trip upriver, stopping at Fertig's ordnance supply depot, six miles distant. Soon Smith and Fertig went further upriver to Esperanza, where Fertig had his guerrilla headquarters. Evans and I stayed at the supply depot with Lt. Bob Crump, the depot's officer in charge, awaiting the lighter with our supplies. When it arrived we would separate our ten tons from Fertig's supplies and set them aside for later pickup, to be taken with us to Samar Island.

Crump was a young American geologist who had surveyed Mindanao for oil deposits. He had completed his survey and was in Manila awaiting transportation back to the States when the war caught him. He turned his survey over to a Filipino, who put it in a safe-deposit vault in a bank. The bank was later destroyed, and three years' work went down the drain. He had returned to Mindanao in search of a hiding place from the Japanese, and there he joined the guerrillas.

To me, Bob's food was much better than the breakfast had been. He had some chickens, and therefore we had eggs. Not necessarily fresh eggs, though. Those we cracked open and found to be free of feathers, we fried. Out of a dozen, we managed to find six or seven that were not occupied. He also served lugao, which one cannot avoid in the

Philippines. I stirred the rice and eggs together, hoping to hide the rice. The mixture was barely edible, but I devoured it.

I now realized that I was going to have to learn to like rice. Meanwhile, I planned to rely on "I Shall Return" chocolate bars as a main course until they ran out. At this point I began to understand that the change in lifestyle represented a major obstacle, on a par with the Japanese Army. Fatigue and the debilitation from jungle accommodations plus alien food loomed large in my view of the future.

That day, I learned how tough it is to move supplies when you are using native labor and worn-out launches instead of GI trucks. In the afternoon, while we were still awaiting the lighter, a native came paddling up the river in a *baroto,* a native dugout canoe with outriggers to keep it upright. He told us that the lighter was stuck near the mouth of the river. One of the launches, the *Liberty Belle,* had run aground on a sand-bar in the bay, and the other launch was not strong enough to pull the fully loaded lighter further upriver than Butuan.

I jumped into his baroto and we went to Butuan, arriving at dusk. I found the lighter anchored offshore opposite the town, in full view of any Japanese planes that should chance to fly over it. While the Philippines are noted for thick jungles and heavy foliage, sometimes with branches reaching across and concealing whole rivers, the Agusan River around Butuan is quite wide, with rice paddies along both shores. No natural cover here. This was not a good place to park an equipment-filled lighter!

Lt. Willard Money had done the best he could to camouflage the lighter with coconut fronds and banana tree leaves. The equipment unloaded from the sub the preceding night was already being put to use, for he had set up one of our 37-millimeter antiaircraft guns on the beach to drive off any inquisitive Japanese planes.

Lieutenant Money was a big man. Even though life in the jungles had assaulted his health, he still towered over six feet and weighed close to two hundred pounds. An Air Corps man who had been a crew member on Colin Kelly's bomber, he had fled to the hills instead of surrendering. (Kelly was among America's first heavily publicized war heroes. At a time when the military and the press needed something positive to report to offset the bad news of the early days of the war, he was reported to have bombed and sunk the Japanese battleship *Haruna,* a feat for which it was recommended he receive the Medal of Honor. He did not receive the medal, and in later years it was revealed that the story was a fabrication, probably started by an overzealous member of MacArthur's staff.)

There was nothing I could do at the time to improve the cargo situation. The only other launch we had available had already been loaded and was on its way to the supply dump. It would not be possible for it to get to its destination, unload, and return before dawn. In the company of Lt. Elwood Royer, a Pennsylvania Dutchman by birth but more recently from Salt Lake City, I went to the mouth of the river, where we found the *Liberty Belle* high and dry on a sandbar. Even though it was midnight, a crowd of Filipinos was working desperately to get it afloat. They knew what a task it had been to capture this vessel from the Japanese and get it operating, and they struggled heroically to get it back into the safety of the river. Everything was going as well as could be expected, so Royer and I returned to the lighter and slept.

The launch we were awaiting to pick up its second load was the *Captain Knortz*. It was named after a guerrilla hero, William Knortz, who lost his life early in the war. He had had another launch out in the bay on the north coast of Mindanao one night. The diesel engine failed, and after working on it for hours and not being able to get it to run, he attempted to swim to shore, a distance of two or three miles, to get help. The men he left behind on the boat said that after he had been swimming for several minutes they heard two shots. Knortz had his pistol with him, and it is presumed he fired the shots to drive away attacking sharks. His body was never recovered. This presumption leaves the manner of his death unconfirmed, a situation not uncommon in clandestine operations.

The *Captain Knortz* pulled in at the expected time, and we sent off the second load. Something had to be done and done in a hurry, because the lighter was in a very bad position and every minute it was in danger of being bombed by Japanese planes. One hundred tons of equipment is not considered very much in normal operations, but when one is fifteen hundred miles inside enemy lines, that much equipment is more valuable than a warehouse full of gold. Moving it was imperative. While we were pondering our next move, the *Liberty Belle,* now free of the sandbar, hove into sight. With that launch plus the *Millie,* which Fertig and Smith had taken to Esperanza and which had just returned, we were able to tow the lighter upriver to Amparo and anchor it in a secure, secluded spot. From there the three launches ran shuttle service to the depot, and within twenty-four hours the cargo was reasonably safe.

I began to separate our equipment from Fertig's while Evans went upriver to Esperanza. He wanted to set up an infirmary immediately because Fertig had told him of the deplorable health of many civilians and guerrillas. The Agusan valley is a malaria sector, and 75 percent of the population was stricken with this malignancy. It was after he saw these people that Evans realized he was needed on Mindanao as a doctor.

"Besides," said Doc, "with you around, Smith doesn't need me as a radioman."

Two days later, I was satisfied with my separation job and had our equipment stowed, ready to be loaded on the launch that would carry us to Samar. Or so I thought. I contacted Major Smith by radio for instructions, and he told me to bring all our gear to Esperanza, where it was to be unpacked, further separated, and repacked. Why? Who's to know? The guerrilla army worked just like the regular army.

Lt. Leonard L. "Bob" Merchant, Fertig's chief transportation officer, had our goods loaded onto the *Liberty Belle,* and we headed up the Agusan to Esperanza. En route he told me why and how this boat had found herself high and dry on the night we arrived. Merchant, in preparation for moving the lighter from the bay into the river, had carefully placed channel markers at the Agusan's mouth early on the day of the landing. He had driven stout bamboo poles deep into the sand along the shallows, attaching flares to their tops as he went. The flares were bundled rags saturated with coconut oil, the local substitute for oil lamps. They would burn for hours. Helping him was one of his most capable Filipino boatmen, Saltoro.

"Do you know what these are?" Bob had asked Saltoro.

"Oh, but yes, Sair!" he replied. "They are *lamparos* to show to you the way to Butuan, Sair, when you bring to the river the big raft!"

"That's right, Saltoro. Now, here's what I want you to do. When it starts to get dark tonight," Bob said very slowly so that Saltoro would understand, "I want you to get Sanchez and Domero and the baroto, and paddle out here and light these lamparos. Do you understand?"

"Oh, but yes, Sair!" Saltoro answered.

"Then tell me what you are to do." It was important to have a Filipino repeat instructions to be sure he understood them, for they would rarely admit that they didn't understand.

Saltoro repeated Bob's words, and Bob was satisfied.

After the lighter was cut loose from the submarine, Bob watched as the pilot of the *Liberty Belle* turned to port, then to starboard, then to port again—obviously unable to find the lighted markers.

Bob yelled to Pedro, the pilot: "What the hell are you doing? Get this tub up the damned river!"

"Yes, Sair!"

Again the *Liberty Belle* yawed, dragging with it the lighter and the *Captain Knortz,* which was serving as a pusher.

"Where the hell are ya goin'," Bob shouted. "The freakin' lights are over there to the left." Merchant, an Air Corps mechanic who had not surrendered, never quite got the hang of this port and starboard stuff. He never docked a boat; he "parked" it.

"No, Sair! They are not our lights! That is not the right way, Sair!"

Bob had a short fuse. "Get the hell outta the way. I'll drive the bastard!"

Merchant grabbed the wheel and lined up on two lights he saw. He still doesn't know what or where those lights were, but he promptly put the *Liberty Belle* up on a sandbar.

He was livid! Fertig would bust his ass for this one. But now there was nothing to do but get the boat off the bottom. Luckily the lighter and the *Captain Knortz* were floating and could proceed at least as far as Butuan.

Two days later, Saltoro sheepishly approached Merchant.

"What the hell happened to the lamparos?" Bob asked.

Came the reply: "But, Sair! I could not find Sanchez and I could not find Domero and I could not find the baroto. So, Sair! I swam out to the lamparos, but my matches, they got wet, and they would not light!"

Esperanza was a much smaller town than Butuan. A large house built of imported milled lumber was the dominant structure. It was surrounded by another large house, made of bamboo, and about twenty smaller bamboo houses of various sizes. The large bamboo house held one wealthy Chinese family. It was large because there were many children, and also because it housed a store, and space to be rented to the government for the post office. The Chinese householder was a rich man of the community.

All the other inhabitants labored for the wealthy or operated farms as sharecroppers. They did, however, have a democratic form of government, and the peons elected a mayor, a council, and a judge. They also had a vote in the provincial and national elections. And they paid taxes!

In prewar times, the large, lumber-built house was the abode of a wealthy Filipino family. From here the Filipino ruled his fief, controlling the lands and the people for miles around. He had recently moved his family farther upriver and loaned his house to Fertig to use as his domicile and headquarters. It was a one-story affair on stilts, as were all the houses, and about thirty feet square in plan, divided into several rooms. It boasted a veranda with wooden front steps instead of a bamboo ladder. Fertig could be found on this veranda most any time he was in town, and it was here I witnessed his sternness with his men.

A Filipino had been brought in on a desertion charge and was promptly ordered confined by the colonel. The prisoner appeared to have been beaten, and Fertig ordered an investigation into possible mistreatment. I later inquired as to what would happen to the deserter and was told he would be brought to trial before a court-martial composed of Filipino officers who were members of the guerrilla forces. The trial would be in accordance with the Articles of War of the U.S. Army. As for the beating, I was told that if the prisoner had, indeed, been beaten, those responsible would also be court-martialed. This was proof to me that the guerrillas on Mindanao were not bandits, as many of the guerrillas groups had become, but were a disciplined military unit. I was not in Esperanza long enough to learn the results of the court-martial.

Fertig had the best of a meager lot of food and drink, furnished by the wealthy Filipino, who recognized the importance of the guerrillas as protectors of his domain. Fertig's troops did not share in this larder.

About twenty-five Americans formed the cadre of Fertig's headquarters. Many were Air Corps men from Del Monte Airfield. Among them was Capt. Robert V. Ball. Captain Ball was chief signal officer, in charge of the radio network. A new bamboo house held the net control station (NCS), through which contact was maintained with Australia. The NCS also had irregular contact with several radio stations scattered throughout Mindanao and surrounding islands. Some, located on mountaintops, afforded a view of the seas, and they reported Japanese shipping movements to Fertig's station, to be relayed to U.S. Naval Intelligence in Australia. Setting up a similar network of coastwatcher stations was our mission on Samar. Other stations moved with the commanders of the infantry patrols roaming the island. At best, these stations operated intermittently, since they had only homemade radios, which were extremely unreliable. With the equipment delivered by the *Narwhal*, these stations would now be able to maintain regular communication.

Ball's station required a 110-volt electrical supply. Since electricity was a luxury not found in these small towns, a power unit consisting of a twenty-kilowatt generator driven by a diesel engine had been installed. It had been moved there from a nearby mine that was abandoned upon the arrival of the Japanese. Since this was more power than the station needed, a crude distribution system carried electricity to Fertig's headquarters and to most of the other houses to provide electric lighting.

Captain Evans converted one building into an infirmary and immediately had a thriving practice, with both soldiers and civilians as patients. His medical skills were sorely needed here, and it was not realistic for him to go north with Major Smith and me as a radioman.

Although he never said so to me, Smith was unsure of my ability to take charge of his radio network. In fact, I believe he was concerned about my ability to cope with the lifestyle we would have to endure and the dangers we faced. Would I "crack"?

While he knew the Philippines and the Filipinos, and was as tough as they come in combat, Smith knew nothing about radio operation. He needed to feel secure about his chief signal officer. True, Doc Evans was no more experienced in jungle life and guerrilla combat than I was, but by having both of us with him, there was a good chance that one of us would be able to handle the job without folding.

Together, Smith and Fertig found the solution. Evans would stay with Fertig, serving both as a doctor and as chief signal officer. Ball, who had gone with Smith to establish the radio station overlooking Davao harbor nearly a year ago, would go north with us.

I was quickly impressed by Captain Ball. He was a handsome man with dark, curly hair, five feet, ten inches tall, and weighing in at 150 pounds, despite the privations of the past two years. He wore a permanent smile. At twenty-eight years of age, he was my senior by about five years. Somewhere he had acquired a supply of vitamin pills, and he made a religion of getting a pill three times a day. He was also an exercise fanatic, jogging and doing push-ups every day. This despite the rigors of a normal life in the jungles.

"Good health is the most important thing for survival in the jungles," he said.

He had a philosophy for budgeting his time, and he taught it to me: Always leave something to do tomorrow.

"In the first place," he said, "it's too hot to do too much work in any one day, and in the second place, with nothing left to do, tomorrow would be a dull day."

Ball and I became fast friends immediately. This was important, for we would soon be spending twenty-four hours a day together. Even a solid friendship could grow thin under those conditions. I looked upon him as a mentor, and he accepted me as a student.

Some of his lessons, I'm sure, kept me alive. He taught me how to recognize which nuts, berries, and roots were edible and which were highly poisonous. Sometimes the differences in appearance were minute—tiny, but not insignificant. Another very valuable lesson came out of his descriptions of his skirmishes with Japanese patrols. When describing ambush setups, he always stressed the need to ensure that a back door was available for emergency evacuation; following this guidance saved my neck on occasion months later.

Fertig was quite aloof and mingled only with a very few select people— old prewar friends, rich Filipinos, politicians. Major Smith, obviously, moved in with Fertig. Doc Evans, though "only" a captain, became a part of Fertig's select group. I rarely saw the colonel, and even more rarely spoke with him.

I joined the lower-echelon Americans for dinner on my first night in Esperanza. Here I had my first taste of *ginamoose,* a slurry of boiled baby shrimp, small enough to qualify as maggots. I've never eaten maggots, but they couldn't taste worse than ginamoose. We also had the usual boiled rice and some boiled fish. I was quite disappointed because I figured that the more Americans there were around the place, the better the food supply would be and the better tasting the meals. Not true.

Almost all of the Americans had their own huts, equipped with native housekeepers of the female variety, and Ball was no exception. After dinner we all went to Ball's house, where I shared with them one of my precious bottles of Mount Vernon whiskey and a bottle of apricot brandy. This was the first stateside booze they had tasted since the surrender. Realizing that the two bottles would not last long, they augmented the bar supply with several bottles of *tuba,* a native drink made of the juice that seeps from a freshly sliced coconut bud. Every day the tuba gatherers scale the palm trees, cut a thin slice from the end of every available bud, and hang a small bamboo bucket under it. The next day the gatherers scale the trees again and collect the juice in a larger bamboo bucket. The bud by this time has formed a thin covering over the wounded end, so another thin slice is taken and the process is repeated.

Tuba has the alcoholic content of beer for the first day. Then it quickly becomes more potent. After five days it is mixed with red beans—what the natives call chili beans—and makes good pepper vinegar. If it's allowed to stand for ten days and then triple distilled, it will run a gasoline engine.

With gasoline in short supply, the guerrillas ran their precious few trucks on tuba alcohol. This would sometimes create a problem. Men would take a truck on an assigned detail with plenty of fuel to complete the mission and return to base. It was not unusual for them to siphon the fuel from the tank along the way to mix a few highballs. Then an SOS would be sent to the nearest distillery for more fuel.

We had a great, though raucous, party that first night. I related the latest news from the outside world. They had heard and read a lot of the propaganda passed out by the Japanese, which was counter to equally exaggerated Allied propaganda being beamed to the islands from short-wave radio stations located in California and Australia. It was only human for them to believe some of it. They were happy to hear first-hand news from someone from the outside whom they considered reliable, as well as my tales of the Allied victories on the islands between Australia and the Philippines. Not so the estimates of when the Americans would get to Mindanao.

My bottles were empty, and I was quite thirsty after my long discourse on the news. I was scared of the water, so I decided to try the tuba. Its bouquet was audacious, and its full-bodied flavor somewhere between presumptuous and nauseating. I did not like it. However, several months later, when all the whiskey I had brought with me was gone, I would sit in a coconut grove and wait for the gatherers to come down from the trees, there to drink the fresh, sweet, yellow nectar of the coconut bud. Even though it was full of dead flies, it was delicious.

After our night of revelry, I was not in shape to find my way to my quarters, so Ball rigged up a place for me to spend the night at his house. I had not yet gotten my head to my makeshift pillow when I felt the building shake. *That must be a water buffalo scratching its back against one of the poles supporting the house,* I told myself. I didn't think more about it and went to sleep in a drunken stupor.

The next morning, Ball said to me, "Did you feel the earthquake last night? That was a big one!"

Sorting our gear again and getting it ready for the trip north took only one day. I then had idle time to fill until we were to depart for Samar. I spent some time helping in the radio room. My skill as a radio operator had become rusty, so I needed more practice at sending and receiving messages. I also worked with the code clerks, teaching them new code systems, keyword programs, and cipher security. The most important factor in cipher security is to not use the same code keys too frequently. Cryptograms can be broken quite easily if one studies a sufficient volume of messages that use the same code keys.

Leaders of the guerrilla infantry units and of the perimeter guards protecting Fertig and the Esperanza headquarters came and went, taking with them columns of *cargadores* bearing a share of the arms and ammunition we had brought in. I talked to as many of them as I could, for I needed to learn something about Philippine geography. Of Mindanao I learned a lot, but that would not help me where I was going. Unfortunately, I got precious little information about the islands to the north. No one I talked to had ever been to Samar.

I was also very concerned about the seeming indifference to the Japanese presence. There was so little discussion of the Japanese Army and its deployment that after several days I became quite complacent; in fact, there were days when I completely forgot that I was fifteen hundred miles behind Japanese lines. Apparently the Japanese were not as unconcerned as the guerrillas seemed to be, and they formulated plans to attack. Soon after the Smith party departed for Samar, the Japanese went after Fertig in force and drove him from Esperanza to a spot deeper in the jungles. By that time, however, the equipment we had delivered had been well dispersed throughout the guerrilla organization, and none was lost.

To Samar

CHAPTER 4

In addition to us three Americans—Smith, Evans, and me—our original party out of Australia included nine Filipinos who were also soldiers in the U.S. Army. They had been handpicked by Colonel Whitney from the ranks of the First and Second Filipino Infantry Regiments in California. All had volunteered for this duty. Most had lived in America for many years and had been educated in the United States. They could speak Visayan and Tagalog—the dialects of Samar and Luzon—in addition to fluent English. They were well-trained radio operators, though lacking in practical experience. This they would soon get. Most were also schooled in gathering intelligence information as espionage agents.

Our coastwatcher network was assigned to cover the sea-lanes between Leyte Gulf and Manila Bay. Geographically, this is a vast area—some ninety thousand square miles. However, there were only about six hundred sea-lane miles to be watched, and there were ten passes or straits through which most of the traffic would pass. We calculated a need for ten stations, located on high ground and with good visibility of the seas, to give the area adequate coverage. In addition, we would need another three floating stations as spares to take over the operations of stations forced to move by Japanese patrols or bombers. We also would have to establish a few stations that would operate only to send out intelligence information. Although we would recruit local radio operators to man some of our stations, our network would not be complete until we got more men and equipment from Australia. We anticipated a rendezvous with the *Narwhal* in several months, after our main station was established on Samar, to augment our supplies and our manpower. The military operating as it does, our game plan was changed from time to time, and our network never grew to planned size.

Major Smith wasted no time in getting parts of our network established. Sgts. Aniceto C. Manzano and Crispolo C. Robles were sent to Bondoc Peninsula in southern Luzon; Sgt. Restituto J. Besid with Pvts. Querubin B. Bargo and Andres S. Savellano went to Masbate Island; Sgts. Gerardo A. Sanchez and Daniel B. Sabado headed for Cebu Island; and Sgt. David D. Cardenas and Cpl. George R. Herreria went with us to Samar.

Captain Ball had replaced Doc Evans on our invasion team. We added Capt. Armato Arietta, a Filipino member of Fertig's organization, who would serve as a courier and espionage agent, and Lieutenant Royer, who had combat skills, especially with .50-caliber machine guns. Two of these weapons were our heaviest armament, for the 37-millimeter antiaircraft guns had stayed with Fertig. Royer would command our mighty army in the event of skirmishes with the Japanese.

Also with us were five Filipinos who proved to be very important to our well-being. Each had his individual skills, which would be used repeatedly in the days ahead. Rodriques, about sixteen years old, was our cook, trained in this skill by Major Smith's wife, Kathryn, when he was their houseboy on Masbate Island. Rodriques stayed with Fertig while Smith was in Australia, and rejoined Smith each time he returned to the islands. He kept us as well fed as possible, given the raw materials he had to work with. Whenever we got a pig to cook, I would hang around his stove as he rendered the lard from the animal. This process produced succulent, crisp, tasty snacks of pig flesh that really hit the spot. Rodriques would use the lard to fry whatever he could—usually fish or camotes, and, on rare occasions, chicken, eggs, or bananas.

Catalina was the major's bodyguard. He had sailed with Smith to Australia, where he joined the U.S. Army as a private when Smith accepted his commission. He returned to Mindanao with Smith, went with him to establish the coastwatcher station overlooking Davao, fought alongside Fertig's troops when Smith returned to Australia, and rejoined him on his return to Mindanao. Medium in height and stocky in torso, Catalina was ever alert to Smith's safety and watched over him like a Secret Service agent would the president of the United States. I felt that he was watching over me, too.

Ochigue and Madeja were two soldiers we borrowed from Fertig. Both were seasoned veterans of guerrilla warfare and had reputations for courage and loyalty. In addition, Ochigue was one of the few Filipinos big and strong enough to carry a Browning automatic rifle (BAR) and two bandoliers of ammo. Madeja, though smaller in stature, kept pace with him.

Federico, another teenager, had been with Captain Ball so long that they were bonded like father and son. Federico took care of Ball's equipment and belongings, while Ball took care of Federico.

Lt. Gerald S. Chapman, an Air Corps man who had joined Fertig's guerrilla force, was transferred to our party. He was already on northern Samar, operating a coastwatcher station overlooking San Bernardino Strait and reporting to Fertig's NCS. Chapman was guarding one of the most critical shipping lanes with antiquated, worn-out radio gear. We planned to furnish him with new equipment when we got to that area and then incorporate his station into our net.

On 23 December we moved downriver to Butuan. With a passenger list of twelve, two crew, and ten tons of arms, food, and radio gear aboard, the *Millie* was overloaded and no longer maneuverable. She obviously was not the vessel we needed for the perilous trip we faced. Also, we wanted to load more ammunition and food. We needed more boat.

In Butuan we located the *Malaria,* a seventy-foot Japanese fishing vessel captured by the guerrillas. Powered by a one-cylinder diesel engine, she was capable of five knots per hour on the sea. She had an aft engine house and a deep hold amidships. When we met with heavy seas the second night out, we learned that she also had a split keel. *Malaria* was not her original name, but she was so dubbed because of the way she shook due to the slow "pub, pub, pub" of her one-lung engine—like a person suffering the chills of malaria.

In Butuan we loaded some rice and fish for our next week's larder. Of more importance, we loaded a twenty-five-pound sack of salt. The major knew how important this would be in trading with the natives in the jungle mountains, where this commodity did not exist. It was almost worth its weight in gold. We also took on the only available meat—two live chickens. Are chickens generally capable of emotional expression? These were. They huddled together, heads low on the breast, each consoling the other.

"Hey, Ball! Look at those chickens! I think they have more sense than we do," I said. "They seem to be scared of the run we're making!"

"They're right," Bob replied. "A man's a damned fool to try to run through these straits. Each time I sail from one island to another I swear 'Never again!' but here I am trusting my luck once more. I've covered damned near every square inch of these islands, and now I'm starting my second round. Ever since I escaped from the Jap camp I've been chasing the greener grass on the next hill. I don't suppose I'll ever find it until I either get picked off or somebody comes around and takes me back home."

I had to agree with him about the grass on the next hill. I had only been on Mindanao three weeks, and I was already looking for the pastures of Samar. But I didn't grasp the fatalistic thought of the rest of his statement, for I had not been exposed to any real danger as yet, and, like any other inexperienced GI, I considered myself indestructible.

Fertig sent the following message to Brisbane on 23 December 1943:

> CMS AND PARTY CLEARED MY HEADQUARTERS TODAY.
> SHOULD CLEAR 10TH MILITARY DISTRICT BY DECEMBER 25.
> WE WILL MAINTAIN DAILY SKEDS [radio contact] WITH HIM.
> LAUNCH PATROLS INTERCEPTING ALL SAILBOATS BETWEEN
> LEYTE, BOHOL.

Whitney's endorsement on this message was sent to General MacArthur on 24 December: "Note enemy patrol activity between Southern LEYTE, BOHOL and Northern MINDANAO. Trip north of Smith party will be a hazardous one."

On Christmas Eve, the Smith party was heading out of the Agusan River into the Mindanao Sea. As dusk seemed to rise in pursuit of the sunset, we chugged away from Butuan, taking advantage of the cover of darkness to sail the first leg of our northward journey. By hugging the west coast of Mindanao's Surigao Peninsula, we could stay reasonably clear of the Japanese convoys. Our main concern was the Japanese patrol boats sniffing like hounds around the shores for traffic such as ours. If we were discovered, our defense would be evasion by slipping into an inlet—if one was available— or engaging them in battle. The latter was not a desirable alternative, because we lacked the speed and maneuverability of a gunboat. The *Malaria* was an old, wooden tub with virtually no speed and no cannon. Her armament was our few rifles, submachine guns, and BARs, topped off with two .50-caliber machine guns.

Dinagat Island, our first relatively safe landfall in the Surigao Strait, the ocean gateway to the southern Philippines, was ninety miles—some eighteen sailing hours or more—away. We would have to put in somewhere en route.

Major Smith was running the show, Ball was helping him call the shots, and we had a captain on the boat. With nothing for me to do, I stretched out on the roof of the cabin and watched the moon playing hide-and-seek with me through some lazy clouds. I thought about home, my family, my friends—what I might be doing if I was home on this Christmas Eve. And, for the first time since I got involved in this mission, I realized what I was doing to the folks at home. Especially to my Mother and Dad! I was one of three sons they had sent off to war, and now I had suddenly dropped completely out of existence! My weekly letters to them, even though delivery was slow, would no longer arrive. Sure, I had written home and said they might not hear from me for a while, but now I suddenly realized that the censors would not pass a letter like that. I was gone! Missing! Dead! Mother and Dad, what have I done to you!

I slid off the cabin's roof to the rail—and puked. For the first time in my life, I was concerned about someone else's feelings. A snot-nosed, selfish young punk had suddenly gotten a conscience.

Four months later the mailman handed Mother an envelope from the War Department. I will never be able to sense the anguish with which she tore open its flap, or the relief she felt on reading its contents. Inside was a letter from me—the last one I had written—all about the deeds of derring-do in the cauldron of Brisbane, Australia. Another letter was included. It read:

Dear Mr. and Mrs. Stahl:

This is to inform you that the writer of the enclosed letter is alive and well. Although you cannot correspond directly, you may send one letter per month, not more than two pages, and one photograph, in a sealed envelope bearing his name only, without rank. The letter must be enclosed in another envelope addressed to: U.S. War Department, Section 14A, Washington, D.C.

Letters from him will be forwarded to you as conditions permit.

To maintain security and to insure his safety, it is imperative that you inform no one of this matter.

Uncle Sam was very kind. He also forwarded my last letter to my girl-friend with the same covering letter.

Letters of this sort were being delivered all across the United States to parents and wives who were almost out of their minds with fear and worry. In most cases, the fears had little substance. For some, though, the horrors proved all too real.

The servicemen and women who actually faced combat seldom gave thought to the red-handed demon of war and what it could mean on a personal level. Such thoughts had a way of unnerving a warrior and could lead to indecision at a critical moment. It was *after* the action that the combat veteran had time to think about what was already history and what could have gone wrong. Even then, we found it best not to dwell on such negative daydreams.

I was awakened by shouting. Captain Arietta was calling to a native onshore, asking him to bring a baroto out to the launch. With our hit-or-miss navigation, we knew only that we were somewhere along the coast of the Surigao Peninsula.

Soon the native was beside us, and after talking to him Arietta said, "There's a barrio along the shore, Bolo-Bolo-Domei. This fellow says there are no Japs there, and it will be a good place to hide today."

We were able to pull into a small inlet near the barrio, where we anchored and concealed the *Malaria* as best we could with banana and palm tree leaves.

The local citizenry were Christians, and with them we celebrated Christmas Day, exchanging gifts of our "I Shall Return" chocolate bars and cigarettes for their native chocolate, *calamai*. Their chocolate had a coarser texture and a stronger flavor than did our domestic chocolate bars. It came in bowl-shaped chunks, molded in halves of coconut shells.

The sudden arrival of Americanos was cause for a special celebration this Christmas Day. From nowhere a pig appeared—alive, but not for long. Soon it was slaughtered, dehaired, scrubbed, and on a spit over a fire. Meanwhile, the women of the barrio gathered herbs, roots, leaves, and whatever else went into the making of the sauces for *lechon,* a pork barbecue dinner. Rice, *palay,* was pounded in a large wooden mortar and pestle, then winnowed and put to boil. After several hours of preparation we sat down to a unique Christmas dinner, the likes of which I would never again see.

"Sat down to dinner" connotes tables, chairs, silverware, china, table-cloths, napkins—the works. All of these were nonexistent. The meat of the pig was sliced off with a bolo, the same one that had been used to kill the pig and to chop the kindling for the fire. The sauces were contained in halves of coconut shells and were ladled out with spoonlike pieces of bamboo, as was the rice from the clay cooking pot. All this was placed on a fresh banana leaf—the plate—and eaten with the fingers while we squatted on the ground. The Filipinos had a way of hunkering down with both feet flat on the ground and their butts resting on their heels. I don't recall ever seeing an Americano who could do this; we just sat down and crossed our legs in front of us.

No matter. The food was delicious. The sauces, made from herbs and roots, gave a unique flavor to the meat, regardless of the part of the pig it came from. And, to my delight, the sauces disguised the taste of the rice. And the best part: no dishes to wash.

Of course, these villagers knew about the wonders of tuba, and one chunky lad brought out the village supply, slightly overaged, which he doled out in the customary coconut shell equivalent of stemware. The locals seemed to think we lacked the social graces of polite guests when we declined the third or fourth servings. However, it was rather rank, and besides, our minds were still locked on the narrow passage of the Strait that awaited us with the setting of the sun.

Throughout the day we all rested as much as possible, and as darkness approached that evening we stripped the camouflage from the *Malaria* and crept out to open water, waving good-bye to the residents of Bolo-Bolo-Domei, our Christmas dinner hosts and hostesses. Storm clouds were blotting out the pale blue of the sky with dark gray masses that looked solidly ominous. With apprehension and mixed emotions, we watched them gather above us. A storm would make our next leg more difficult to sail, but the gray, elemental confusion might very well conceal us from the Japanese patrols. If we could maintain a five-mile-per-hour pace (almost flying, for our doughty *Malaria*), we could reach Dinagat before daylight.

The rains came. And so did the winds. And that is when we discovered the rift in the *Malaria*'s backbone—the split keel. At times it felt as if we would separate into two pieces of boat, but the captain yielded to the wind and the currents, enabling our noble vessel to remain intact. Thoroughly drenched, we reached Puerto Princesa on Dinagat Island and were able to put in and camouflage the boat before dawn. We lucked out, since the Japanese had left the town the previous day.

Eighteen miles to the west, across the Strait, lay Panaon Island and the southern tip of Leyte, where Lt. Truman Heminway had set up a coastwatcher station as a part of Fertig's network. Major Smith and Captain Ball loaded new radio equipment and codes in a baroto and paddled across the Strait to deliver them to him. Meanwhile, the rest of us spread out our cargo to dry it as best we could. Smith and Ball returned late in the evening, and since none of us had slept in more than twenty-four hours, we stayed in Puerto Princesa overnight.

Seventy miles of open water across Leyte Gulf separated us from our primary destination—Samar Island. We had no choice but to cover this leg by sailing day and night, hoping we would encounter no Japanese patrol boats. We would be passing Homonhon Island on our starboard side, but we could not risk a stop there, not knowing whether it was occupied by friend or foe.

We sailed at dawn, and everyone on board kept a constant watch for other vessels. Royer had set up our .50-caliber machine guns on deck and had spread belts of ammunition on top of the *Malaria's* engine house to dry. The ammo had gotten wet on the run to Dinagat, and we were afraid it might misfire. The combination of the sun's heat plus the heat from the engine did a good drying job—so good, in fact, that some of the rounds started to explode. When the first few rounds went off, almost simultaneously, we were all sure we were under attack. Only after we could locate no enemy vessels in sight did we realize what was happening.

Again we were lucky, for we encountered no enemy patrols and reached a small bay at barrio Guiuan on Samar Island late on the night of 27 December. Only a narrow peninsula and bay separated us from the town of Pambujan Sur.

As the year drew quietly (we hoped) to a close, we had at last reached our new home. True, we were at the southern tip of Samar, and our appointed destination was at the northeast corner, overlooking San Bernardino Strait and the Japanese using that route; but at least we were now on land and no longer exposed on the open sea.

Establishing Smith's Network

PART 2

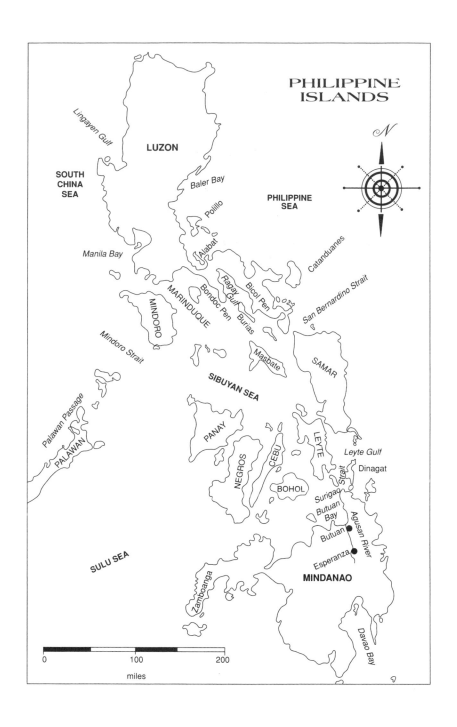

PHILIPPINE
ISLANDS

LUZON

SOUTH
CHINA
SEA

Lingayen Gulf

Baler Bay

PHILIPPINE
SEA

Polillo

Manila Bay

Alabat

Catanduanes

MARINDUQUE

MINDORO

Bondoc Pen

Ragay Gulf

Bicol Pen

Burias

San Bernardino Strait

Mindoro Strait

Masbate

SAMAR

SIBUYAN SEA

Palawan Passage

PANAY

LEYTE

Leyte Gulf

NEGROS

CEBU

Dinagat

PALAWAN

BOHOL

Surigao Strait

Butuan
Bay

Butuan

Agusan River

SULU SEA

Esperanza

MINDANAO

Zamboanga

Davao Bay

0   100   200

miles

To Palapag Mesa

CHAPTER 5

Ten tons of equipment does not sound like much, but put it into a small vessel in a shallow bay with no chance of unloading at a dock, and it becomes a large problem. Add the strong possibility of being spotted by enemy aircraft and bombed off the map, and the problem becomes enormous.

At Guiuan we began to off-load our cargo onto outrigger canoes so small that they would have difficulty staying afloat with more than two people aboard. It was a slow operation, but that was just as well, for we still did not know if we could stay there. Were we in friendly territory? If not, we would have to reload our gear in a hurry and "haul ass" to more friendly climes.

Major Smith made his way to Pambujan Sur to determine the local attitude toward Americans. Meanwhile, Captain Ball and I proceeded to stash our equipment on the shore. It was a relief to have Smith return with a favorable report. We emptied the *Malaria* of its cargo and sent it on its way south. Then we began loading our gear onto a beat-up old truck to haul it over a mountain to another bay, where it was loaded onto a sailboat to cross the bay to Pambujan Sur. Repeating this process over and over made for a couple of sleepless days and nights.

Why didn't we sail right into the Pambujan Sur harbor? It had deep water up to its pier, and we could have off-loaded very easily. The answer is simple. We had to bide our time until Smith determined that we were welcome. More important, the Pambujan Sur harbor's narrow entrance could have been easily blocked, trapping the *Malaria*—and us. We would have had no escape route.

By 30 December we were established in the largest house in the town. Time for radio station MACA to hit the air for the first time. Ball, using one of our small radios, relayed the transmission to KAZ, the AIB radio station in Australia, through Fertig's station, KUS. I encoded the first message, saying we had arrived safely on Samar. We also tried to contact some of our net stations, but met with no success, because they had not had time to establish themselves at their destinations.

On 31 December a guerrilla leader, Maj. Manuel Vallei, arrived at our headquarters, along with several local politicians. Success in the islands depended in large part on a good relationship with politicians. We tuned in a news broadcast from San Francisco—the first news they had heard since the islands had fallen, except for the constant Japanese propaganda broadcasts. Seeing us—real, live Americans who had come from Australia—and hearing the news of the Allied offensive in New Guinea and other islands to the south brought tears of joy to their eyes! They had been waiting for General MacArthur to send THE AID, and it had finally arrived.

To show his appreciation, Major Vallei quickly organized a New Year's Eve party—a dance complete with live band in the local school building. Makeshift decorations were made and hung; a buffet of many varieties of native and Spanish delicacies was spread. And instead of having coconut oil lamps to light the festivities, the town's electric generator was fired up for the first time since 1942.

Of course, we had first choice of dancing partners, for if any man made a move toward any girl in the hall before we had selected our partners, he was ushered out immediately.

To climax the festivities, Major Vallei gathered the Americans together and said, "I have a surprise I have been saving for the first Americans to return here."

With that he led us to his house, opened his electric refrigerator, which hadn't been in operation since the generator had been shut down, and broke out a case of Coca-Cola.

"This was bottled in Manila," he said, "before the Japanese came, and I have been saving this one case for our first American guests."

Needless to say, the dance was over as far as we were concerned. Ball and I fought for the privilege of carrying the Coke to our house, where we had several fifths of stateside whiskey begging for a chaser.

It was a *very happy* New Year's Eve.

*　　*　　*

The New Year's celebration continued into the next day. Ball, Royer, and I were more than a bit hung over. Smith had soaked up as much of the booze and Coke as we had, but he recovered more rapidly.

The town of Pambujan Sur boasted an industry—a machine shop that used to supply parts for the mining industry. It stood idle now, except for reloading cartridge casings with black powder and lead bullets for Vallei's guerrillas. They had the tools to make arms. What they lacked was raw materials.

Major Vallei had one more surprise for us—a homemade cannon! Fashioned from a piece of six-inch cast-iron water pipe, it was mounted on a wheeled carriage. Vallei had the piece rolled into the town square, and after much ceremony he personally touched the flame to the fuse.

It went off. How it went off! Eager to demonstrate their military capability with a bang, the cannoneers had used too much black powder. When the smoke cleared, the cannon was intact—except for a split down the barrel from end to end.

The noise didn't do my headache any good, either.

We were still far from our ultimate destination, a position on a mountaintop near the north coast of Samar, on Palapag Mesa. There, in the jungles high above barrio Gamay, near the town of Oras, we planned to establish station MACA, our NCS.

Ball, Royer, and I had the happy task of manhandling our gear about a hundred miles up the coast to Gamay, and then up the mountainside to an uncleared site in the middle of nowhere. Smith had an equally difficult task. He had to deal with the *politics* of guerrilla warfare.

There were good guerrillas—and there were bad guerrillas. Some, like Fertig's organization on Mindanao, actively resisted the Japanese occupation and strove to make life a bit more tolerable for the Filipinos. Others were mercenaries who saw the Japanese occupation as an opportunity to rob and plunder under the guise of resistance. They operated, in effect, a protection racket, but only feigned protection.

The mercenaries quickly became enemies and warred against each other for control of portions of the various islands—the areas they wanted to loot. For the Filipinos, life under the heels of these robbers was little better than it had been under the control of the Japanese.

Part of our mission was to evaluate the guerrilla bands, then try to combine the worthwhile groups under a common command. Selecting a commander acceptable to all the guerrilla chiefs on an island was rather difficult. Egotists all, each was "the best" and therefore felt he should be the overall leader. Our trump card in this game—our power play—was the promise of THE AID, a submarine loaded with arms and ammunition, which we would call for if they would cooperate with us and with each other in subversive activities against the Japanese. We offered them arms for the price of unity of purpose—ultimately under our direction.

On Samar there were only two guerrilla organizations worthy of consideration. Major Vallei controlled the southern portion of the island, and was not against a cooperative effort—if he could control the whole island. The northern portion of the island was controlled by Capt. Pedro Merritt. Captain Merritt was a mestizo born of a Filipina and a U.S. Army black man of Spanish-American War vintage. Merritt was not about to give up his domain. He was not interested in surrendering his power on the mere promise of some arms to be brought in on a submarine that, to him, was nonexistent because he hadn't seen it.

Smith, our diplomat, spent much time during the next several weeks running back and forth between Vallei and Merritt, trying to resolve the issue. Meanwhile, Ball, Royer, and I struggled to move our equipment northward. We cleared Pambujan Sur on 3 January, leaving Sergeant Herreria there with a small radio as a rear guard. Smith also sent Sergeant Cardenas to the west coast of Samar to observe shipping on the Samar Sea and to keep us informed of any Japanese land activities while we were establishing the main station.

Some gear was shipped in three *bancas,* small sailboats, moving along the coast. Royer, Ochigue, and Madeja each rode one banca, armed with BARs. Each boat carried about a thousand pounds of gear. The rest of our equipment went by land. Four *carabao,* water buffalo, and their owners were hired to pull heavily loaded vehicles—two carts and two sleds. We still had the truck we had used earlier, but its engine objected to the diet of alcohol it was being fed and was very unreliable. The monsoon season had begun, and with it our labors were multiplied. The constant drizzle made the road feel as though it had been greased, and the bridgeless stream crossings became deeper and more treacherous. The truck wallowed in the jellied mire or tobogganed from the road. We soon found it best to depend on the carabao carts and sleds and on cargadores, who backpacked heavy loads mile after mile on the one-lane, muddy road running close to the coast. Reverting to methods long since rejected in America, we abandoned the truck.

Our train of cargadores resembled an old African safari, some with

Carabao and cart for moving cargo. *(U.S. Army Military History Institute)*

backpacks, others with loads balanced on their heads, still others with heavy loads suspended on long poles with a man toting each end. Although the constant rain made life generally miserable for us, it did have a plus side. The carabao sled runners moved more easily in the mud, permitting heavier loads. Yet, if we covered five or more miles in a day we were happy.

Which is worse—clothing saturated with rain, or clothing saturated with sweat under a poncho? I soon got a native-style buri palm leaf hat, a wide-brimmed woven affair that, like an umbrella, shed the water from my head and sent it down to my shirt. I folded and packed my poncho for future use during lesser rains.

Thirty miles up the east coast of Samar sits the town of Borongan, and it proved to us that the "bamboo telegraph" worked well in the Philippines. Before we started moving north the people of Borongan knew we were coming, and when we arrived they were ready for us. This town was in Captain Merritt's area, and he had ordered a reception that would outdo that at Pambujan Sur. Whether it did or not is debatable. We enjoyed the food, the drink, and the fellowship. What we needed, however, was an assemblage of volunteers to help us in our move.

Despite our transport problems, we encountered some very wonderful and loyal people in Borongan. Here lived Mrs. Emma McGuire, the Filipina wife of an American mestizo who had lost his life in a motorcycle accident in 1942. She knew where her husband, who had been the manager of a mine, had hidden some equipment back in the hills when the invasion began, so she led us to one of his caches, where we found what we would need in our camp—a diesel engine and a ten-kilowatt, 110-volt generator.

We had brought with us a big, clumsy, but *powerful* radio, one with a fifty-watt output. According to Doc Evans, that was enough power to reach Australia from anywhere in the islands. It was this monster that required a 110-volt power supply. When we left Australia, our equipment included several small, gasoline-powered generators, two to supply 110 volts and the rest to charge six-volt storage batteries. During a test run on Mindanao, one of the 110-volt generators had thrown a connecting rod, making it useless to us. We left it with Evans for spare parts.

We were glad, therefore, to get this spare power supply. We were not overjoyed, however, to add another ton to our hauling burden. A smaller rig would have been our choice, but we were shopping in a tropical jungle, not at Sears.

Mrs. McGuire fed us three good meals a day during our stay in Borongan, her table always adorned with foods from her capacious larder of prewar canned goods. I loved her for her vittles, for she served a variety of mixes and sauces to conceal the taste of that hated staple—rice. A few weeks later she moved up to our camp with her family and kitchen staff. What a blessing! Few people have remained in my memory as solidly as Mrs. Emma McGuire. She had been Miss Philippines in her younger days, though by this time she had spread to amazing proportions.

Dr. Arturo Victoria was another helpful Boronganian. He and his wife were extremely knowledgeable and furnished us with many lively conversations during our short stay. He took on the chore of furnishing us with medical treatment, something we sorely needed and deeply appreciated. Amazing to me was that he and his family spoke none of the Filipino dialects in their home. The only languages allowed within its walls were English and Spanish, and their children were extremely fluent in both. Of course, they all spoke Visayan, too.

We dismantled the diesel engine as much as possible, removing the two flywheels and miscellaneous parts. Still, the cast-iron block assembly weighed more than five hundred pounds. The cargadores suspended it between two long poles, and four men shouldered the ends of the poles to carry it. Each flywheel, weighing about two hundred pounds, was also slung from poles, with a man shouldering each end. The miscellaneous parts were backpacked. The ten-kilowatt generator, unlike those manufactured with today's technology, was large and heavy. It could not be easily dismantled, and required a two-pole sling arrangement. Twenty men, working in shifts, were needed to move the engine and generator.

Of course, "McGuire's Monster," as we had labeled the recently acquired diesel engine and generator, required additional cargo: diesel fuel. Coconut oil burned well in diesels and was universally used for this purpose. We picked up three large drums of it in Borongan, and these, suspended from stout poles, required six more bearers.

We did not have a permanent team of cargadores. Almost daily we had to recruit a new crew from a local town or barrio to move us farther up the road. To protect us from a surprise attack by a Japanese patrol, we sent out an advance scouting party of three or four soldiers, led by Captain Arietta. This party would also recruit laborers—sometimes, I fear, with a bit of "persuasion."

The cargadores and the carabao teamsters were paid daily. They were afraid to accept our real Philippine currency lest they be caught with it by the Japanese and be unable to offer a satisfactory explanation for where they had gotten it. But they accepted our APA currency, even though we were passing out higher-denomination bills than the Japanese ever printed. Some of our large-denomination currency was later known to have been used by the Japanese troops.

Each evening during the move, Ball or I would hang a makeshift antenna and set up a radio to make contact with Australia, relaying through Fertig's station on Mindanao. We used a small, portable set for these contacts, the kind of radio that would be used by our satellite stations. With three or four watts of output, the transmitter was barely powerful enough to send a signal to Fertig's station, now more than two hundred straightline miles away. In addition, we tried to contact our agents, who had gone their separate ways from Mindanao. They did not respond to our calls.

We were also unsuccessful in contacting Sergeant Herreria in Pambujan Sur, where our safari had begun. While we were at Borongan I decided to return there to determine the problem. This was not an unthought-out decision on my part. We still faced forty miles of sloughing through mud to reach Oras, where the road, such as it was, ended, and then thirty more miles on a muddy trail to Gamay. But Mrs. McGuire had a motorbike, and if I could get it running I could use it to return to Pambujan Sur—and then ride all the way to Oras on return. This would be much better than hiking.

I was able to get the bike started, and set out the next morning, arriving in Pambujan Sur later the same day. Deep in the recesses of the condensers, resistors, and tubes of the radio at Pambujan Sur I found a broken wire. After I connected the ends together the radio worked.

But another problem had developed on my trip south. The clutch was slipping on the motorbike. My knowledge of the mechanics of motor vehicles and engines of the gasoline and diesel varieties was almost nil. I could fix radios, but machinery had me buffaloed. Major Vallei had a mechanic who spent three days making the repair. It would have been done in an hour in America, but speed was never the order of the day in the Philippines. There was always "mañana."

The repairs completed, I returned to Borongan, arriving around dusk. The rain, instead of being a slow, constant drizzle, had become torrential. It rained hard for about a week, making it impossible for me to travel northward. I divided my time between Dr. Victoria's and Mrs. McGuire's homes so that the burden of feeding me did not fall too heavily on either family. After a few days I had read all of their old magazines and books, and time hung heavily on my hands. I knew that Ball was waiting for me to help him—in Oras or somewhere. There was still lots of work to do.

It was the rain that had made the jungle on these volcanic islands. Through the aeons, the dripping moisture had eaten away at the lava rock, slowly chipping it into bits of sand and dust until, eventually, there was a pocket of soil that could nourish a seed. This was the start of the lush forests in which we hid and carried on our coastwatching. The rain. The ever-lovin' rain. The rain that made our lives a soggy struggle as we tried to haul our tons of equipment and supplies up the slippery trail that we chopped from the jungle. It was the rain that slowed the Japanese patrols, just as it slowed us. It was the rain that chipped away at our strength, our energy, and our determination, just as it wore down the lava rocks. The rain was our enemy and our ally.

Finally the torrents of rain diminished to a slow drizzle once more. I hit the road. It was a mess of muck. Many times that day I slid off the road and found myself knee-deep in mud. In one spill the motorbike was on its side completely under water and silt.

I got to Oras the next day. Despite the rain, Ball had somehow moved the equipment out of Oras to Gamay, and from there to the base of the mountain. I spent the night in the home of the mayor of Oras.

Early the next morning a runner from Borongan arrived with a note from Dr. Victoria. It read: "The Japs landed here yesterday about one hour after you left. They were looking for you and your party. We directed them to the south." Thanks, Doc, for sending them the wrong way. By the time they get to Pambujan Sur and back up here, we will be well hidden in the hills.

But what about Herreria? He was in Pambujan Sur with a rifle, a radio, and a duffel bag full of U.S. Army clothing and gear. Would warning of the impending arrival of the Japanese reach him by bamboo telegraph in time to escape? There was nothing I could do but hope and pray—and wait.

Ten days later he arrived in our camp. He had set up his radio station about a mile to the north of Pambujan Sur, on a bluff about a half mile from the coast, giving him a view of any passing ships. From there he could also see the inlet to the Pambujan Sur harbor. When he saw the Japanese launch entering the harbor, he and the two soldiers Major Vallei had assigned to him abandoned the camp and took off to the west into the jungles. After the Japanese left, Herreria returned and found his camp intact. This experience unnerved him, and he packed up his equipment and came looking for us.

Meanwhile, Sergeant Cardenas had run into a hotbed of Japanese activity on the west coast of Samar. His station was captured before he was able to get it operating, but he, fortunately, was able to escape and make his way to our location.

Herreria was not unnerved for long, however, nor was Cardenas intimidated by his experiences. Together they soon headed north to the Manila area, where they became one of our best operative teams. En route they tangled with the Japanese and lost their radio equipment, but managed to avoid capture. While in the Manila area they each made several trips into the city, where they were able to penetrate the Japanese headquarters and bring out much valuable information. They carried this information to Sergeant Robles on Bondoc Peninsula, from where it was radioed to us and relayed to GHQ.

Major Smith had divorced himself from his diplomatic duties long enough to reconnoiter northern Samar and select the site for our station. He was somewhat familiar with Samar, for as a mining engineer he had worked on Masbate Island, located immediately to the west across the Samar Sea. From there he had, on occasion, visited Samar.

Smith selected Palapag Mesa, on the northeast corner of the island. Rising to thirteen hundred feet above sea level and faced with steep mountains, it provided nearly perfect terrain for protection from attack. It lay between almost impenetrable jungles to the north and the south for several miles in each direction. At the base of the mountain to the west was the town of Catubig. We could be warned of any Japanese approach from that direction by runner. The east face of the mesa was almost a sheer cliff, easily defended, Ball and I agreed, but a bitch to scale with our equipment.

An overgrown trail led from Gamay to the top of the mesa. The first mile back from the coast was flat, then the mountain began abruptly. We had to hack the growth away with machetes to make it usable. The steep trail whipped back and forth across the face of the mountain, much like the path of a switchback railroad. From the top of the cliff, a four-mile, fairly level path led to the site.

Of course, during our backbreaking labors up the mountain, the rain continued. The trail up the mountainside was a three-foot-wide slough. In the dry season the cross slope would have been reasonably flat and stable, but now there were about six inches of gooey soil underfoot, resting on a sloping base of volcanic rock. With each step we would slide toward the downhill side of the path. We could not use carabao to haul loads up the trail; it was much too narrow, and a carabao is not a sure-footed Grand Canyon mule. Everything was moved on the shoulders and backs of diminutive, but surprisingly strong, Filipinos. With a really heavy load, they would gather together to the task, grunting, shouting, lifting, pushing, and pulling—all the while joking, laughing, and making a game of their toil. They lost much of that esprit de corps when moving the diesel engine and the generator, though.

Meanwhile, the site was being cleared and bamboo-and-thatch structures were being built. Although Captain Merritt resisted Smith's efforts at guerrilla unification, he assigned many of his "subjects" to the task of helping us get situated. Had he not been embroiled in a territorial battle with Major Vallei, he might have been a much greater asset to the American cause. Unfortunately, he could not swallow his pride.

Our equipment moved up the mountain at a rate of about one ton a day. I stayed in Gamay, dispatching the cargadores with their loads, while Ball and Smith received, sorted, and placed things as they arrived at the camp site. Ball and I kept in touch by radio, using the voice capability of the sets and speaking in the only tongue we knew—English.

This wasn't as risky as it might seem, for the radios were not very strong and the Japanese were far away, we hoped. This was, though, a violation of all army regulations. But—Hey! Will the MPs come from Australia to arrest us? We sort of hoped so. Meanwhile, Royer, Ochigue, and Madeja led small groups of soldiers on patrol to protect us from unexpected visitors.

Occasionally I would wander a few miles up or down the coastline, where several farmers had cleared *caingains,* small truck patches. I was surveying their crops. When would the maize and *piños*—pineapples—be ripe? Food was always on my mind. It wasn't exactly an obsession, but it wasn't far from one, either. And then, one day, I made a quite different discovery.

Why an illiterate farmer, living along a dirt road, the front of his hovel facing the ocean and the back bordering on a jungle, would have such a device is beyond me. Nevertheless, amid a pile of junk behind one of the farm houses I found a commode. A "porcelain pony"! For months I had been wearing two side arms. One was a .45 automatic, the other an entrenching shovel. Diarrhea was my constant companion, and I used that tool many times a day. Wouldn't it be great, I reasoned, to have an outhouse complete with a flush commode in our camp? I couldn't wait to make a deal with the guy. The negotiations were weird, since neither of us spoke the other's language, but somehow the commode became mine. What a joy! I felt like a man who had just rediscovered "The Lost Dutchman" mine or a buried chest of jewels in an inherited basement. Real American civilization had been unearthed in this primitive jungle.

I sent it up the trail on the shoulders of two cargadores. Soon Ball was calling me on the radio. He was chuckling.

"Bob," he giggled. "I'd stay away from the major for at least a week if I was you. By that time maybe he won't shoot you." In the background I could hear Smith raving.

Crestfallen and embarrassed by my own lack of thoughtfulness, I returned to my chores, vowing to restrain my creative urges in the future. Just the same, it seemed that Providence had smiled on me at the time.

Certainly, after these many years, our campsite has reverted to an indistinguishable part of the jungle. But somewhere among the trees, the vines, and the rotted remains of past vegetation lies a moss-covered plumbing fixture, a monument to my stupidity.

Smith's savvy showed in the location he had selected for our station. At about a thousand feet above sea level, we were not at the absolute top of the mountain. To the south, several square miles of land rose about two hundred feet higher than our camp. It was a veritable rain forest, and here the jungle moisture collected and sent a small stream—the beginning of a mighty river, I suppose—through our camp. The stream provided us with drinking water, bathing water, and laundry water—in that order—as it flowed along. His savvy also showed in the layout of the camp. He ordered construction of a shack for radio operations, a cookhouse with a mess hall of sorts, and individual lean-tos for the officers—himself, Ball, Arietta, Royer, and me. And, of course, there was a dormitory for the enlisted men. He knew we needed some privacy—a chance to get away from each other for part of each day, even though we were confined to a cleared area of less than a half acre. He also ordered a pit toilet to be built. It did not feature my treasured commode.

You may have noticed that I just listed myself with the officers. Before we left Mindanao, Colonel Fertig had cut orders making me a second lieutenant in the U.S. Forces in the Philippines (USFIP). In our situation this was quite necessary, for the class distinction between officers and enlisted men was very important to the Filipinos. An American who was not a commissioned officer was automatically considered by the guerrillas to be the lowest of the low—a misfit to be ignored completely. There just were no capable American military men who were not of rank. It was also important for an American to outrank the Filipino guerrilla leader he was dealing with at the time. (This may cause some confusion for the reader, who will find the same American carrying a different rank at various places in this book.) I found myself voicing a personal promotion to captain, major, or colonel when my situation dictated. I had a problem when I encountered Lt. Gen. Gaudencio V. Vera, but we'll get to that later.

Station MACA

CHAPTER 6

Before we left Brisbane, Major Smith had chosen "MACA" as our call sign. The letters represent the way MacArthur scrawled his initials on papers: "MacA." Smith was not the military sort, but he had quickly recognized the importance of skilled maneuvering in Army politics. Kissing up was rife in the services, in the AIB, even in the guerrillas. He knew he had to do it if he wanted to get what he wanted and needed—adequate supplies and good manpower.

Although Bob Ball or I had set up a small radio each evening as we worked our way northward on Samar, station MACA did not become stationary until the second week of February 1944. "Temporarily stationary" would be a more apt description.

We weren't completely moved in, but we had set up the fifty-watt transmitter and the diesel engine and generator we had hauled from Borongan. We had lots of extra wattage available from our generator, so, like Fertig, we ran electric lights into our few buildings. Overhead, and certainly in full view of any curious Japanese airplane pilots, was the antenna, stretching about a hundred feet between two tall trees. Our location near the top of the highest point in the area was fine for transmission and reception of radio signals, but it did not do much for concealment. This was a problem at all of our stations.

One by one our satellite stations came on the air. We had established time schedules for contact with each of them, but we soon realized that they were not in as secure a position as we were and might not find it safe to call us at the scheduled time. Therefore, we maintained a continuous watch on our assigned frequencies. This meant that Ball or I had to sit in front of the radio from 6 A.M. to 10 P.M., awaiting a call. The headphones grew very heavy.

We, of course, had other operators with us. They had been taught to send and receive Morse code in the AIB camp in Australia, but they were inexperienced. So many stations—Army, Navy, and civilian—communicated on our assigned frequencies that the interference was, at times, horrendous. It was not unusual to hear a very powerful stateside station "working" an equally powerful station halfway around the world. They would blanket the frequency, burying the signals of our low-powered radios. Little could be done except wait until they ended their transmissions, strain again to hear the MACA call, then vary the signal's pitch ever so slightly to make it different from the pitches of the other signals. This was not taught in school. It was a skill learned through experience, and our operators learned rapidly.

Ball and I worked out a deal. Occasionally, one of us would do double duty, working the whole shift, while the other took a break. I liked ocean bathing, so I would often hike down the mountain to the coast, where I would ride the waves and lie on the beach—not a tan, sandy beach like those I knew in New Jersey, but a black, sandy beach, for these were volcanic islands. Ball would head for a quiet spot in the surrounding jungle, take to a book, and get away from it all. These were our simple pleasures on a day off.

Sergeants Robles and Manzano had reached Bondoc Peninsula on Luzon. We made our first contact with them, station MAA, on 28 January 1944, when we were still on the move. One day later we successfully contacted Sergeant Besid and Privates Bargo and Savellano, station MAB, on Masbate. Theirs would be strictly a watcher station, observing shipping on the Sibuyan Sea.

Sergeants Sanchez and Sabado, station MAD, reported sporadically. They were on a military intelligence mission to Cebu, an extremely "hot" area. Cebu City was a transportation center, the site of a major airfield, and a port of call for cargo ships. Learning the makeup of the cargoes was their main interest. A radio contact with us to send out this information had to be brief, for their peril increased in direct proportion to airtime. We wanted to respond to them promptly on call, no matter when.

The satellite stations had ATR4 radios, a collection of resistors, condensers, vacuum tubes, and wire packed as neatly as possible into a compact unit—about the size of a lunch bucket for a person with a huge appetite. While the unit itself was quite portable, moving a whole station in a hurry was not easy. One problem was the power supply. The ATR4s used a dry-pack battery furnishing low voltage for the filaments of the vacuum tubes and a higher voltage to push the signals out into the ether. The battery packs weren't large—they were smaller than the radio—but they weighed at least five pounds each. With a one-time life of about five transmission hours, the average watcher station would eat them up at the rate of one every ten days. A six-month supply was a ninety-pound burden.

An even bigger problem was the antenna. Before we left Mindanao, Larry Evans, our expert radio technician, gave us instructions on antenna installation. According to the latest theory, the most efficient signal output would be obtained by using half-wave antennas, that is, antennas cut to a length one-half the wavelength of our signals. Operating on five frequencies between 4,010 and 8,020 kilocycles would require five different antennas, varying in length from 58 to 116 feet. Also, the desired height was at least thirty-five feet off the ground, and the ideal orientation was perpendicular to the direction of the station being contacted.

So much for theory. Our agents cut wire about eighty feet long, strung it between the two biggest trees they could find, regardless of direction, and hoped for the best. Technical perfection was a luxury that was not ours. When it came time to "haul ass," they yanked the antenna down if they had time, or left it there for posterity. They could always find more wire.

It was a foregone conclusion that, in the event of enemy attack, we would have to destroy the massive radio installation we had built up. So, we had to set up in advance alternate locations we could move to if we were driven from Palapag Mesa. A few days after MACA was in operation, Smith and I went on a burial mission. We went off into the rain forest to set up the first of these alternate sites. The location of these sites was to be known only to him and me. We could not take cargadores or guards (except the ever-faithful Catalina, the major's bodyguard). Ball had no need to know the locations, for he would be leaving us soon to go north. Royer spent much of his time along the coast road, so he would be one of the first to face enemy invaders and also among the first to be captured if the Japanese came. It would be better for him, and for us, if he didn't know where we were.

Smith and I each carried a pistol, rifle, machete, jungle hammock, backpack of food, and entrenching shovel—mine for two purposes, for I still had diarrhea—chronic, bordering on dysentery. We rigged up two small sleds, like miniature carabao sleds, and on them we pulled the three pieces that constituted a 3BZ radio, the two storage batteries required for its operation, a gasoline-powered generator, two five-gallon cans of gasoline, and three cans of real pesos.

Surprisingly enough, hacking through the rain forest was not all that difficult. Being on a mesa, we were on what amounted to gently rolling terrain. Wet, yes, but the overhead growth was so dense that the smaller, bush-type plants had difficulty surviving. By working our way around the bigger trees and the fat vines that climbed them, and by chopping down some underbrush, we were able to cover several miles per day. We took turns in the lead, one chopping away with his bolo while the other two followed behind, pulling the sleds. On my first turn at the front, my left arm (I'm a lefty) soon told my right arm that it was time for it to get to work. In less than a day I was ambidextrous with that wicked blade.

As we went along we had to mark the trail with something distinctive. In a month our makeshift trail would again be overgrown, so the usual trailblazing signs, such as notches on trees, would then be indistinguishable. We had no choice but to use pieces of cloth tied around vines. We could only hope that if we ever had to use the trail we would remember to remove the markers en route.

On our third day out, the major sat down on a fallen tree and said, "OK, boys. This is it."

I sat down beside him. I didn't say anything to him, but to myself I said, This is *what?* This spot didn't look any different from any other place I had seen in the last three days. I didn't argue, for I was glad for the rest.

We cleared a small area, perhaps twenty feet square. Smith and Catalina went off about fifty yards beyond the clearing with the sleds and the radio gear. There they quickly built a sort of shelter with palm fronds to conceal the equipment and protect it from the rain. Meanwhile, I moved off in another direction and dug a hole about two feet deep and large enough around to take a five-gallon can. This was difficult digging, for the ground was mucky humus threaded with a thick mat of twisted tree and plant roots. Into it went one of our three cans of pesos. I drove a stake close to its heart and marked it with a piece of cloth. Not far away I buried another can, and, still another short distance away, a third can. I had just put sixty thousand pesos—thirty thousand American dollars—into an earthen safe-deposit box.

When we were leaving the burial site, I asked the major, "What made you pick that location?"

Came the reply, "I was tired of walking."

Months later I recognized the value of the money I had stashed in the jungle. I was in the Army's finance office in Manila, collecting my back pay—$3,088.22 for fifteen months' work. I had buried the equivalent of twelve years' pay! I often wonder what happened to that money. I know *I* never dug it up.

On the way back to camp, I stumbled and fell against a bush. As I fell, a branch hooked onto my eyeglasses, pulled them off, and flipped them into the underbrush. I was so nearsighted that I had to put my glasses in a special place each night before going to bed so I could find them by feel in the morning. Had I been alone I would have been in deep trouble. Fortunately, Catalina found them rather quickly, and we continued our hike.

This event gave me something to ponder as we trudged along. My vanity had kept me from being fitted with GI glasses. They were, to me, ugly. Nature had not endowed me with great looks, and I didn't need any adornments that made me look worse. In the bustle of getting ready for this venture, it had never occurred to me to get an extra pair. This was an example of my poor planning. Now here I was, fifteen hundred miles from the nearest U.S. Army unit, with one pair of civilian glasses, not even the sturdy, unbreakable kind. Should something terminal happen to them, I would still be able to operate a radio, but how would I locate it? I thought of trying to have another pair sent to me if a submarine ever brought us more supplies. That was a great idea, except that my medical record in Australia did not include the information from an eye examination and fitting. How would they know what prescription to send me? From that day forward my glasses were treated with tender, loving care.

Major Smith was not one to sit around idly. Two years of roaming through the jungles with the constant threat of an unknown Japanese presence had him constantly looking over his shoulder for trouble. He maintained a mental picture of what lay in any direction from his present position, be it in a camp or on a trail, and he was almost animal-like in his maneuvers. One thing was certain; he would never be caught off guard. This constant alertness was, no doubt, a big factor in his survival. He didn't itch for a fight, but he had no fear of a battle if one was in the offing.

His ability to read the thoughts and the intents of the Filipinos was no less uncanny. He could seemingly pick up the scent of an enemy, despite protestations of loyalty. He had determined that Major Vallei, the leader of the guerrillas in the southern portion of Samar, was loyal to the Americans and to his Philippine homeland. As a fighting force, Vallei's guerrillas might not decide the outcome of future hostilities against the Japanese, but at least they would be on our side. Smith was not so sure of the loyalty of Pedro Merritt and his army.

"Bob," Smith said to me, "Let's go down to Catubig and talk to Merritt. Let's see what he's doing."

"OK, Major," I replied. "Ready whenever you are." I wasn't exactly thrilled about slipping and sliding down and then clambering back up a tortuous ten-mile trail, although I had never been to Catubig and was interested in seeing the town. But he was the boss, and I did his bidding.

Catubig was situated on a stream that became a full-fledged river in a hurry by collecting water rapidly from the mountains and jungles surrounding Mount Capotoan and its encircling hills. The river was navigable by small boats for about twenty miles and spilled into the Philippine Sea at Laoang, near the east end of the San Bernardino Strait. Here Captain Merritt spent most of his time. His organization didn't include a headquarters, so his headquarters was wherever he happened to be at the moment.

The town was a collection of about twenty bamboo shacks situated along the west side of a road that paralleled the river. Their fronts faced the road, and their backs abutted the river. Extending from the rear of each house was a catwalk on stilts leading to an outhouse, which discharged directly into the water. It wasn't hard for me to see why Filipinos had such a problem with disease, for this river was also the source of water for cooking and drinking. The connection between drinking water, sewage, and disease never seemed to register with the natives.

What interested me most, I suppose, was that there was no door on the outhouse. This, too, I soon learned, had a purpose. One could see when it was occupied and should await his turn. The catwalk and the outhouse were so rickety that they would not bear the weight of two people.

Nature has a way of protecting people from themselves. At least twice a year this river was subject to flooding. Then it would churn its silty bottom, overflow its normal five-foot-high banks, and spread the fertilizer-rich water and silt across acres and acres of nearby fields. Thus, the toilets were flushed and the crops fed.

Merritt learned through the bamboo telegraph that we were coming.

When we arrived, preparations were already under way for a fiesta. The Filipinos used any excuse to have a fiesta, and we didn't object. This one, however, did not end on a happy note, for the meeting between Smith and Merritt was anything but cordial.

Smith was seeking a commitment from Merritt to join in a united front against the Japanese. He knew that Merritt preferred to keep his options open. Merritt would go with the side that did the most for him, and he hadn't yet heard the Japanese offer. Smith had also warned me that this meeting might become a confrontation, and that I should be ready, as he put it, to "fight our way out."

This was the first time I had seen Merritt, although I had heard much about him. When I saw him, his ancestry was evident. He was much larger in stature than any Filipino I had yet seen. His skin color and negroid facial features belied any Filipino heritage. Filipinos are brown. He was black. In addition, he had the curly hair of an African Negro.

Smith and Merritt discussed the pros and cons of the guerrilla movement, and of the American aims, for a long time. I noticed that both ate a considerable amount of the available food, yet neither touched any of the alcoholic drinks to be had. I had partaken of both. I also noticed that each of them was becoming more exasperated by the other's position.

Finally, Smith stood up and slid his hand down to his pistol. I stood up and cocked my tommy gun.

"Listen to me, you *black bastard!*" Smith shouted. "I'm in control of this island. If you do anything to try to stop me, or to help the Japs stop me, I'll cut your balls off and ship them back to Africa!"

Not one of Merritt's men moved. None of them wanted to face a tommy gun or the BARs held at the ready by Ochigue and Catalina on the edge of the group.

From that day forward, Merritt gave Smith very little help. Nor did he ever give him any trouble.

A few weeks before we had embarked from Darwin, the *Narwhal* carried a small intelligence party to Mindoro Island. This party, eight men with Maj. Lawrence H. Phillips, Corps of Engineers, in charge, set up a small coastwatcher network overlooking the shipping lanes from Manila into the South China Sea. Their NCS call sign, ISRM, was politically equivalent to ours. It stood for "I Shall Return—MacArthur."

Late in February, the *Narwhal* was to deliver more men and supplies to Phillips. Phillips did not keep the appointment, for he and several of his men were ambushed and killed by the Japanese while taking a bath in a stream near the rendezvous site. The submarine discharged its cargo and passengers on Mindanao a few days later instead.

As usual, the full story of the ambush and its possible cause will never be known. However, Phillips and his men may have been careless in maintaining code security, sending too many messages using the same keys. Information gathered from Japanese files after the war indicates that the enemy had broken his codes and knew of the planned supply mission.

We did not learn of Phillips's death immediately. He was in direct contact with GHQ, so we had no code system established with him. We noted, however, that we were no longer hearing his signals on the air, and were more or less prepared for the sad news brought to us by a courier returning from the west coast of Samar. The courier did not have any details, and several weeks passed before we learned how Phillips had died. Smith was the one most affected, for he had known Phillips in Australia. To the rest of us, ISRM was just another coastwatcher station that no longer existed.

I know it sounds callous, but to Ball and me this meant that we now had to expand our network to include at least one coastwatcher station somewhere in northwest Mindoro. We would have to spread our operators and equipment thinner so that the sea-lane from Manila to the South China Sea would be covered—and this meant sending men and equipment we could ill afford to give up.

By March 1944 we had a pretty smooth operation going. Our satellite stations were sending in many ship sightings. We had been able to recruit several native civilians who were radio operators for the Philippine postal system, sort of like our Western Union. It didn't take long for them to learn the Army's systems on the air. In addition, we had recruited a few brave Filipinos who undertook intelligence missions for us. The Japanese were not bothering us, and we were able to obtain food regularly from the natives.

Then our troubles began. The constant high humidity and moisture got into the bowels of our radio and shorted out critical parts. We had spare parts—condensers, resistors, tubes, wire, and a soldering iron to be heated in the embers of a very hot fire—and I was able to find the affected parts and replace them, but when the main transformer went out we were in trouble. We didn't have a spare. Fortunately, we had Benito Moya working for us. He was one of the radio operators we had recruited—

a very quiet little man with unlimited patience—a person who could sit down and "pick the fly shit out of pepper," and he undertook to repair the transformer.

For several days Benito unwound the wires inside the transformer, carefully coiling them so they could be returned to the core after the burned spot was found. Once he discovered and fixed the break, he painstakingly rewound the coils, layer by layer, each layer separated from the next by paper impregnated with a waxlike substance, until the transformer was whole again. Alas, the moisture got to it again and again, and he repeated the task several times until we decided it was a lost cause.

Without that transformer, our big radio transmitter was useless. And without that radio, we no longer had need for a 110-volt generator. McGuire's Monster, which had been so laboriously moved from Borongan to our camp, was no longer needed. As far as I know, it still sits somewhere in the jungle on top of Palapag Mesa, amid a tangle of decaying vines. Beside it lies a fifty-watt radio transmitter, next to a commode.

We had only one backup transmitter that was powerful enough to reach Australia with regularity. It was standard equipment in the Netherlands East Indies military units, so we labeled it "The Dutch Set." This radio resembled the ones I had built when I was a teenager and radio ham. It had a metal chassis on which was mounted the usual array of radio parts, and was faced with a piece of Bakelite through which protruded the knobs for tuning and operation, the markings for the dials being crudely drawn by hand. Its electrical power came from a generator mounted on a stationary bicycle.

We scoffed at this piece of equipment, calling it a piece of junk we were sure would never be of any use and wondering why we had bothered to bring it with us. We soon knew. Despite its crude appearance, "The Dutch Set" had one great advantage over its professional-looking American and Australian counterparts: it was waterproof! All of the guts of the set had been coated with a paraffin-like substance that was not affected by the heat of the resistors and tubes. Moisture was sealed out. It had another plus: its weird-toned signal was much different from that of American or Australian radios. Its signal cut through and overpowered competing signals, making us much more readable to the receiving stations.

We relied on this set while the transformer for our big radio was being repaired, and when that set was no longer operable "The Dutch Set" became our mainstay. Ochigue, Madeja, and Catalina did not like it. Because of their size and strength, they were called on to pedal the bicycle. When we were receiving a message, the pedaling was like riding a straight, level road, but when we were transmitting a message much more power was required, and the ride on the bicycle was "uphill all the way."

Once in a while, Federico or Rodriques, both wiry little fellows, would try to demonstrate that they, too, were strong and powerful by taking a turn on the bicycle. When they faltered, they were subjected to a lot of good-natured kidding from the bigger fellows. I think it was kidding, but I'm not sure, since all the jabbering was in Visayan. This was the sort of high-level entertainment that broke up what was otherwise a dull life for all of us.

In mid-April, Ball left us to go north to establish a radio station on the east coast of Luzon, about a hundred miles northeast of Manila, near Baler Bay. There, at the south end of the rugged Sierra Madre mountains, Maj. Bernard Anderson, a veteran of the Bataan fiasco, had organized a guerrilla army. He was in a very strategic spot for subversive activities against one of the largest concentrations of Japanese in the Philippines. Of course, this meant that he was in a most hazardous location as well. Ball would supply him with radio capability to get his intelligence information out to us and on to Australia, and also would be in position to arrange for a submarine rendezvous in the area.

On 2 May 1944, the extreme perils of what we were involved in came home to me. Sergeant Besid and Privates Bargo and Savellano, our team sent from Mindanao to establish a station on Masbate, were discovered by the Japanese. Bargo and Savellano were captured and executed. Besid escaped and later rejoined us on Samar. Until now, our "invasion team" had been intact. Suddenly my complacency disappeared. Although I had yet to see a Jap, I now realized that what happened to Bargo and Savellano, and to Major Phillips and his men, could happen to me.

When a young man thinks of combat, be it sports or war, he sees himself the victor, the hero. Never does he envision himself the vanquished—the occupant of an unmarked grave. Could this be why we continue to have wars?

We had planned supplies and manpower for the first six months of our mission. Now it was May 1944, and the U.S. Army was still dillydallying around far south of the Philippines. We had used up the supplies we had brought with us on the *Narwhal* six months earlier. Several radios had been captured by the Japanese patrols, our generators were wearing out, and we needed more arms and ammunition, medicine, cigarettes (we had been rolling our own cigars from native tobacco for months), and, above all, shoes.

For weeks we had been sending GHQ our shopping list of items. Finally someone in a cushioned chair in Brisbane decided we were due for a supply run. A rendezvous was arranged and accomplished; the *Narwhal* arrived in Gamay Bay on 24 May 1944. Aboard were twenty-two men and fifty tons of equipment.

Again we lucked out, for the Japanese were nowhere around when the sub arrived. We had no launches, no lighter. Instead, we had a sea full of large barotos shuttling between the submarine and the shore, each loaded to within inches of shipping water. But the weather was good to us; the sea was especially calm, and by dawn the cargo was spread along the beach close to the water's edge. The submarine was long gone.

Two *paraos,* large bancas, were anchored offshore, one to be loaded with men and equipment to move up the east coast of Luzon to Captain Ball at Baler Bay. The other was mine, for Smith had determined my schooling under him to be complete. It was time for me to graduate and go out on my own. He had decided that we needed a sub-NCS on southern Luzon to improve our operations in that area and to serve as an alternate NCS should MACA be lost to the enemy. This station would also be important in relaying Ball's traffic if he should be forced to use a low-powered transmitter, and it would serve as a relay station for radio stations being established by other guerrilla units on northern Luzon. The *Narwhal* had just delivered the necessary equipment. I was to take a penetration team to Bondoc Peninsula on the west coast of Luzon, about one hundred miles southeast of Manila Bay. With luck I could land near Robles's station. Smith and Royer would stay on Samar.

We picked through the equipment on the beach and loaded about five tons' worth on the parao destined for Ball. Before nightfall it sailed away, with six of the newcomers on board: Lts. Vincente V. Labrador and Carlos F. Ancheta; S.Sgt. Cipriano L. Miguel; Sgt. Pete L. Luz; and Cpls. Agrifino J. Duran and Rudolph B. Santos.

Another five tons of equipment were loaded on my sailboat. With me would go four newcomers: S.Sgt. Gerardo B. Nery, Sgt. Jack Montero, and Cpls. Eddie C. Holgado and Julio C. Advincula. In addition, I had "adopted" Ochigue and Madeja. If Smith could have his Catalina as a bodyguard, these two were mine.

While all the activity of loading the paraos was going on, a steady stream of cargadores was toting the other forty tons of gear up that tortuous trail to MACA.

Early on the morning of 27 May, we had the beach cleared of equipment. I shook hands with Charlie Smith, who had by now become one of my dearest friends, boarded the sailboat, and headed into a new life. I wondered if either of us would survive, or if we would ever meet again. I think Charlie had the same thoughts.

I think we both had another thought. Was my training really complete? I still had not encountered a Jap!

Among the twenty-two new arrivals were two Air Corps meteorologists, Sgt. William R. Richardson and Cpl. William Becker III. America's island-hopping forces had advanced to a point midway between Australia and Mindanao. P-38 fighters, stripped of their armament and fitted instead with aerial cameras, were beginning to map the area. Soon B-24s would be based close enough to reach the Philippines with a full load, drop their bombs, and return home. To the Photo Joes and the bombers, weather information was very important.

Richardson and Pfc. Jerry D. Pascua, another of our new men, set up a weather observatory along the east coast of Samar. They had to move frequently, for making weather observations required that they release hydrogen-filled balloons into the air daily to determine wind currents. Obviously, this activity drew attention to their location and aroused Japanese interest.

Corporal Becker, with Sgt. Raymundo E. Agcaoili and Pvt. Isaac Z. Aguila, went to Sorsogon, Luzon, to set up another weather station. They had problems similar to Richardson's and Pascua's, but they, too, succeeded in their mission.

Until now the Japanese had not paid much attention to northeastern Samar. They soon did.

Establishing My Network

PART 3

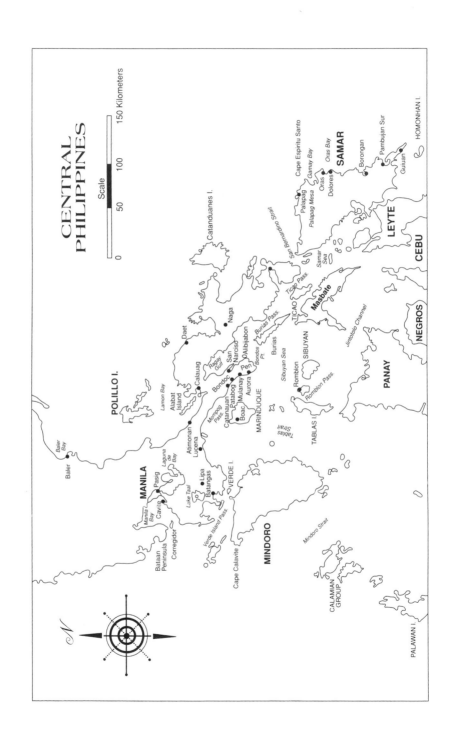

To Luzon

CHAPTER 7

We had a favorable wind at the outset of our voyage to Luzon. Within several hours we had reached the northeast coast of Samar and turned west toward the San Bernardino Strait. As we were rounding Cape Espiritu Santo we saw two launches moving toward Samar from the east side of Luzon. They appeared to be heading into the area we had just left—where the submarine had surfaced only a few nights ago.

I had two choices. I could proceed, knowing that Smith had observers watching the waters we were in and would be aware of the launches. Or, I could set up a radio on board, call MACA, and warn Smith. Our sailboat would pass as a normal native commercial vessel, we hoped. Using a radio would only draw attention to us. I decided to remain quiet, because getting established on Luzon was very important.

We moved into the current of the Strait. The Pacific Ocean feeds the South China Sea through the waterways between the various islands. East-to-west currents prevail, and the flow through the Strait runs for eighteen out of twenty-four hours in that direction. Even though we were becalmed for much of the afternoon, we were still making ten to twelve knots because of the current. As we were passing through the Strait I wondered if Lieutenant Chapman, located high above us on Luzon, was watching us.

By the morning of the twenty-eighth we were well through the Strait and in the pass between Ticao Island and the Luzon mainland. By noon the wind had died. We were again becalmed, a condition that was, I soon learned, a virtual certainty every afternoon. With little, if any, current, we sat in one spot for hours. The native crew sat on the stern, whistling at the sail. This, they said, would "call up the wind." Apparently the wind wasn't listening. When the captain sensed that I was getting irritated, he put a long oar over the stern and began to *leo-leo*—in the States we call it sculling. Back and forth he stroked the blade behind the boat. He knew what he was doing was useless, and so did I. Yet, he was trying. And, of course, it did no good for me to become irritated. My emotions didn't make the boat move.

This was exasperating, not to mention worrisome. Here we sat, within sight of land on either side, with no way of knowing who was watching us. I took all of my people below deck and left only the regular crew topside, not wanting to draw attention to ourselves by having many people on deck. Down in the hold, among the stowed gear, it was hotter than hell.

Finally the sun reached the horizon, and, as the air cooled, the breeze began to blow. Darkness allowed us to get up on deck, where we spent the night.

Morning came, and by my feeble navigational skills I calculated that we had covered thirty nautical miles in the past twenty-four hours. It was now the twenty-ninth, and we were in Burias Pass. By midday we

Banca used for interisland travel.

were again within sight of land on both sides—becalmed. A repetition of the day before. Back into the hot hold we went.

Bad navigation on my part put us several miles off course into Ragay Gulf that night. We maneuvered back to our planned course and rounded Bondoc Point early in the morning of the thirtieth. We were low on drinking water and considered trying to pick some up there, but the water was much too shallow for the parao to near the shore. We had no small boat, so someone would have to swim to shore, borrow a baroto, and bring out the water. When a pair of sharp eyes spotted a shark fin, we abandoned the swimming plan. We would do without water.

We sailed on, but before we lost sight of the Point a launch came out toward us. I had a premonition: *I was about to meet the enemy for the first time.*

The parao on which we were traveling was of rather crude construction. It appeared to be built on top of a baroto, a dugout canoe. With that as its base, ribs were added about three feet apart, and the hull was covered with wide boards. I think they call this "lapstrake" construction, but I may be wrong. I'm not a shipwright, nor am I a marine architect. I'm a landlubber trying as best I can to describe a boat I once rode in.

Just below the deck was a six-inch-high slot that extended completely around the perimeter of the boat. I suppose this was to ventilate the hold. Through this space ran the long poles to the outriggers. (This space soon had a much more important function for us.) The end result was a sailboat thirty feet long and eight feet wide, not counting the outriggers, with two masts and sails.

On seeing the launch, I immediately took my men below deck. I placed Ochigue at the center of the boat along one side. Here, through the ventilating slot, he could see and shoot at the launch should it approach on his side. Madeja occupied a similar position on the opposite side. Both had their BARs at the ready. The others were spaced at other points on each side. I told them all to remain absolutely quiet, and not to take any action unless I started it. My plan was to allow our captain to do all the talking and try to get us through without being boarded. Should this fail...

The launch pulled up alongside the outrigger on Ochigue's side. No breathing was audible in the hold of our parao. Through the ventilation opening, I could see four armed men on the launch. They were not Filipinos. I did not understand any of the conversation that took place between our captain and the person who boarded us from the launch. I did hear what I thought might be the accent of one who normally spoke Japanese, although I was not sure.

The discussion seemingly became more heated. Suddenly the hatch cover was lifted, and a head came through it to look below. The owner of the head had sealed his doom. Immediately, Ochigue began to spray the launch with his BAR. Madeja leaped to his side and opened up as well. All was quiet within ten seconds—a seeming eternity.

No part of my body, internally or externally, was *not* trembling. I had to appear to be a strong leader, although doing so required a superhuman effort. Somehow, despite the uncontrolled flow of adrenaline, I pulled it off.

I ordered the Jap dragged from the sailboat to the launch. But now what? Should we just set the launch adrift with its inanimate crew and hope that when it was recovered by someone we would be far removed? I wanted a more positive way of disposing of the evidence.

I dug through our gear and found some plastic explosive, a fuse, and a detonating cap. We set the explosive in the launch's hold at the base of the transom, rigged to go off in five minutes. We then started the engine, lashed the wheel, and pointed the launch toward the southwest into the Sibuyan Sea. It headed on an erratic, yet reasonably straight course. We heard it explode. We watched it sink. We cheered! But it was a hollow cheer, at best. None of us liked the narrow confines of the sailboat as a combat arena, least of all me.

It was not yet noon, so we still had some wind pushing us to the northwest along the coast of Bondoc Peninsula. The captain hugged the shallow waters offshore as much as he dared. I sat below deck with my binoculars glued aft through the ventilating slot. I was certain we had been seen and would encounter more problems.

Suddenly, around a headland several miles behind us loomed a Japanese naval vessel! I don't know what class or kind it was, but it was *big!*

"Head for the shore!" I screamed.

The captain turned to starboard and promptly ran aground. The crew and everybody else went overboard to push the boat back into deeper water. Meanwhile, the Japanese ship motored on its merry way past us, ignoring us completely. They didn't know or care that we existed.

"That's enough of this shit for me," I announced. "We're putting in *somewhere* tonight."

I didn't hear a dissenting voice.

But where? For navigation I had a 1933 edition of the *United States Coast and Geodetic Survey Chart of the Philippine Islands,* covering all the land masses and seas from Borneo and the Celebes Sea north to the Batan Islands, roughly a thousand miles. The scale was about twenty miles to the inch. It gave much information about the depths of the water in the major seaways, but didn't show any rivers, inlets, or anything else about the land. So much for detail. I also had a 1940-edition *Socony-Vacuum Oil Company Road Map*. Why that was published I'll never know, for there were precious few roads in the Philippines. This map, too, lacked any indication of coastal topography. My pocket compass rounded out my store of navigational equipment. I doubt that Columbus was equipped any better—or any worse.

With these navigational aids I had a fat chance of finding Sgt. Crispolo Robles on Bondoc Peninsula, Luzon, Philippine Islands.

The sun set. Dusk sped by in good tropical fashion. You could almost hear a clunk when night fell. To the northeast the dark mountains of Bondoc Peninsula were silhouetted against a light blue, starlit sky. Dead reckoning told me we were near the town of Mulanay and Robles's station, but was it opposite us, ahead of us, or behind us? I searched the profile of the mountains and noted a clue. Just ahead of our course, the mountains dipped to what could be a river valley. It was a chance, and had to be taken.

I pointed it out to the captain and told him to try to find a channel we could use to get close to the shore in that area. We moved in that direction and soon found ourselves in dangerously shallow waters. He dropped the sails and we began to pole the boat, now this way, now that, cautiously working our way closer to what might be a river.

Still afloat, we came to a mangrove swamp. We still seemed to be in a sort of channel, but I feared grounding the boat and decided to try to wade ashore. Madeja went overboard with me, and together we sloshed our way knee- to hip-deep through the tangle of mangrove tree roots. In this mass of foliage we were in what could be called absolute darkness. We had coated ourselves with insect repellent, but within minutes we were both covered with literally thousands of mosquitoes. They were in our eyes, our ears, our noses—we had to breathe through clenched teeth to keep them out of our throats. Loyal Madeja would have suffered through this torture with me forever, but I couldn't take it, and we returned to the boat.

Meanwhile, the captain had been checking the depth of the water around the boat. "Sair," he said. "We are in a wallow."

"What's a wallow?" I asked.

"It is, Sair, where the carabao take the bath. It is deep enough for our boat, Sair. We can go in here."

I doubted that we were in a carabao wallow here in the swamp. I suspect he used that term because he didn't know the English words "muddy channel." I didn't argue. He was the boss of the boat, and I allowed him to move closer to land. I wanted to get us and our gear off the boat, and if this was the way, great.

We were in a ditch of some sort, a path through the mangrove swamp that almost seemed to have been dredged. Slowly, cautiously, we moved inland. Soon we were clear of the mangrove trees, still afloat in a narrow but relatively deep ditch. In fact, the ditch was so narrow that there would have been barely enough room to turn the boat around to get out.

Still fearing that the boat would run aground, I told the captain to get as close to the bank as possible so that we could unload. This we did. Using the outrigger supports as a gangplank, we piled the gear on the riverbank. We were now on terra firma, and I already felt more comfortable, despite not knowing where I was or what might lie ahead.

My concern now was to conceal where we had landed. If our parao had been under surveillance and was now seen returning to the south, even the village idiot would know where we had debarked. I told the captain to move out of the river and continue to sail northwest for another day or so before returning to Samar. The captain was a pretty sharp cookie and understood what I was trying to do. He agreed.

I gave him a tip of a thousand pesos. Real.

Memorial Day, the thirtieth of May. The day for placing flags on the graves of departed veterans, and flowers on those of loved ones. On this day in 1944 such a hallowed spot beckoned to me, and although I was well aware of it, I managed to ignore it. It was not yet to be.

Benito Ampiloquio rose with the sun, slipped on his damp shirt and pants, and headed for the bay. He would net some fish, then return to his house for breakfast. His wife would have the palay pounded and winnowed by that time. After he finished eating, he would carry some of the rice and fish to the U.S. Army radioman who lived on top of the mountain three miles to the northeast of Benito's coastal barrio, Patabog. He would carry enough for three meals so that the radioman would not have to leave his station today.

As he walked along the path beside the river, the morning sun still low behind him, Benito noticed that the cogon grass had been trampled in one area. *Must have been some wild cattle here last night,* he thought. He made a mental note to bring his rifle, the rifle he had concealed from General Vera, tomorrow. Perhaps he could shoot one of the cows and drag it home to slaughter. It had been a month since he and his family had eaten *baca.*

He saw a man appear on the path a short distance ahead of him. The man had a rifle. He was not wearing the telltale cap of a Japanese soldier, so he must be a guerrilla. Benito gave no thought to fleeing, for he knew that if he tried to run the guerrilla would shoot him. The local guerrillas were as much to be feared as the Japanese.

On this morning, the soldier was Ochigue. They approached each other while Madeja stepped onto the path behind Benito, ending any chance of retreat. I watched from the tall stalks of cogon grass as they conversed. They were having difficulty, for Ochigue and Madeja spoke the Visayan dialect, while Benito spoke Tagalog. There are many dialects in the Philippines, and while there are some similarities, the vocabularies are quite different.

Sergeant Nery stepped up to join them, for he knew Benito's tongue. Soon he returned to my side. "Lieutenant," he said, "you ain't gonna believe this, but that fellow knows Robles, and also knows where he's at!"

I didn't believe it. No one short of a *saint* could be so lucky, and there wasn't a saintly bone in my body. I sent Nery and Madeja with Benito to find Robles and bring him to me. After yesterday's escapade I was taking no chances.

They returned before noon. I believe Robles was glad to see me. He and Sergeant Manzano had departed Mindanao in December, and Manzano had moved farther north soon after the two had gotten to Bondoc. Robles had been alone among the natives since January, and, being Americanized, he needed company. Yet, something seemed to be bothering him.

Benito had prepared a "buckwheation," a place to hide in the hills if the Japanese should appear. It, too, was three miles northeast of Patabog, but along a more southerly trail out of the barrio. A mile of dense forest separated it from Robles's station. A more visible trail near the hiding place led to the town of Mulanay, on the coast five miles south of Patabog. I told Benito I needed to use his hideaway for a short while. I had no idea if that meant a few days or a couple of months. He was glad to let us use it when I handed him a few .30-caliber cartridges for his rifle. I left to Nery and the others the job of moving our equipment and gear to Benito's hideout. It would be the location of our station, S3L, for the immediate future.

Robles led me to his station. From there, on 31 May, I contacted Smith by radio.

CHASED EN ROUTE BUT ARRIVED OK. ANDERSON'S MAN HERE SO WILL DISPATCH MONEY AND CODES IMMEDIATELY. WILL INSTRUCT HIM ON RENDEZVOUS WITH OTHER PARTY.

*   *   *

About two hours later, I received the following message from Smith:

GOOD GOING. CONGRATS. SEND TWO RADIOS TO ANDY. NIPS
ARE AFTER US. KEEP CONTACT WITH BALL.

The launches we had seen moving toward Gamay Bay when we were departing Samar had been loaded, as I suspected, with Japanese troops to go after Smith and station MACA. Smith was about to utilize one of the alternate sites we had prepared.

June was hell. But, in turn, I was to find out that so would be July…and August…and September…etc.

When I was on Samar with Smith I had the equivalent of a nine-to-five job. He called all the shots and made all the decisions. My only responsibility was to keep the radio station operating. Otherwise, I just did as I was told.

Now things were different. I was in command, in a situation where plans I made had to be changed almost minute by minute, or so it seemed to me. Smith was on the run, and he was on the air only sporadically. My station had suddenly become the NCS. Instead of simply sending information to Smith to be relayed with his big transmitter to GHQ, I had to find another route through the ether to Australia. I tried going through Fertig's station, KUS, on Mindanao. The Japanese were giving him fits also, however, and KUS couldn't be of much help to me.

That was only one of the problems. In addition, I soon had a daily flow of agents coming in and going out. I had agents losing their radios—or worse, being captured. I had stations coming on the air, only to disappear and never be heard again. I had really important ship sightings that I could not get through to GHQ because the Japanese were jamming my signals. The Japanese were using direction-finding equipment to locate my station. And guerrillas to the north were depending on my station to handle their radio traffic to and from Australia.

A young kid whose only responsibility as a civilian was to sell tires and household appliances to the retail trade suddenly was in over his head. For all the problems, however, there were two good things going for me. First, Bondoc Peninsula was not an important bit of real estate to the Japanese, so it was not occupied. Second, we had brought at least five hundred pounds of rice with us from Samar, so we would eat for a while.

General Vera

CHAPTER 8

It was about ten o'clock of a humid morning when Jack Montero came to the station. Gerardo Nery was operating the radio. Montero had gone to Mulanay the day before, shopping for *viands,* vegetables, and *manók,* chickens. He returned with neither. But he had a message.

"A 'General Vera' is in town and wants to meet you there," he said.

"Where is he?" I asked.

"At the schoolhouse. And so's his army."

I strapped on my .45 and slung my carbine over my shoulder, and we headed down the trail.

"We've got company," I mumbled to Montero. Spaced every quarter mile or so along the trail was a soldier standing in the bushes. There were probably others I had not noticed.

"You got *that* right, Sir," Montero replied. "There's lots of beady eyes on us. This could be trouble."

"Just stay calm—but be ready." I saw Montero feel for the clip in his submachine gun.

When we reached the schoolhouse, we found about twenty men lolling about. Their "uniforms" consisted of whatever they could find to provide coverage with some measure of decency. Some bore small arms, others had bolos strapped to their waists. One wearing a semblance of a military uniform and carrying a pistol approached me.

91

"I am Colonel Figueras, the chief of staff for the general," he said, rather haughtily. "Come. I will introduce you to him."

As Montero and I entered the schoolhouse door, someone yelled, "Attention!"

Everyone inside stood—except the general. He just sat sprawled in a chair behind the teacher's desk, toying with a pencil over a pad of paper.

What in the hell is this? I asked myself. *A rehearsal for a grade-B movie?*

Colonel Figueras said, "Lieutenant Stahl. I have the honor to present to you" (he pointed with arm extended and his hand palm up, and with a slight bow) "Lieutenant General Gaudencio V. Vera, commander in chief and judge advocate of Tayabas Guerrilla Vera's Party!"

Without standing, the general nodded, then directed us with his pencil to five seats, front row center. Obviously, he was expecting others to join us. He then passed an extended arm across the room much as would the pope from his balcony to the crowd in Vatican Square. Everyone sat.

My God! I thought. *With all my other problems, now I have a Hollywood grandstand psycho to contend with!*

Still seated, the general introduced the others at the head table. On his right was his wife; on his left his other wife. Seated at one end of the desk was his "friend." She was obviously the one he was screwing, for she wasn't hard to look at, while both his wives were considerably less well favored. Her name was María. Colonel Figueras took a chair at the other end of the desk.

I looked around. Behind me seated at the several rows of student desks were what appeared to be local townspeople. They could have been dignitaries. I had no way of knowing. More important, around the perimeter of the room armed men stood shoulder to shoulder, obviously there as a threat to me.

Now the general stood. It made little difference, for his head didn't rise much higher. He was about five feet, two inches tall, exceedingly thin, gaunt, sunken cheeked, hollow eyed. His teeth were much too large for his mouth, giving him a constant snarl. His eyeballs were very large, adding to his proper appearance as the madman he was. He stared at me as he spoke.

"Welcome to Bondoc Peninsula, Lieutenant Stahl. My guerrilla forces have kept this entire peninsula free of the Japanese. The United States Army and the Philippine Army may have surrendered, but *we* did *not* surrender! Bondoc Peninsula has not surrendered to the Japanese! We are still a free country!"

He went on and on. His troops had attacked the Japanese garrisons to the north and had "established a front, preventing the Japanese from moving down the peninsula." He was maintaining civilian government in all of the towns and barrios. His troops were enforcing the laws. And much, much more was claimed.

His tirade ended with, "And when my supreme commander, Gen. Douglas A. MacArthur, sends me enough guns, Tayabas Guerrilla Vera's Party will drive all of the Japanese from the Philippines forever!"

He sat down. There was a murmur of conversation throughout the room. I had no idea what was expected of me, so I just sat there and waited. Finally the general said, "Colonel Figueras. Bring in the proof that we have the power. Bring in the Americans we have rescued from the Japs!"

Figueras left, but he was back almost immediately with three new-comers—three light-haired, white-skinned Americans. They stepped up to me and introduced themselves in turn: George McGowan, Eldred Sattem, and Chester Konka.

If the general thought that his show would go on, he was about to receive quite a jolt. Ignoring the general, the four of us shook hands, patted backs, and began talking all at once, no one listening to the others. It was a bedlam that went on for about ten minutes. The three extra chairs in the front row were never occupied.

Everyone moved outside, where a table had been spread. Party time. Barbecued pig, many flavored sauces, rice, fried camotes, and fried bananas. My three new friends and I conversed through full mouths.

Soon George McGowan maneuvered me away from the rest. "Bob," he said. I don't recall George *ever*, in our more than a half year together, calling me "Lieutenant." "Bob. You got trouble."

"What do you mean?" I asked.

"That son of a bitch is gonna kill you and the rest of your guys. He wants your guns."

"Oh, shit! What do I do now?" I said this out loud, but I was talking to myself.

"Soft-soap the dumb bastard," George replied, "And play for time."

Suddenly, for me, the party was over. I thought of the soldiers Montero and I had seen when we were coming down the trail to town, guessed at how many there were. I added those I could see here in the school area. We were outnumbered at least ten to one. We didn't have a chance.

I ate some more food—although my appetite had gone somewhere else. I had to do something distracting while I considered what the next move was to be. Fleeing was impossible. To fight was to invite disaster. I needed time to think.

I walked to where the general was holding forth with the local politicos, at least that's who I thought they were. George wandered over to join us. We chatted, with the general doing most of the talking, telling me of his prowess as a military leader.

At a lull in the conversation, I looked at my watch. Then, loud enough for all to hear, said: "General. I must go to my station now, because I must call Australia at four o'clock. I will see you tomorrow."

If Vera was surprised at this maneuver, he didn't show it. He probably thought that if he didn't kill me today, he would do so mañana.

I turned to George and said: "George. Would you like to go with me and see my station?"

"Sure."

The general said nothing. He could kill George tomorrow, too.

The trail to station S3L was rather steep. Not nearly as bad as the one up the face of the cliff at MACA, but steep enough that talking en route wasn't practical.

By the time we got there I found I had not lied to the general, for I had some messages to send, and, luckily, Doc Evans at Fertig's station was able to relay for me. That done, George and I sat down on a couple of makeshift benches at a makeshift table. We now had time to talk.

"George. Have you got any ideas on what in the hell I can do?"

"Shit, no," was the reply. "Konka and Sattem and me have been with this bastard for a couple of months, and can't get away. We wanna go south and try to get to Australia somehow, but the prick won't let us go. I think he's holding us hostage, hoping to trade us to someone for some guns or something."

"How'd you come to be with Vera? Did he spring you from the Japs?"

"Shit, no. The three of us were taken out of a Jap prison, luck of the draw, kinda, and sent to do coolie labor for a Jap patrol. Konka and me, we was Air Corps mechanics, and mostly we kept their trucks runnin'. Sattem, he was from the Coast Artillery, and since they didn't have them kinds of guns, they made him do all the shit details, like—ya know—cookin', scrubbin', and all that kind of crap. We did all their dirty work, but it was better than being in prison. Until they started beatin' us."

George paused, and sort of cringed as he thought about what they had been through. Then he continued: "The patrol got a new commander, and he really hated Americans. So, every time we moved into a new town, like every two or three days, he'd drag us into the town square in the evening. He'd make all the people in the town watch while his men beat the shit out of us with their belts—and clubs. And once in a while one of us would be clobbered with a rifle butt. All the time he kept tellin' the Filipinos that we were rotten dogs—didn't deserve to die—just to be tortured. Finally, we got sick of that shit and took off one night. We ran and ran and ran for hours with them chasing us. But we got away."

Again he paused. I could see that he was thinking of some of the details of that night.

"While we was runnin' in the dark, we came to a kind of a old fence or somethin'. Konka and me ran right inta' the son of a bitch, and it tore the hell outta' our legs. We wanted ta' get away so bad, we stepped back and ran inta' it agin', and it tore us apart some more. Then Sattem went up and stepped right over it. It was only about a foot high! Then we stepped over it, too."

He lit a cigarette, and went on. "We wound up with a farmer in the mountains who took us in and fed us. That's where Vera's people found us and took us to him."

His story was interrupted by a call on the radio. It was something routine, so I copied it and put it aside for the time being.

"Look," he continued. "Old 'Pancho'—that's what we call him—he's been good to us. Feeds us, treats us like humans. Not like the Japs did. But he won't let us go. And I guess you noticed, we don't have guns."

For a long time, we hashed and rehashed my situation and possible solutions. All the ideas we had came to the same end. Disaster. I was about to just give in to the general and hope to get out alive.

George, though, did not give up so easily. He was a gambler. When asked where he was from, he would reply, "I lived behind the post office in Reno, Nevada—seventy miles behind it."

"Bob," he said, "don't give in. This guy is a kook, but his ego is so big that he thinks he's in direct line of command behind General MacArthur."

I sneered. But I liked George's suggestion. Play on the son of a bitch's ego.

"I'm not shittin' you, Bob. Make up some cock-and-bull story to feed to him, and he'll buy it."

What's to lose? Give it a try.

I composed a message "to General MacArthur." I even went to the trouble of encoding it. Of course, it wasn't sent. Then I wrote a reply from MacArthur, again complete with decoding, which was never received.

TO MACARTHUR FROM STAHL. MET GENERAL GAUDENCIO V. VERA ON BONDOC PENINSULA. HE HAS STRONG GUERRILLA FORCE HERE WHICH CAN AFFORD ME AND MY STATION PRO- TECTION FROM THE JAPANESE. BUT HE NEEDS ARMS. CAN WE SUPPLY?

*   *   *

The reply:

> MACARTHUR TO GENERAL VERA THRU STAHL. APPRECIATE
> YOUR CONTRIBUTION TO THE LIBERATION OF YOUR HOME-
> LAND BY FURNISHING PROTECTION TO ONE OF MY MOST
> IMPORTANT SOURCES OF INFORMATION. YOUR OFFER TO
> ENSURE SAFETY OF STATION S3L WILL BE REWARDED BY SUP-
> PORT AS SOON AS POSSIBLE.

Early the next day I went back to Mulanay with the phony radio-
grams. I located the general and handed him the messages. *This is it,* I
told myself. *If he buys this baloney we're home free. If he doesn't, its "adiós
amigos!"* I was not a mountain of confidence.

Vera handed the papers to a young man who served as his secretary.

"I cannot see these. My glasses got broken in one of our battles," Vera
said. I guessed he was illiterate.

The secretary read my "message" to MacArthur. At first Vera beamed,
then seemed to scowl a bit after conversing in Tagalog with Colonel
Figueras. The secretary then read MacArthur's "message" to Vera. His
chest expanded so much I waited for the explosion!

"My commander has acknowledged me!" he shouted for all to hear.
"He is sending us arms!"

The scheme worked! Moral: When you're dealing with a nut, think
like a nut.

"Do you want to send a reply to General MacArthur?" I asked. I
wanted to spread the lard on thicker. Then I had second thoughts, and
said to myself, *You dumb bastard! Shut up! Quit when you're ahead!*

"Yes, Lieutenant. Yes! I will write one immediately."

A half hour later he handed me his reply. I glanced at it but didn't
read it. It was so long it would have required a four-part message if it
were sent.

I put it in my pocket. Upon my next call of nature, the paper was put
to good use—then buried with the rest of the crap.

Next I had to find Robles. Where was he yesterday, when I met with the
general? Why had he been less than enthusiastic about our arrival several
days ago? I wanted some answers—fast.

I hiked up to S3L. Nery was sitting at the radio, ready to answer if any calls came. McGowan was with him, for we had planned for George to help move the station if things did not go well with the general.

"It worked! It worked!"

"I told ya it would," said George. "That dumb shit will believe anything if it fits his ego. And there's lotsa' room in that ego."

"Yeah. So far, so good. But how am I going to explain the delays—'Why ain't the submarine coming in? Where are the arms, and why ain't they here?'"

"One thing at a time, Bob. We're OK today."

George went with me to Robles's station. Rather than walk three miles back to Patabog and three miles more to Robles's station along a more or less parallel trail, we decided to cut through the forest. It was a pretty tough mile, for we had to hack away lots of underbrush and cross several narrow but deep streambeds to create a path. All things considered, the direction we took was not bad. We intercepted the main trail within a quarter mile of Robles's station.

As we worked our way through the forest I reflected on the events of the last several days. I had seen Robles only once since we landed. Where had he been? Had he been avoiding me? Why wasn't he at the schoolhouse when I met the general? Why didn't he warn me about the general—tell me what a nut he was? To put it mildly, I was developing a very dour mood.

"George," I said, as we took a break from our labors, "I'm gonna jump all over Robles as soon as I see him."

"Why?" George asked. "He didn't do anything."

"That's right. He let me get damned near killed and didn't do a freakin' thing about it. I oughtta shoot the bastard!"

"Calm down, Bob. You need that guy, so don't go off half-cocked. At least hear him out before you explode on him."

I thought of his advice. George was going to be a good man to have around. Still, Robles had a lot of explaining to do.

We encountered two of Vera's soldiers as we approached Robles's shack. Fortunately, they recognized George and let us pass. From here, high on a bluff overlooking Mompog Passage, shipping movements could be observed and the information quickly radioed out. Robles was doing just that when we arrived.

We chatted. Talked about the radio equipment—the war—the food—the people. Robles and I both knew that I had not hacked a mile-long trail through the forest so we could have a social visit. Each waited for the other to get to the subject.

Finally, I got down to the serious business. "Cris," I said (Crispolo was his first name), "what's going on here? Why didn't you warn me about the general?"

"I don't really know," he replied.

"What the hell do you mean, you don't really know! I damned near got killed—all of us damned near got killed, and you didn't do a damned thing to help us."

"I don't know how I could have helped. I have no influence with Vera."

"But you could have been there. You could have said something. You could have done . . . well, something."

We sat there in pregnant silence, each weighing our next words very carefully. George was right. I needed Robles. And he needed me. Smith needed us both.

"Lieutenant," Robles finally spoke, "Let me try to explain. I don't know if I can or not, but let me try."

"OK, Cris. I can't be any angrier than I am now, so go ahead."

"When Manzano and I arrived here six months ago, we ran into the same buzz saw you did, only, I believe, worse. Vera was even crazier then than he is now. He had a very small 'army' and almost no arms. The guerrillas to the north around Lopez and across Ragay Gulf on Sorsogon were anxious to wipe him out, and he was constantly running from them.

"Actually, none of these guerrillas are worth a damn against the Japs. If they should accidently encounter a Japanese patrol they would run like hell. The leaders are not military people. In peacetime most of them were politicians. Now they have 'armies' made up of their friends and relatives. They roam the countryside like nomads trying to find and kill each other. They have to eat, so they force the civilians to give them food. They've already confiscated most all the guns and any other useful articles they could find."

I passed around a pack of cigarettes, and we all lit up. Then Robles continued. "Vera grabbed Manzano and me as soon as we landed here. He would have killed us for our guns immediately, except that one of his wives interfered. She has a few grains of brains and got him to weigh the value of our guns—two pistols, two carbines, and two tommy guns—against a radio that could make contact with the Americans to the south. The radio won, but even then it was a swap.

"Manzano was going to move closer to Manila and into densely populated areas where guns would be a burden. So he took only his pistol, and we gave Vera his carbine and submachine gun. Vera was happy, and I had a spot for the radio. It was a good deal for me."

"Yeah. But I still don't see what all this has to do with me," I said.

"Look, Lieutenant. My radio hasn't done Vera a damned bit of good yet. I'll bet he gives his wife a lot of shit about it. I figured that I should lay low, so the dumb bastard didn't realize that you, too, came here with nothing but arms and a radio—and that he already has a radio. If I had tried to help you he might have killed us all. We need at least one watcher station on Bondoc Peninsula."

What he said made sense—ugly, sickening sense! Sacrifice whatever or whomever so that the radio network survives. A wonderfully patriotic gesture, except that it was *I* who would have been sacrificed. Not a pleasant thought.

But what about my departure from Samar—the launches moving toward the submarine rendezvous spot I had just left—my decision not to warn Smith by radio, lest our move to the north be compromised. I had made a like decision then.

But it seems so different when the shoe is on the other foot!

The Turkey Shoot

CHAPTER 9

For several months, Lieutenant Chapman had been covering the San Bernardino Strait as a coastwatcher from a spot on Samar, as a part of Fertig's network of stations. Now, assigned to our network, he moved to southern Luzon near the town of Santa Magdalena, where he had a much better view of both the Strait and the surrounding waters. But the Japanese presence in that area made his operation much more difficult—not to mention dangerous. As a result, he had to limit his airtime, lest he be detected and captured.

Although I had copies of Gerry Chapman's codes, we had limited communications, for he found it best to make direct contact with the NCS, MACA, Smith's station on Samar, or else communicate with KUS, Fertig's station on Mindanao. I relayed for him only on rare occasions. One of those occasions was in the late afternoon of 15 June.

I heard Gerry trying to contact MACA and KUS. I had no idea of the content of his message, but I noticed that the Japanese "jamming"—sending out interfering noises to keep his message from being heard—was more intense than usual. He tried repeatedly to get through to both stations, but neither could read his signals. I could read bits of his message through the jamming, and decided to try to get a complete copy. If I could do so, I might be able to help. A sixth sense told me it was important. By listening in on his repeated transmission attempts, I finally was able to get an accurate copy of his coded message.

100

Gerry's transmitter had about a four-watt output. Mine had twelve. I thought I might be able to blast through the interference with my more powerful signals. I called MACA to relay Gerry's message on another of our regular frequencies, but the Japanese jamming was covering me like a blanket. I called KUS. Same result. I tried calling KAZ, although I had a history of limited success in reaching Australia with my equipment. I couldn't raise a soul. Meanwhile I listened to Gerry on another receiver. He was still trying, but it was a losing battle.

Suddenly I heard someone calling my station. I couldn't read the caller's ident, but through the din I finally understood a request for me to change to another frequency. "QSY 10,800. QSY 10,800," the caller said. Whoever was calling obviously knew something about my equipment, for he was asking me to switch to 10,800 kilocycles. Only a station that knew what frequency crystals I had would request this, for it was a doubling of my 5,400-kilocycle crystal, a frequency I rarely used, but a good one for long-distance communication.

I made the change. The Japanese apparently hadn't been listening, for they didn't move in on the new frequency. The station that called me was KFS, the Mackay Radio station in San Francisco! Mackay Radio was a commercial communications network with stations around the world, and was now furnishing relay services for military radio. With their supersensitive equipment, they had heard my calls to KAZ and offered to relay for me.

Soon the message reached Naval Intelligence in Australia via two different routes. KFS sent it direct to KAZ, and also sent it to Fertig's station, KUS, which relayed it to KAZ, too.

Now that the message was sent and received, I took to decoding it to see why Gerry had deemed it important enough to fight so hard to get it through. His message read, "GOING EAST, TWO SMALL PATROL BOATS, TEN CRUISERS, THREE BATTLESHIPS, ELEVEN DESTROYERS AND NINE AIRCRAFT CARRIERS." Gerry had spotted a flotilla of Japanese naval vessels heading eastward through the San Bernardino Strait, out of the island waterways into the Pacific Ocean. This was one hell of a large portion of the Japanese Navy!

Why was this significant? At the time, U.S. forces were invading the Mariana Islands. The Fifth Fleet was standing off the shore of Saipan, having bombarded the island to clear the beaches for the amphibious landing. Now the fleet was supporting the landing, and Adm. Raymond A. Spruance was unaware of the approaching Japanese fleet—unprepared

Forty years after he reported Japanese fleet movement through the San Bernardino Strait, Gerry Chapman (*right*) meets with the author.

for a sneak attack from the rear. With the information Chapman supplied, Spruance had time to steam westward to engage the oncoming Japanese flotilla. The result: the First Battle of the Philippine Sea, the "Marianas Turkey Shoot," in which the U.S. Navy virtually destroyed the Japanese Navy, especially its air arm. The Allies now had supremacy on the sea and in the air, a power we never relinquished. Had he done nothing else, Gerry Chapman had earned, and rightfully deserved, the "Well Done" he received from the U.S. Navy.

The radio contact with KFS had a deeper significance for me. With my twelve-watt transmitter I could rarely send a readable radio signal the fifteen hundred miles to station KAZ in Australia because of ionospheric problems, a part of the technology of shortwave radio I never did fully understand. Yet here I had made contact with a station some seven thousand miles away, across the Pacific Ocean! Again, that mysterious ionosphere came into play. Apparently something called "skip distance" was involved. At any rate, I discovered that when darkness covered the Pacific between me and San Francisco, a period of about one hour each night, I could communicate with KFS, a powerful relay station. I now had an unseen ally who would provide a much-needed new path to KAZ.

Vera's Camp

CHAPTER 10

There were repercussions to our success in relaying Chapman's sighting report to Australia. When Chapman saw the Japanese fleet heading through the Strait, his report turned a possible naval disaster into a major victory for the United States. The significance was not lost on the Japanese. We began to observe evidence that they were taking our operations seriously.

Launches carrying strange-looking gear, which we described as "Chinese clotheslines," were sighted both in Mompog Passage and in Ragay Gulf. Our radio station was between them on Bondoc Peninsula. I suspected that these were crude radio-direction-finding rigs seeking a fix on our station. My concern was great enough that we ceased radio operations for several days until they moved away, shifting our radio relay work to one of the other net stations.

We were too close to the coast and were vulnerable to attack by Japanese patrols. We were not high enough in the mountains to be able to make best use of our limited signal strength. We did not have a good view of the seas. In short, we were in a lousy location.

Leaving the station in Nery's hands, I went off in search of General Vera. When I found him and told him I needed to relocate to a safe, high spot that afforded a view of both shores of the peninsula, he was eager to help. The general had taken the "message" from General MacArthur seriously. He would have shelters built for the station in or near his camp. Since finding him had not been easy, and since this location seemed to provide the other things I needed, I agreed. I saw in this two pluses. First, mercenary or not, he had some armed men who *might* fight to protect us from the enemy if the need ever arose. Second, he could feed us along with his troops, eliminating our problem of searching for food. I realized that the food would be stolen from the civilians, but perhaps I could supply him with APA money to buy the food instead of forcibly taking it.

Moving in with him was a horrible mistake. The problem was sanitation. Here was a "military unit" that had never heard of a straddle trench or a latrine. Imagine more than one hundred men, women, and children living in a jungle camp where every call of nature was handled as an animal would—drop it anywhere and don't even cover it catlike! I now knew why they lived the nomadic life that Robles had described. The stench was unbearable.

I discussed this with the general and even showed him diagrams of a straddle trench as depicted in my *Soldier's Handbook*. I could see that he didn't take to the idea.

"Lieutenant. Do not worry. I have a squad of twenty men who are already building the houses for the new camp. We will move again in a few days."

And move we did. Again and again, when the land around the camp was polluted, we took up residence on another mountaintop, and as soon as we had moved, the construction crews were put to work building the next camp.

There was no shortage of locations for camps, for Bondoc Peninsula, save for the very narrow coastal plains, is a mass of forbidding jungle mountains, each of which a prudent person would deem inaccessible if that person were not engaged in a war. They are not high mountains— they range only to about fifteen hundred feet—but scaling them is a nightmarish task. There were few ridges connecting the peaks, and the usually steep trail, if a trail existed, descended almost to sea level before rising to the new heights. These were rain forests—damp, sloppy, and uncomfortable, even without the contribution of the frequent monsoons.

This nomadic life rendered the operation of an NCS a near impossibility. In effect, we had to have two stations, one operating while the other moved, but we had neither the equipment nor the manpower to do this efficiently. In addition, many of the sites were completely buried in the forests, without a view of the waterways. In desperation, I confronted Vera.

"General," I said, "I cannot be moving my station every week or so. Australia is complaining that I am not doing what I was sent here to do, for my operations are interrupted too often."

"Lieutenant Stahl," he replied, "I am only doing what my supreme commander, General MacArthur, ordered me to do. I must protect your station, and we must keep moving so the Japanese cannot find us."

"Yes, General, you are doing that, and well. Australia knows. But I need a permanent location. And it must be where I can see the ships."

It galled me to be forced to patronize this character. Yet I needed his support in order to keep my station operating. This was a touchy issue, for in his little mind he believed he was doing a great job of following the instructions given to him by his "supreme commander." He was ensuring the safety of my station, just as he had been ordered to do when we were in Mulanay. Yet, in reality, he was a psychopath, with a hair trigger on his temper. I had witnessed his violent rage, seen it terminate in the execution of real or assumed enemies. I had not yet endeared myself to him, and I and my men could easily be the objects of his next maniacal rampage.

To my advantage, I had learned to read his facial expressions for signs of the level of his anger. This talent I had picked up by conversing with him frequently, for we invariably ate together. The measure of his rage was reflected in the rapidity of his eye movements and the tenseness of his lips surrounding his oversized teeth. Neither of these signs was now evident, so I pursued the idea of a permanent—as far as permanent was possible in enemy territory—camp for my station. After much persuasion, he agreed to help me get set up wherever I wanted. He also agreed to supply me with four soldiers for perimeter guards, plus a cook. The magic of General MacArthur's "message to Vera" was still working.

The next day, Eldred Sattem and I roamed the hills nearby and selected a spot midway across the peninsula, between the towns of Catanauan on the west and San Narciso on the east. From here we could walk to three bluffs, all within a mile, from which we could see the coasts and both towns, each about ten miles away, and the town of Mulanay as well. Vera had a radio shack, a mess shack, and several lean-tos built there in two days. We dug our own straddle trench.

Handy to the selected location for our camp was a free-flowing, clean-watered stream. It was not ours exclusively, for we had several neighbors on local ridges, small family groups who had "buckwheated" from nearby towns for fear of the Japanese, fear of the guerrillas, perhaps just plain fear. Each family had cleared a small area on which they could live and grow some crops for sustenance. This ample source of water was their primary reason for selecting the locations to which they had moved.

We had no shortage of water.

The stream came out of the ground and flowed immediately into a sort of steep riffle, almost a waterfall, and it was from this portion of the stream that water for drinking and cooking was collected. The ledges, about eight feet high, ended in a rather large pool serving as a bathing and laundering area. Here the women would do the family's washing (and ours for a small fee), beating the clothing on large, flat rocks at the pool's edge. That task finished, they would bathe in the pool, washing their bodies without removing the wraparound garments they were wearing. Children before puberty wore nothing but shirts, which grew shorter and shorter as they grew bigger and bigger, so bathing, for them, was not a problem. Passing that age, the girls adopted the wraparounds and the boys adopted shorts, neither of which were removed for bathing. After the women and children left the pool area, the men would assemble for their baths.

Noting that the riffles dropped at about a forty-five-degree angle, Sattem took a long bamboo pole, rammed a long stick through it to break out the diaphragms dividing the pole's sections, and created a water pipe. He then stuck the pipe into the source of the water, propped it up with other poles so that it carried some water straight out from the top of the riffles, and voila! A shower bath!

We uninhibited Yankees would strip to the altogether and cavort under Sattem's contraption, unheeding, or uncaring, of who was watching us. It wasn't long until the native males began to approach us, asking for some of our soap, a commodity they did not have and one that, for some reason or other, we had been supplied with in a quantity we would never, ever, use up. The natives would work up a huge pile of lather on their heads, then share the lather with their friends.

Soon we began to hear female tittering in the bushes surrounding the pool. We had an audience. Finally, one of the bravest girls approached for a head full of soap, all the while trying to avert her eyes, yet not being able to do so because she would then be looking at our nudity. With a head full of suds, she ran off to share it with her friends on the other side of the pool. In just a few days everybody was showering with us—but they didn't remove their shorts or their wraparounds.

Being away from Vera's constant presence would be good, but now we had an added problem: he no longer would be supplying us with food. This would not be an immediate burden, for we still had a hidden stash of rice. But we now had fifteen people to feed; the six Filipinos who had sailed with me, the three Americans who had moved in with us, four perimeter guards, a cook, and myself. This would soon become a problem.

The New General Vera

CHAPTER 11

Station S3L was soon operating as a well-knit organization. Major Smith had successfully evaded the first set-to with the Japanese and somehow, miraculously, not lost his equipment. MACA was again the NCS, although sporadically, because the Japanese were nearby and would occasionally send a patrol in Smith's direction, calling for another fight. When he was off the air I could relay through my newly found friends in San Francisco—station KFS. Sergeant Nery and the other radio operators were doing a very efficient job. Chester Konka had taken over as cryptographer, encoding and decoding messages. Eldred Sattem kept the generator operating and the batteries charged. Ochigue and Madeja handled the posting of the guard. George McGowan sort of hung around with me. I had little to do but recruit agents and give them assignments—and sweat until they returned.

For several days I roamed the mountains surrounding our camp, making a mental map of the lay of the land. George and I had set up an alternate location for emergency use and had stashed food and equipment in several other spots, but I needed to know as much as possible about the terrain in all directions—a lesson I had learned from Smith.

On one of my early walks I became disturbed because I did not encounter any of the perimeter guards. I returned to the camp and located Ochigue. "How come there aren't any guards out there?" I asked.

"But, Sair, they are there," he replied.

"Then why didn't I see any?" I persisted.

"Come with me, Sair, and we will find one."

We walked perhaps a half mile. Ochigue stopped and made a half whistle, half guttural sound. I can't really describe it, let alone make it. Out of the bushes stepped, like a cat, a pygmy-sized, bushy-haired, extremely dark skinned native, naked except for a loincloth. He was not carrying a rifle. He had a small bolo tied around his waist, a bow in his hands, and a quiver of arrows on his back. An Igorot!

"This is a guard?" I stormed. "What good would he be if the Japs came after us?"

"Let *him* show you, Sair," was the reply.

Ochigue spoke to the guard, and pointed to an odd-looking tree some one hundred feet away. Immediately the Igorot whipped out an arrow and zinged it into the tree. And again, and again. Three arrows in not more than ten seconds, all without the attention-gathering noise of rifle fire, and if there had been a six-inch-diameter bull's-eye on that tree, all three arrows would have been in it! I could do no better with a carbine.

"Where did this guy come from?" I asked.

"Sair. Between here and Lopez is a small but very deep jungle. It is from there he came. He and his family moved there from the north a long, long time ago."

"Is he one of Vera's soldiers?" I asked.

"No, Sair. He heard that the Americanos were here, and he wanted to see one. I hired him. And I also have his brother."

I was wrong. Instead of fifteen, we had seventeen mouths to feed.

Getting to know the territory required visiting the nearby towns and barrios. Good relations with these people would pay off in warnings of Japanese arrivals and in procuring food.

Years of association before the war had demonstrated to the Filipinos that America was a nation of heavy drinkers. We didn't have to struggle to keep this idea alive. Consequently, many of the people in the surrounding towns who wanted a favor from me would introduce the request with a gift of something alcoholic. *Prascos,* about a quart, of various unidentifiable alcohols were often sent. More appreciated were gifts of Japanese beer, brewed in the San Miguel Brewery in Manila, a reasonably good substitute for stateside beer. Occasionally, Japanese soldiers would use the brew as a bartering incentive in dealing with the Filipinos. Eventually, after several more trades, the beer would arrive at S3L with the compliments of a mayor or other influential citizen from one of the surrounding communities, accompanied frequently by a request for a copy of the latest radio news. I would send the messenger back with a typed copy of a news summary, to be proudly displayed by the beer's donor to everyone within sight for weeks and weeks, until the paper was tattered and torn beyond recognition.

This led me to establish a newsletter. I began to send out frequent news summaries to the mayors, with the request that they make copies and distribute them to towns and barrios more remote from our area. Result? The citizens became reasonably well informed of the progress of the war. Copies of our newsletter were found in the files of Japanese military units when the islands were secured by the American forces.

More immediate was the flow of gifts of Japanese cigarettes, candy, and other items, purchased by the Filipinos from the Japanese neighborhood association stores and sent to me. Most appreciated were the Akedonos cigarettes, not a bad-tasting Japanese cigarette, and much better tasting than my poorly hand-rolled native tobacco cigars.

Among the townspeople there was an aura of ill feeling concerning Vera. He was not so much feared as he was despised and loathed. He was a blowhard and a braggart, and there were numerous rumors of his mistreatment—and even execution—of his political enemies. In addition, the people placed no stock in his offer of protection from the Japanese if they should appear in the area.

Of the towns I visited, San Narciso was by far my favorite, and I hiked there—ten miles each direction—frequently. The mayor, Jesus Medenilla, was a successful businessman, and also well educated, as were his wife, son, and three daughters. This showed in their conversations, their living standards, and their dress. They were quite Americanized. The mayor was well known and very well liked, and his popularity extended as far as Manila. Vera knew better than to tangle with this man. Vera catered to him.

This family's demeanor and lifestyle had rubbed off on the other citizens of the town. The houses, on stilts as was the custom throughout the Philippines, were better built, better kept, and had neater yards than in any other town I had seen in the islands. The ever present pigpens and chicken coops sat empty under the houses. To keep the guerrillas and the Japanese from confiscating the livestock, the mayor had ordered all the animals taken to a well-concealed community caingain, a farm, deep in the woods, there to be tended by the citizens on a rotating basis. He ordered frequent distribution of meats to all.

Dogs roamed freely in the streets. These were not pets. One or two would disappear from time to time when the mayor cut the meat ration.

Many men wore cotton trousers and shirts instead of the more common coarsely woven *abaca* shorts and sleeveless tops; women wore dresses, not wrappers, and carried umbrellas to keep the brilliant sunshine from giving their skin an even darker shade of brown. Most, though, both men and women, were barefoot, for shoes and clogs were in short supply and were saved to wear to church or to fiestas.

"I understand you met the general," the mayor said to me as we sat on chairs on his veranda. It was our first meeting.

"Yes. It was quite an experience." I had emphasized the words.

The mayor smiled. "I take it from your reply that I need not ask your reaction to him."

"I've met quite a few guerrilla leaders, but he certainly is one of a kind." I was unsure of the relationship between the two. Was I saying too much? Was I talking out of turn?

"My son, Juan, is a lieutenant in Vera's army," he continued. "He says you have had quite an effect on the general."

"How come?"

"Juan says Vera is—how do you Americans say it?—cleaning up his act."

"What do you mean?" The last time I had seen Vera was in that pigsty I had refused to live in. It would take a lot of cleaning before anyone noticed.

"Well, Lieutenant, since he received a message from General MacArthur he has decided to convert his bandits into a trained army."

Surely the mayor was too smart to believe my sham. Deep inside he certainly must be laughing. It didn't show.

"Yes," he continued. "They now have inspections, drills, even combat practice—no shooting, of course, for they have very little ammunition for the few guns they have."

"I hope they dug some latrines," I replied. "That's what they needed most."

"Oh, yes, Lieutenant. They have. Juan says the camp's so clean they won't have to move every week anymore."

We chatted on, while his wife brought us drinks. Rather potent drinks, and midway through the second I felt a bit woozy.

"Mayor, what's in this drink?" I asked.

"Alcohol. Distilled nipa palm juice. We call it nipa wine. It's not bad

Guerrilla platoon leader preparing troops for inspection.

mixed with good, strong papaya juice. It's about 170 proof, the way you measure it in the United States. Hard to get, though, because we don't have many distilleries around here."

An idea for a future use of nipa wine began germinating in my mind. Perhaps this wine would be useful in case of a gasoline shortage.

After several days of rest and relaxation while getting to know the people of San Narciso, I undertook the trek back to our radio station. In nice weather, the hike from San Narciso to S3L was a pleasant constitutional. The first five miles—to barrio Abuyon—ran through a narrow stand of coconut trees that lined the shore of Ragay Gulf. Here, if the time of the day was right, one could buy a bamboo container of tuba.

Whenever possible, we would time our travel to arrive at about four in the afternoon. The tuba gatherer would have a fresh supply then, and after sipping a bit of the nectar we would carry a three-quart container to the camp to add a bit of splendor to the evening's ration of rice.

At Abuyon the trail turned away from the shore. The first mile of this leg of the journey traversed a large, flat cogon grass field to the base of the mountains. This stand of grass ranged from eight to ten feet tall. All that could be seen from the trail was the sky above. Here a long-sleeved shirt and trousers were essential, for cogon grass has narrow, sharp-edged leaves that cause painful scratches and cuts on bare skin. Except for one small area near the center of the field, the path was usually dry. Even the wet area was easily crossed.

Then came about four miles of rather steep climbing in a deep forest. As trails go, this one was not bad, except in the rainy season, which had begun soon after we arrived there. With the rains it became a muddy "bitch." It ended at a cleared, level area, about a half acre in size, where our camp was situated. We were not surrounded by a jungle. We were in a mahogany forest with heavy underbrush. Rotting stumps gave evidence that the area may have been logged many years previously. To fade

Guerrillas ready for inspection.

into almost impenetrable jungle, we needed to go not more than a quarter of a mile to the north. The whole journey—San Narciso to S3L—could be made in about two and a half hours.

When Vera's men built the structures in our camp, they had erected one rather large headquarters building. It was a two-room affair, bamboo framed with buri palm leaves for roof and siding, all tied together with rattan around a dirt floor. The main room, about ten feet wide and twelve feet long, served as both a radio room and a mess hall. A small table and bench in one corner held the communications equipment. Down the center of the room ran an eight-foot-long mess table with benches. All were made of bamboo and rattan. Added to this room was a smaller one furnished with a bamboo platform padded with a woven buri palm mat for a bed. Atop this was my jungle hammock, the bottom resting on the palm mat, the top tied off on four corners so I could be protected from the oversized mosquitoes by its netting and from the leaks in the roof by its top. This room was my private quarters. Nearby was a cookhouse, and surrounding all were many individual lean-tos so that everyone had a place of his own. Each of these had a roof over a bed similar to mine. The Igorot preferred to sack out away from us, in the woods.

When I arrived in camp from San Narciso, I found everything in order. Sergeant Nery had no problems to report in operating the radio; code clerk Chester Konka had been able to decode all the incoming messages, and none of them required major quick decisions; Eldred Sattem had the generator working—the batteries well charged; and George McGowan was biding his time awaiting my return. Our "army"— Ochigue, Madeja, and the guards—had set up a good security program.

With dinner, everyone got a small but much appreciated ration of tuba. We had no meat, no fish, no camotes. Just rice, and tuba to wash it down. Food was becoming a problem.

After dinner we gathered around the mess table. Under the light of homemade lamps sitting on the table—halves of coconut shells or flat tin cans from army ration packages filled with coconut oil, with rolled rags for wicks—McGowan, Sattem, and I played poker, gin rummy, single and double solitaire, and cribbage. Sattem had made a cribbage board and taught us the game. We spent many evenings in a running competition for high stakes, which none of us took seriously. When this activity got boring we would bet on whether or not the gaku lizard climbing the wall would catch the fly it was stalking. We read books borrowed from people in neighboring towns. Konka wasn't much for drinking, cardplaying, or betting on lizards, so he sat around reading, or honing and stropping a straight razor he had come upon in his travels. I'm sure he constantly thought of the use he could have made of this instrument if he'd had it when he was a prisoner of the Japanese. These were the activities that kept us from going stir-crazy.

Tonight we had a special treat. Mayor Medenilla had given me a prasco of his precious nipa wine. I poured a small amount in tins for each of us. This was valuable "drinking whiskey" and would be rationed out over several evenings. With each sip we screwed up our faces, for without a mixer or a chaser it was pretty bad stuff, but we liked the effect.

Sattem, always concerned about running low on fuel for the battery charger, said, "Egads! This stuff would eat the varnish off a bar. I wonder if it would burn."

He touched a match to his tin. Immediately it began to glow with a pure, blue flame, not unlike the flame of canned heat. Sattem was sure this liquid would serve as fuel in an emergency. The germ of an idea I'd had when visiting the mayor in San Narciso now had sprouted. I made a mental note to get some nipa wine from Medenilla to stash away for use if we should run short of gasoline. Eventually we got some, but we drank it all. It wouldn't have been enough to charge a battery, anyway.

While Sattem and I were engaged in a hot cribbage game, George left the room. I assumed that he was going out to "wring out his sock."

"Bob," he said when he returned, "the general sent you a present."

"OK." He was disturbing my concentration on the game.

"A new cook."

"What's wrong with the old one?"

"Nothing. But he thought you'd like this one better."

With that he beckoned to someone beyond the doorway. In stepped the general's concubine!—the young girl who had sat at the end of the desk in the schoolhouse.

"What the hell's going on here?" I exploded.

"Say hello to María, your new cook."

With all my other concerns when I met the general at the schoolhouse, I had not really looked at her. I had noted that she was better looking than his wives, but that was all. Now here she stood. About sixteen years old, five feet, two inches tall, about one hundred well-arranged pounds—a dark-haired, light-skinned dream. This was just the kind of trouble I didn't need in my camp!

I gulped. "Hello, María. Welcome to S3L. Glad to have you here."
What the hell else could I say?

This was no dowdy, rotund Mrs. McGuire, who had lived with us on
Palapag Mesa. This was a voluptuous young thing who would have all
of my men at each other's throats trying to get next to her. Now I had
a reason to find Vera's camp *tomorrow*, to thank him profusely for his
kindness, but to refuse his generosity.

What did I ever do to have General Vera thrust upon me?

Later, when I was safely inside the netting separating me from the flying
insects, María appeared at the side of my bed.

"Lieutenant," she whispered, "I come in?"

"No, María. I've walked a long way today, and I'm very tired. Perhaps
tomorrow night."

"Please, Sair. The mosquitoes. Very bad, and I have no net."

What's a gentleman to do? Let a lady be eaten alive by mosquitoes?

At dawn, Dominador "Doming" Trafalla brought my toothbrush, razor,
soap, towel, and a mess cup of hot water for my morning toilette.
Doming was my houseboy. I don't know where he came from. He just
sort of appeared in our midst one day, and gradually attached himself
to me. The arrangement was sealed when I fitted him with a pair of jungle
boots. Now he was mine forever! Fourteen or fifteen years old, short and
skinny, he was surprisingly strong and very eager to please me. We got
along well. Our only problem was that his English was practically
nonexistent, as was my Tagalog. We communicated in sign language or
by having one of the other Filipinos serve as an interpreter. This arrangement became somewhat exasperating at times, but all in all he was a
good kid and I was glad to have him with me. Gradually he learned a
smattering of English, which helped considerably.

After breakfast, María, Doming, George, and I set out to find Vera's
present camp. I felt that I might need George's diplomatic skills when
talking to the general. I knew about where Vera was located—some
twenty crow's-flight miles north of our camp, several miles inland from
Ragay Gulf near Buenavista. It would be a circuitous thirty-mile hike—
a ten-hour walk I wasn't anxious to take.

Barefoot María kept pace with us on the hike, although she was reluctant
to return to Vera's camp. When we stopped to rest along the trail, she said to
me, "I am afraid to go to that place, Sair. The general he will punish me."

"Why? You did nothing wrong."

"Oh, but Sair, he will think I not try to please you in bed. He will tie me to tree again."

"Tie you to a tree?"

"Yes, Sair. He is very mean to me. Many times he say I do not obey. Sometime he say I sleep with soldier. But I not do that! But he punish me anyway. He tie me to tree with no clothes on! Everyone look. He makes me shame!"

I began to have second thoughts. Should we return to S3L? Was there a way to keep her in our camp without creating havoc? Impossible. With a camp full of horny males? Inconceivable. She had to go back. But, she also had to be protected from the general. I hoped that "diplomat George" could pacify Lt. Gen. Gaudencio V. Vera.

As we neared Vera's camp, a guard with very military bearing stopped us on the trail. With his rifle at port arms, he told us we must await permission to approach the camp. This soldier recognized McGowan and María, but, unlike our approach to Robles's radio station several weeks earlier when a rather lax guard recognized George and allowed us to pass, he did not have the authority to allow *anyone* past him. He had to send a runner to Vera's camp to get that permission.

The runner returned, and we proceeded. As we approached the camp I found myself sniffing the air—expecting the stench I had encountered at the general's previous camps. My nose encountered no discomforting smells.

Vera had come down the trail to meet and greet us. George and I shook hands with him, and María faded into the bushes.

"It is good to see you, Lieutenant Stahl," he said. "And George. Do you like being with the lieutenant?"

"Sure do, General. But we ain't eatin' as good as we did in your camp." George always knew the right thing to say. He had a career awaiting him back in the States—as a politician.

"We will eat good tonight," said the general, "And tomorrow I will show you my camp."

And eat good we did. In addition to the ever-present rice, we had baked camotes, barbecued manók, and a dessert of grated coconut covered with a sweet syrup.

We sat around the table after dinner drinking nipa wine. Tired and well fed, the booze got to me rather quickly. Meanwhile, Vera's wife number one had moved to a spot next to me, while wife number two sat near George. María was present and stayed near the general. She dodged my glances, as I did hers. I was worried about her, but figured no harm would come to her—at least overnight.

Doming had prepared a place for me to sleep. I was woozy from the drinks, and he led me to my bed. He had help from wife number one, who wanted to, or had been ordered to, join me. Whether she did or not I don't know, for I passed out. I couldn't ask Doming; after all, he didn't speak much English.

An excess of nipa wine will guarantee one the granddaddy of all hang-overs. That is what I had when we sat down to breakfast. Obviously, Vera had pulled out all the stops for the previous night's dinner; in the morning we had a weak slurry of rice—with no trimmings. He had wiped out his larder.

Vera led George and me through his camp. It was different. There were no soldiers lolling about doing nothing, as had been the case in the previous camps I had seen. Everyone in sight seemed to be engaged in a chore of one sort or another. He had, as Mayor Medenilla had said, cleaned up his act.

Through the fog that surrounded my brain I noticed that this camp was clean and well organized, and the general made sure he pointed out all the improvements he had made in the living conditions. He made a special effort to show me the straddle trenches, which he now thought were an excellent idea.

Back in his headquarters we sat to talk. Gradually my mind was getting back in focus, but it wasn't easy.

"General," I said, "I'm impressed by your camp. It is so different."

I didn't want to say that he was no longer living in a pigsty. Yes, this was a different camp—and this was a different man than I had met a month or so ago. No longer was he a braggart, a boor, a horse's ass. He appeared to be interested in preparing to fight a war rather than in killing his family's political enemies and robbing the civilians. Quite a large order!

Then he chopped me off at the knees with flat-out truth.

"Lieutenant," he said, "I have thought a lot about our first meeting. I was going to wipe out your little group and take your guns. You did not fool me with your message to General MacArthur and his answer to me."

I gulped, and had nothing to say.

He continued, "When the war began I was in the Philippine Scouts. Sure, I was not a soldier with a gun. I was a cook." The Philippine Scouts, formed in 1899, was a part of the U.S. Army. The Philippine Army was created in 1935, with General MacArthur as military advisor. In 1936 MacArthur became field marshal of all Philippine military forces. As tension mounted in the years following, MacArthur's command was expanded to include the

Philippine Department of the U.S. Army, the U.S. Forces in the Philippines (USFIP). MacArthur's command became the U.S. Forces in the Far East (USAFFE) in 1941, encompassing all the U.S. and Filipino military forces in the Pacific. Many of the American troops became a cadre assigned the task of expanding the Philippine Army by training raw recruits in a hurry. War against Japan was imminent.

"When the Japanese overran my country," Vera continued, "my Scout battalion was wiped out. I ran to my relatives in Lucena. Then the Japanese came there, and we all ran to the hills. We would be a guerrilla army. But with no money we soon became bandits in order to survive."

This conversation was getting a bit heady for me, and it was rapidly clearing the fog from my brain. I began to feel like a priest must feel when hearing a confession.

"You made a fool of me in front of everybody with your fake messages. I was very angry then and I *really* wanted to kill you! But I couldn't, because everyone would know I did it because you made me a—how do you say it?—a dunce."

"General," I began, "I did not mean to—"

He held up his hand and continued, "You also ended my career as a bandit, for no one would take me seriously any longer. I had to change my army into a real guerrilla army."

He went on with hardly a pause. "That was good. I want to get back at the Japanese for what they have done. After all, I am a Philippine Scout! I will fight them."

One of my assignments on this mission was to try to organize the guerrillas into resistance forces. Here was one falling into my lap. *Don't louse it up now, Bob!* "General, you made a wise decision," I blurted. I didn't know what to say next.

George bailed me out. "General Vera," he said, "how can we help you? And how can you help us?"

Before Vera could answer, I said, "If you *really* want to help, fighting the few Japanese in the area is not important right now. This will make them mad and send them patrolling to find us. Then I will have to go on the run with my station. That would not be good, because we would be off the air a lot. Spying and getting information is much more important. Can your men do this?"

"Oh, yes, Lieutenant. But they need to know that they have support. They need evidence that General MacArthur is behind them. The only evidence they will understand is arms."

Filipino and American guerrillas.

"I will get you arms. Not tomorrow, but soon. I will give you whatever arms I can spare, but they are only a few. And I will try to get more."

I could see that my statement did not sit well with Vera. He was not happy with an unsecured promise.

"General. Do you have a man you can really trust—one with courage—to go on a mission?"

"Colonel Figueras will go."

"Good. Send him to Samar, to Major Smith. I will ask the major to supply him with arms for you, and if he has none I will arrange for Figueras to go to Mindanao to get some from General Fertig."

I didn't know if I could come through on this promise, but why not take a chance? There was, however, one promise I could make and keep.

"If you are willing to have your men gather information, you will need a radio station. I will send a man and a radio to you, to send the information to me, and then to Australia."

Now the general was happy.

"And General, when the time comes to fight the Japanese and help the Americans return, we will have plenty of arms, I promise you."

The subject of María still remained. This was a ticklish problem I dreaded to face, but face it I must.

After dinner, a meager meal much like breakfast had been, I said to

Vera in a confidential way, "Thank you, General, for sending María to me. She was delightful." This I said with a knowing leer. "But, I have an eye on one of the Medenilla girls in San Narciso." I hadn't yet *seen* the Medenilla girls. "She would be very unhappy if she knew I had a beautiful young woman like María in camp with me. Don't you agree?"

The general, with a leer better than mine, said, "Oh, yes! But if that does not work out, you can take María back."

I felt relieved. María was safe—at least for the time being.

By mid-July we were hurting for many of the essentials of our existence: food, clothing, medicine, money—not to mention everything needed to keep a radio station operating and an espionage network going. These problems would not begin to be fully resolved until November, following the landing at Leyte on 20 October.

Obviously, no one, guerrilla or Japanese, knew the timing or the location of the American return to the Philippines. Some submarine supply runs went to Fertig in northeast Mindanao; others went to the guerrilla groups located along the east coast of central Luzon, led by Col. Bernard Anderson, Col. Russell Volckmann, and Maj. Richard Lapham. These were diversionary tactics to keep the Japanese thinking that these might be the landing sites. I was directed to go to the east coast of Luzon, near Alabat Island, and take soundings of the depth of the offshore waters, not a pleasant assignment because of the Japanese presence extending there from the Manila area. I was certain to be seen; just what GHQ wanted, I later learned. This was another diversionary tactic.

The heavy shipments of arms and ammunition went to the guerrillas on Leyte and Samar. None came to us. We were not supposed to be actively engaged in warfare against the Japanese. Our mission was still one of gathering intelligence information, reporting ship, aircraft, and troop movements, and pinpointing military installations. It would have been nice, however, to get some noncombative supplies, which we desperately needed.

Somehow, however, we managed to muddle through. Many times, when I became most depressed and was certain we could not continue to operate because of some shortage or equipment failure, we would find a way to circumvent the problem—a substitute or an ersatz material that filled the need. My NCS was never off the air, not for one day! Most of the credit for this feat belongs to my American POW friends and to the high-class Filipinos working with me.

Many months later, when I was back on our side of the line, I greeted with mixed emotions the news that we had intentionally been omitted from the supply operations to keep our activities low key in the eyes of the Japanese. It was small consolation to learn that we had purposely been left high and dry—that our miserable existence had been *planned* by the top brass because, they alibied, we were doing such a fine job on our assigned mission. I couldn't help thinking: *With friends like that, who needs enemies?*

Remaining low key and avoiding physical contact with the Japanese, while very desirable, was not possible. I recognized our limited ability to carry out an armed confrontation, and the occasional threat of enemy action against us gave me spates of emotion. Fortunately, these events were not frequent.

We would undergo occasional days of turmoil when the Japanese would try to put us out of operation. With a pair of launches equipped with their "Chinese clotheslines," they would try to determine our location by reading directional azimuths from each launch. By plotting these on a map, they could pinpoint the location of our station. Usually we spotted these rigs when they moved into position, so we would go off the air at the main station until the launches departed, temporarily turning the net control activities over to one of our other stations.

Occasionally, however, we were not as diligent as we should have been, and before we shut down our station they would zero in on us and put ashore a party of Japanese troops, perhaps twenty or thirty in number, to seek us out. When this happened we would call on General Vera (fortunately I had supplied him with a radio), and his men would "discourage" the Japanese, sending them packing. When Vera's men were not nearby, it fell upon me and my small "army" to set up an ambush. Always in our favor was the reluctance of the Japanese troops to penetrate very far into the jungles. The Japanese occupation army was made up of conscripts, not regular army troops, and they were not the bravest of soldiers. A few bursts of rifle and submachine gunfire from a concealed position would disperse them quickly.

On one occasion, however, they came after us in force and routed us completely. We were able to hide our main station equipment quickly, albeit effectively, and then we scattered in many directions. Doming and I went with one of our Igorot guards to his tribe's barrio, a full day's hike away, where we spent the night. Primitive is primitive, but this was unbelievable! Situated along a small stream similar to the one that ran through our camp on Palapag Mesa were lean-tos that would barely afford shelter to a small animal. Only one was of decent size. It was the home of the tribe's leader, and it served as the cooking, eating, and social center.

When we arrived, I was quickly surrounded by a horde of nearly nude pygmies who stared at and touched my white skin and felt the clothing I was wearing. The chief, probably the patriarch of a very inbred family, did a lot of talking and made much fuss over the tribesman who had led me there.

Eventually we ate. I have no idea of what the food was. All I know was that it tasted good to someone who was very hungry, as was I. Added to the food was a drink that wasn't bad and had a great alcohol content. There was much revelry, and I smiled, not knowing why, and ate and ate. Not understanding their language did not assuage my hunger.

Doming was able to understand their dialect with help from our guide, but with difficulty. He tried to keep me aware of the gist of the conversation, but, as usual, Doming and I had problems "in the translation."

It came time to retire, and I told Doming to sling my jungle hammock between a couple of trees.

Doming said, "But Sair. The *teniente* [head of the barrio] say you sleep in house."

"No, Doming. I will sleep in the woods in my hammock."

"But, Sair," he continued. "The teniente say you to sleep with she," pointing to the chief's daughter. "You make white *sanggól* for he!"

Now I had a problem. His daughter's face, shape, and size were anything but enticing. More important, this was headhunter territory. Was this an offer meant only as a gesture, one that was to be politely refused? Was it a sincere request, perhaps even an order, which could *not* be refused? Did he really want a mestizo grandchild? A wrong guess could result in the loss of one's head—mine!

We left the barrio early the next morning, heading back to see what was left of S3L. I pondered the decision I had made the previous night. Obviously, I had made the right choice.

Our Cupboard Is Getting Bare

CHAPTER 12

Our supply shortages grew more serious. Fuel for our battery charger was a major headache. I had brought from Samar one fifty-five gallon drum of gasoline—enough for two months of operation, at most. That drum took on a hollower sound each day.

I was awaiting a sailboat from Samar with more supplies, including gasoline, which *Colonel* Smith (yes, he had been promoted) had promised to send to me. I doubted it would ever come, for Smith was being chased all over Samar by the Japanese. He would have great difficulty getting the supplies through enemy lines to the coast and into a sailboat. I began to look for alternate sources.

Whenever I wearied over the pauperlike existence we were leading—depression sessions that were becoming more frequent by the week—I would take a long walk to try to get my thinking straight. Doming and I took one of these strolls along the black sands of Tayabas Bay, north of the town of Catanauan, in mid-July. We spent the day checking the stash of fermenting coconuts we had planted along this beach from time to time on previous hikes. "Drinking whiskey" made this way is really not too hard on the taste buds. It's not as smooth as Kentucky bourbon, but not nearly as harsh as nipa wine.

The recipe is simple. Take one well-matured coconut. Strip off the husk down to the hard shell. Locate the spots that indicate where its three umbilical cords had connected it to the mother tree. Punch small holes at these spots, penetrating the shell and the meat to the liquid-filled center. Blow into one of the holes while allowing the air to escape from the others to ensure the presence of air inside. Insert a small amount of sugar (a tablespoonful does the job nicely) into the center. Fashion three plugs and fit them snugly into the holes. Bury the coconut six inches below the surface of the warm sands. Wait at least a week before removing it from its "oven." Remove the plugs and pour. Or, if you are in a hurry, drink directly from the container. Voila! You have a cupful of sweet-tasting alcohol not unlike Southern Comfort (if you have enough imagination).

We dug up several of the well-aged nuts to take back to camp, replacing them with a new batch. Then we continued to walk along the beach. We were opposite the north end of Mompog Passage, a portion of the seaway traversed almost daily by Japanese merchant and naval ships and frequented with regularity by our submarines. Apparently a ship had been sunk there recently, for I spotted two drums floating offshore that looked suspiciously like gasoline containers. One was quite far out in the deep water; the other was close to shore in the shallows. I waded out to the nearer one, floated it to shore, and rolled it up on the beach. We had no trouble concealing it in the underbrush, and I was elated when I found that it was what we needed—gasoline. We now had a reserve supply.

Not a half hour later we met a Filipino carrying a one-gallon can on a pole over his shoulder.

"What have you there?" I asked him.

"Gasolina," was his reply.

"Where did you get it?"

"It was given to me by the Japanese, Sair, my pay for my work for them, Sair."

"But what will you use it for?"

"I do not know, Sair, but I will take it home because this is my pay and perhaps I can trade it for some rice for my family, Sair." It seemed that every sentence a Filipino said to me contained a liberal sprinkling of the word "Sair."

"I will give you five pesos for it."

"Japanese pesos or Philippine pesos, Sair?"

"Either kind."

"Then, Sair, I will sell it to you for five Philippine pesos or fifty Japanese pesos, Sair."

That was about the going rate of exchange, although a very high price for gasoline. I bought it.

Our fuel problem now seemed to be settled, for that Filipino passed the word, and soon other natives who worked for the Japanese sold their gasoline to us. I was overjoyed at the stockpile of fuel we were collecting.

Before long we were forced to use the Japanese gasoline.

"Goddammit!" I heard Sattem say as the charger sputtered and stopped. Soon he came into the radio shack.

"Bob," he said, "Remember the guy that brought two cans of gas in the other day?"

"Yeah, I remember. We said he must have worked extra hard."

"Well," said Sattem, "That so-and-so didn't work hard. He just took his gas and poured half of it into an empty can, and topped both of 'em off with water."

We had been conned by an illiterate native.

Our cache of gasoline helped for only a short while. Unfortunately, it was 100-octane gasoline—airplane gasoline—and not suitable for our battery charger. It was too powerful. Result: A blown head gasket. Problem: We had no spare gaskets.

We were forced to fall back on an emergency steam-powered charger, which I despised because it was such a problem to transport. I would gladly have had it captured by the Japanese. Smith, over my objections, had insisted I bring it with me. I had a disloyal suspicion that he wanted someone to take it off his hands.

The copper boiler was about eighteen inches in diameter and stood five feet tall. To a Kentucky moonshiner it would have been a dandy part for a still. The bottom housed the firebox; a copper tube ran from the top to an independent steam turbine connected by a direct-drive shaft to the charger. A steam-powered pump sucked water from a bucket and forced it into the boiler to maintain the water level. Attached to the top of the boiler was a safety valve—which never worked. A pressure-controlled, steam-driven blower was supposed to keep the fire at the proper intensity to maintain constant steam pressure. It, too, never worked.

A complex piece of poorly conceived machinery, this abomination, although it did the job of charging the batteries after a fashion, required constant manual control of the fire and, when the pressure got too great, of the safety valve. I had visions of it blowing up. Eventually it did.

Sattem, meanwhile, went off in search of gasket material. This seems to be such a common item in our present society. But in an area without roads, cars, engines? We found engine gasket material nonexistent in our local neighborhood jungle. In Catanauan, Sattem found a Chinese merchant who had a source of asbestos. In his *bodega,* warehouse, he had a kitchen range—a gas stove! Like the "porcelain pony" I had found on Samar, here was another true Oriental anomaly. Why would anyone have a gas stove a hundred miles from the nearest gas line? Bottled propane was not exactly a household item in the jungles, either. Sattem negotiated a price of one hundred Philippine pesos for the stove. He didn't even remove it from the premises. He just tore it apart and brought all of the asbestos back to camp.

At best, this was a poor solution to the gasket problem. The asbestos was more or less laminated, but it lacked a strong binder and did not lend itself to use as a gasket. Sattem, though, would not be defeated. He carefully cut gasket after gasket of the shape needed, and when one blew he would pull the head of the charger's engine and replace the gasket. This was a daily chore—sometimes requiring two replacements for each charging. Konka pitched in to help him.

Bernard Anderson was an Air Corps officer who had been around when the islands fell. He now had a guerrilla organization in the Sierra Madre mountains in east-central Luzon. Bob Ball was with him, or at least nearby, but he could not send messages directly to Smith on Samar or to Fertig on Mindanao, and reaching Australia was impossible. Ball's 3BZ radio had died, and he was limited to using one of the small radios—an ATR4. We took over relaying for him.

Anderson promised to send me gasoline, for Ball's radio was Anderson's connection with the outside world, and he depended on us for relay services. Like the gasoline promised by Smith, it never arrived. Over a period of three months, each shipment from one or the other was lost to the Japanese or to hostile guerrillas—usually the Hukbalahaps, a growing Communist third party—or was purposely ditched by couriers, who were, justifiably, afraid to try to move so bulky a material past the Japanese.

Maj. Richard Barros had been with Anderson almost continuously since the surrender to the Japanese in 1942. Recently he had moved from the Baler area in east-central Luzon to the Bicol Peninsula in southern Luzon, there to set up a guerrilla unit under Anderson's command. He had selected a location directly east across Ragay Gulf from my station on Bondoc Peninsula.

From there, he and his group of sixty guerrillas, former Philippine Scouts, ranged along the coast as far south as Balacan. They made hit-and-run forays against the Japanese moving along the highway and railroad in the vicinity of Naga, one of the larger towns in the Bicol area.

Anderson had received a submarine load of supplies in early August—a rendezvous we had been instrumental in arranging—and sent some supplies to Barros. Among these supplies was a radio with which he planned to set up a coastwatcher station, with messages to be relayed by us. Barros sent an operator to my station to arrange codes and schedules.

Several days after Barros's operator left us, we still had not established radio contact. I considered visiting his camp to help him get the station in operation. Naturally, I had an ulterior motive. He had supplies—food, I should hope. Perhaps even some cigarettes! I might as well see what I could scrounge from him. While I contemplated this visit, Barros sent a guide to my camp with a message asking me to come to his camp to help his radio men get on the air.

Sattem and I hired a banca and crew in San Narciso and, with Barros's guide, set sail for the east across Ragay Gulf. A favorable wind from the northwest put us across the bay, some fifteen or twenty miles under the darkness of night, to a sheltered cove on the Bicol side of Ragay Gulf. As the sun appeared over the mountains we were already hiking down the beach to "Ohio Headquarters, Calayan Command." I never did learn the source of this moniker for Barros's hangout. As we neared a particularly rocky scarp pressing on the beach, Pablo Montalvo, our guide, said, "We will go up here, Sair."

And up we went! Straight up the side of the cliff, hundreds of yards up and up, winding through the boulders that formed this rocky crag. We had not had breakfast. In fact, missing meals was almost a daily occurrence during this period, and physical stamina was not my long suit. We hadn't climbed very far before I had to take a rest break. I peered over the edge of the cliff to see how much progress we had made. I couldn't see the beach from which we had started the climb, for the cliff extended out over the bay. All I could see was shallow water with rocky ledges showing mere inches below the surface—sure and sudden death if one should slip and fall. I shrank from the edge, and for the rest of the climb the wall of the trail and I became one.

Two more intervals of climbing, broken by short rest pauses, brought us to the top of the cliff and onto a small plateau boasting a cornfield, a fast-moving stream, and a small hut.

"Whew! What a climb!" I exclaimed. "That's enough work for me for this day!"

"But Sair," panted Pablo, who, besides being our guide, was Barros's number one agent, "We are not yet there, Sair. We must go farther."

"How much farther is this place?" I couldn't see anything but clouds above us, and surrounding the field where we stood were what looked like impenetrable jungles. Surely this must be the end of the trail.

"It is very near now, Sair." Pablo could see that I was worn out, and I'm sure he knew that if he told me we still had more than a mile to go I would surely give up. "Perhaps we can get some food here, Sair."

The hut—a guard post on the only trail into the camp—was occupied by some guerrilla soldiers. They had breakfast rice on the stove, and we invited ourselves in for a helping. Then out into the jungles we headed, following a trail through vines, bushes, trees, and dense undergrowth. It was, however, less steep and only a mile long, and all at once we were out of the jungle and into another clearing, which proved to be our destination. Here, at last, was "Ohio Headquarters."

At the door we were greeted by Barros—six feet, four inches of man thinned down by the privations of the jungles to a bony framework. But even without the weight he had lost during the past three years, he was *big*. With him was a much smaller, elderly American, Ted Suttles, who had been held prisoner by the Japanese for a long time at Naga but had been among a group that was sprung from the prison by guerrillas. He had been employed by a mining company in Camarines Norte when the surrender came. Along with many others, Americans and Filipinos, he had been sure it would be only a question of a month or so until the Stars and Stripes would again fly over the Philippines. That was more than two years ago.

Our walking into this camp was like Stanley meeting Livingstone, only there were two Stanleys and two Livingstones. Handshakes and greetings—all of us taking unsurpassed delight in seeing fellow countrymen. We sat there most of the morning swapping stories about our escapades and accomplishments over some day-old tuba. Barros broke out a pack of Luckies, and Sattem and I both vowed to ourselves that as long as there was a cigarette in that pack we were *staying*. The smokes alone made our trip worthwhile, climbing the cliff included.

Our conversation drifted to the main purpose of my visit, and my use of the word "radio" triggered Barros to action. He was all for heading out to his radio shack then and there. He obviously was irritated.

"Why does GHQ send half-trained radiomen from Australia?" he griped. "They might be good code clerks, but what's the good of that if they can't get the damned radio going?"

"Let's wait awhile until I rest up," I said. There were still some cigarettes in the pack. "Then we'll see what's wrong."

So we sat and chinned some more. To a stranger it would have appeared to be an old ladies' sewing circle. Barros told us of having just picked up a native who had turned information about his location over to the Japanese and that he was expecting trouble soon. About a week later the Japanese did come after him, and even though he had set up in this seemingly perfectly defendable location, he had to abandon it and make several quick moves until the enemy patrols gave up the search.

After having a bit of rice for lunch, Barros said, "Now, let's get up to the shack and see if you can get us on the air."

"Did you say 'up'?"

"Yes. The station is on top of that hill behind us. It's only about a mile."

Another mile of hiking and climbing, if anything like what we had done earlier in the day, would do me in, I feared. But off we went, climbing and crawling through more jungles until at last we reached the pinnacle. I was sure there wasn't a higher spot on the entire island of Luzon. For a defensive position this was "the tops," I told myself, and laughed to myself at the pun.

The radio station was situated at a perfect spot for coastwatching. It commanded a view of the eastern portion of the Sibuyan Sea and many of its islands: Burias, Romblon, Sibuyan, Tablas, and, in clear weather, a portion of Mindoro. In fact, from this vantage point they would be reporting many of the convoys we were reporting. Also, from here one could see where we had sent a Japanese launch to its doom in the Sibuyan Sea on Memorial Day.

The radio operators were trying to make some contacts, but with no success. It wasn't their fault. They hadn't been schooled in proper operation of the type of equipment they were using. In fact, they had never even seen this kind of equipment in their training, nor had I ever seen a radio like this before. This was not an unusual situation, for the Army sent a lot of equipment to us that might be classified as junk—equipment long ago labeled unfit for combat use. Here was a perfect spot to dispose of these purchasing mistakes, for we were not in a position to complain.

This radio was a low-output field radio powered by a hand-cranked generator. After tinkering with it for a short while, I found that both the transmitter and the receiver would drift off frequency without warning, and radio contact would be lost. I had learned with "The Dutch Set" on Samar that it was necessary to maintain a steady speed when operating the bicycle-powered generator, or else a similar frequency fade would result. As soon as we had mastered the equipment's idiosyncracies and established the steady cranking rate for the hand-powered generator, we were able to get it working fairly reliably. I was satisfied after I contacted Nery at S3L and later reached Ball, who was up north with Anderson. These were the two stations Barros would need to contact with regularity.

Now it was late afternoon. Time for us to head home. We had had our cigarettes. Barros's station was on the air. The purpose of our trip was fulfilled. With a couple of packs of cigarettes and precious few packs of Army field rations in our possession, Barros sent us on our way. I had hoped his generosity would extend to include a tommy gun or two, or perhaps a new pair of shoes, but that was wishful thinking.

Now we had to climb down those dangerous cliffs. I hoped I would be surefooted on the trail, because in my mind I could still see those shallow waters below the cliff, and falling into them was not exactly how I would like to die. Pablo skillfully led the way, though, and soon we were back to our sailboat.

Night was well upon us. The wind had shifted and was now coming from the northeast. The boat's skipper said that was good—almost perfect for the return trip.

We moved out from shore. The night grew darker. The stars disappeared behind a bank of clouds. The wind grew stronger and quite chilly. I grew sleepy, and was soon slumbering in the hold, stretched out on a board, with a buri mat for a blanket.

I don't know how long I slept before I was suddenly awakened by a loud "Crrraack!" I heard the Filipinos shouting to each other, and louder than the rest was Sattem's voice yelling to them in English. They understood very little English, but he must have thought that by yelling louder than they he could make them understand him. I scrambled out of the hold and onto the deck by the mainmast.

"What's up!" I shouted to Sattem. He didn't have to answer, for no sooner were the words out of my mouth than a great wave rolled across the deck. I grabbed the mast to keep from being washed overboard.

"Typhoon! Typhoon!" I heard someone shout. And it was. The rain was coming down in torrents, and the monstrous waves were picking up our boat and tossing it at will across the heavy seas. I dived back down into the hold to see what had made the noise that awakened me. Two large beams ran from each outrigger, connecting it to the boat, but the forward beam of one was no longer fastened. The waves had pounded it loose from the supports. I knew we would capsize immediately without outriggers, so I grabbed some heavy rattan and worked furiously to lash the beam fast, then searched out some stout rope with which I fastened it even more securely.

This done, I went back topside. The wind was bending the mast almost to the breaking point, the supports creaking under the strain. Sattem was aft on the tiller with one of the natives, while two other natives held the boom into the wind.

"Crrraack!" Another outrigger support let loose. Again I jumped down into the hold, grabbing a piece of rope as I went, and lashed another beam fast.

But in the hold I was now knee-deep in water. *She's going to be swamped!* I said aloud to myself. I went back up on deck to man the pump—an inefficient gadget consisting of a bamboo tube with a smaller bamboo pole inside and some sort of makeshift flapper on its end to suck up the water. I pumped feverishly while two natives lay on and clung to the outriggers to keep the boat balanced as she rolled over the crests of the waves.

And the rain continued its downpour. The sky was black, the water was black. It was impossible to see anything even from one side of the sailboat to the other. *Keep pumping! I told myself. Keep pumping! Tell them to run free. No. Save your breath. They can't hear you anyway. Save your breath and keep pumping! Look at those outriggers bending. They're going to break and we'll capsize—sure. But keep pumping! Keep her afloat! The sail's ripping. Hang on! Here comes another wave!*

After an eternity the rain stopped, but the waves rolled and the wind blew gales. I pumped and pumped—how long I don't know, but I wasn't tired any more. I was too scared to be tired. Then the wind began to subside, the waves ebbed. The sky began to clear. Dawn was approaching.

I looked aft and could see Sattem and the native—it was Pablo—frozen to the tiller. Both were too tired to move—too tired to care if they moved or not. The natives came in from the outriggers and fell on the deck, exhausted. My pump sucked wind, and I, too, fell on the deck.

The sun rose, and we all crept out of the stupor we were in. There, to the west, was Bondoc Point. We were forty miles off our course. The sail was ripped to shreds, and the outriggers were barely hanging on, but the storm was gone and we were still afloat. Thank God!

All morning long we lay fitfully sleeping on the deck of the boat, adrift in the middle of the mouth of Ragay Gulf. One by one we stirred to life and surveyed the damage. Without a sail we were powerless. The captain put the leo-leo oar off the stern, and we took turns applying the back-and-forth motion that moved us ever so slowly toward the shore. When we ran aground on the shoals, we were still a quarter mile from the beach. Here we spent the night.

When morning came, Sattem and I waded ashore and began the long trek north to San Narciso, where we stayed the night. This had been my first move over water since my encounter with the Japanese launch on 30 May. I vowed to stay off boats—a vow I didn't keep.

The bamboo telegraph told me that another radio station, not of my network, had been established at Bondoc Point. Although I had made an unscheduled landing near the Point at the end of the ill-fated trip to Barros's station a month previously, I had not seen or heard of this intrusion on my territory. I had developed a possessive attitude toward Bondoc Peninsula. It was *my* domain, and I didn't take kindly to interlopers. I decided to go there to investigate.

This was in early October, just a few weeks before MacArthur's landing at Leyte. The Army and Navy were flooding the area with radio stations. Security needs kept us oldsters from knowing of the impending landing. The station at the Point was a part of a new network based on Negros Island and specifically a part of the Leyte landing operation. They weren't anxious to tell me what they were doing, although they admitted they knew of the existence of station S3L and had been told to relay through my station in an emergency. I told them there was a fat chance of that happening unless I got a battery charger somewhere.

They had a spare gasoline battery charger they lent me—insurance that my emergency relay service would be available if they needed it. I sometimes think they gave it to me to get me out of their hair. With it and a drum of regular gasoline, I headed back to my station.

We were to be back in business soon. But not as soon as I expected. En route to the Point, Doming and I had been able to "book space," that is, hitch a ride, on a banca headed our way out of San Narciso—this despite my vow to stay off of boats. We were not so lucky on the return and had to hike the forty-mile trip. In itself that would not be so bad, for hiking was our one dependable mode of transportation, but we encountered bad weather. The wind coming from the northeast carried with it torrential rains, which promised to be our weather for some time. With this storm, I was glad we had not been able to get a boat for the return trip.

I had hired four cargadores to tote the generator and the gasoline. We planned to take an existing path that was more or less on a straight line inland from the coast between Bondoc Point and barrio San Andres to eliminate a roundabout shore route and shorten this leg of our journey. From there we would follow the shore, passing Alibijaban Island to barrio Sabang, then to San Narciso, and finally to our camp. We were hoping for a decent meal in each of the stopovers.

We set out on the hike to San Andres. In dry weather this would be an easy half-day's walk. The rain made it slightly more difficult. It created a sucking mud that grabbed the foot on each stride, making it slow going. Normally small streams had become swamps, knee to hip deep, that we had to cross. Bypassing them would require hacking a new trail—for who knows how far?—to round the swamp and get back to the existing trail. By late afternoon we had finally reached San Andres—muddy, wet, and weary.

The barrio's teniente took Doming and me into his home, sending the cargadores to a nearby house. Doming rigged rattan clotheslines around the firebox to hang our clothes to dry. Our backpacks were relatively waterproof and our spare clothes dry. Packing like this was an art we had learned the hard way a long time before.

I stripped off my clothes and began to towel off. Then I saw them. Leeches! I had heard about these slimy, slithery, blood-sucking bastards, but never met up with them before. They had latched onto me in the damned swamps we had waded through earlier. I grabbed my jungle knife and began to shave them off my legs.

"Alto! Alto! Stop, Sair!" Doming cried. No Tagalog here. His shouts were in Spanish and English.

He tore my knife from my hand. Never had I been disarmed by anyone before, but he did it so quickly I didn't realize it happened. He threw the blade to the side and took a small stick from the fire, one end glowing, and touched it to a leech. I could feel the burning on my skin under it. Slowly the leech withdrew its head from the hole it had burrowed into my hide and fell to the floor. Again and again Doming repeated this act until I was free of them. They had gotten into my pants and attached themselves to my legs, my ass, and to other more personal and pain-sensitive parts. And how the spots where they had taken up residence stung—burned—bled!

I took some sulfanilamide powder and dusted it onto the spots as best I could. I did the same for Doming after he had removed them from his body. Now he showed me what I had been doing wrong with my knife. I had been decapitating them, leaving the problem part, the head, embedded in my flesh. Now there was no way to extract the head. The infecting germs were there to stay.

By the time we reached San Narciso two days later I had more than thirty boil-like sores to contend with. Most healed, eventually, but I still had some of the sores when I got to the Army medics in Manila, months later.

I stayed with the Medenilla family in San Narciso for several days while Doming took command of the four cargadores to transport the charger and gasoline to our camp. I was a pretty sick pup, but good food and rest made for a fast recuperation, except for the boils, which by now had become tropical ulcers.

Seven thousand islands and rocks make up the Philippine Islands. Of these, less than half have names, and only four hundred are occupied. In the 1940s there were few urban centers: Manila, the capital, on Luzon; Zamboanga and Davao on Mindanao; and Iloilo on Panay. This list might be stretched to include Cebu on Cebu Island, and Baguio, the resort city located high in the mountains 130 miles north of Manila. In these metropolitan areas, modern buildings, paved streets, utilities, public transportation, and a host of other conveniences were the rule, and cultural and social activities were as varied and interesting as those of modern cities of comparable size throughout the world. Away from these urban centers was "the great beyond," where 90 percent of the population resided. There these amenities did not exist.

San Narciso, the town I most liked to visit, was a typical major center in a rural, remote location. To call it a commercial hub would be stretching the truth, yet it was the only place where trading took place on the western shore of Ragay Gulf. There stood forty to fifty houses, some built of milled lumber, but most framed with bamboo. All had thatched roofs. Set quite far apart and randomly scattered, they formed two erratic streets paralleling the shore. The only public utility was a water supply font in the center of the town, the water piped in from a mountain stream a half mile away.

A one-room, wood-framed schoolhouse with a corrugated-steel roof was the site for education for all grades through high school, but without extracurricular activities. Desks and benches would be moved to positions along the walls to provide a hall for social activities.

The town boasted a Roman Catholic church with a full-time priest, who was always available for confessions and other pastoral duties. The church observed all religious holidays, including, I suspect, some conceived locally, for they usually concluded with a fiesta.

Along the shore was a rickety municipal pier where, on occasion, a passing merchant in a parao would stop to vend his merchandise. I can only remember one sailboat tied up there regularly, available for rental if someone could afford it.

Surrounding the town were small farms where rice, corn, pineapples, and vegetables were grown. One of these tracts was a cattle "ranch" where a few scrawny cows and an equally decrepit bull were penned in a small area. The bull had long since lost the desire to copulate and no longer needed to be separated from the females. There, also, were several carabao available for hire for moving cargo.

There were no stores. Manufactured items such as clothing and furniture were supplied by cottage industry. There was one restaurant, a house where the mistress provided meals for travelers, and it was there one could rent a space to sleep for the night. Money did not change hands, except for the services provided the travelers or for dealing with the vendors who brought goods to the dock. By bartering, goods and services were traded. We, of course, had little with which to barter, so people accepted money from us.

Few could remember when Mayor Medenilla first took office. The citizens of the town, and of the surrounding barrios under the town's jurisdiction, found him to be a fair and impartial leader. Thus, he served as mayor, secretary, treasurer, tax collector, and justice of the peace, all without pay. His tenure was limitless.

Social life consisted of visiting with friends and neighbors, an activity that can become tedious in a hurry, so to break the monotony people would visit friends or relatives in adjacent barrios from time to time. However, this was a major undertaking, for there was no public transportation available. To make such a visit, one must walk, or else paddle a baroto along the coast to get there. With luck, one could get a ride on a sailboat that happened to be going in the right direction, or ride a carabao that was returning home after toting a load to some distant location. Such luck was a rarity.

Small wonder, then, that a fiesta was the big thing in the lives of these people. These simple get-togethers added a semblance of zest to an otherwise extremely boring life. Any excuse at all was ample reason for a fiesta.

First came the food: rice, camotes, exotic coconut dishes, papaya, pineapple, bananas both fried and raw, surrounding a suckling pig roasted on a spit, complete with uniquely flavored herbal sauces. Next came the entertainment: surprisingly good home-grown talent sang, danced, and played solo instrumental offerings. One young man played classical guitar selections on what would be considered, anywhere, a professional level. Proud parents would steal sly glances at us to sense what we Americanos thought of their children's talents.

Then it was time for the dancing. A live band played tunes for the native dances, one involving jumping over bamboo poles to a rhythm I could never master. They also played waltz music and American jazz of sorts. We soon learned that, while dancing with the local girls, it was not wise to hold them too closely. The parents on the sidelines liked to see a bit of daylight between the partners. Married couples did not join in the dancing; they did not partake of displays of this nature.

While there was much comic byplay between the young Filipinos and us Americans, we were not beyond being observed with suspicion by the mothers of the maidens in our corner of the hall. They needn't have worried, for we were just there for a chance to relax from the everyday stress of the times.

Assignations were not a part of the game. The young ladies were under constant surveillance, for their mothers considered virginity the principal participant in a wedding procession to the altar. In a town so small, it would be nearly impossible to carry out a tryst. But, young love being what it is, there were some unexpected pregnancies on occasion. Fortunately, none of my men were involved.

At the fiestas, we Americans gravitated to a cluster of girls who were the socialites of the town—the mayor's daughters, Fe, Nacling, and Esther, their cousin Polly, and several others. We were joined by a few young males who, had we not been there, would have been considered the local swains and the eligible bachelors. Fe, sweet sixteen, was the standout, for she was a vivacious coquette whom everyone admired. George McGowan was her choice. Nacling, a bit older but only slightly less comely, liked Sattem. Esther was a child. The rest of us played the field, although I was attracted to cousin Polly, who seemed to be an enigma. Perhaps I was the one who sought a challenge.

Policronia "Polly" Fontanilla was several years older than her cousins. She had gone to college and was now the local schoolmarm. While her skin was a darker brown than that of her cousins, she was, nevertheless, very attractive. Quiet and demure, she was overshadowed in a crowd by her more effervescent cousins. Yet, she displayed a certain coolness and poise that no doubt came from having spent several years in the urban atmosphere of the University of Manila. I enjoyed her company because we were able to converse about things other than the earth-shattering events of the day in San Narciso. Since leaving Mrs. Victoria, the doctor's wife at Borongan, Samar, Polly was the first woman I had met who had been educated beyond the three Rs in a rural school. We spent hours together in conversations on subjects sometimes far beyond my comprehension. To me, this was a purely platonic friendship, and I never came close to making a move on her, for I feared that such an approach might queer our good relationship. Besides, she showed no indication that she considered me more than a pleasant conversationalist who would be moving out of her life as soon as the war was over.

How wrong could I be? In Gilbert and Sullivan's *The Mikado,* Nanki-Poo laments that Katisha "misconstrued my customary affability into expressions of affection." Polly, too, did this. As a result, she gave me a silver ring much like a wedding ring. How was I to know that this was a Filipino custom in which, by accepting the ring, I was indicating that we were engaged, and that I was to give her this ring when we were wed! I had been stateside for a while when I received a letter from a cousin of hers explaining all this to me and asking me to return the ring.

Food and clothing shortages, too, became a major problem. In June I had looked on five hundred pounds of rice as a goodly supply. It wasn't. By mid-July we were getting close to the bottom of the pile. Though we had previously been able to purchase small amounts of this staple, we could no longer buy rice even at highly inflated prices. We augmented our food supply with camotes and some edible roots, and on rare occasions with overpriced chicken or fish purchased in one of the nearby towns. A salad delicacy in today's markets was a staple for us—coconut palm heart. Yet, every tree chopped down for its heart was one less to supply both green and ripe coconuts, which were also a large part of our diet.

Green coconuts were an especially good source of sustenance on the trail. You could quickly quench your thirst by chopping off the end with a bolo and drinking the sweet liquid inside. Then, splitting the nut with a whack of the bolo, you could scrape out the thin layer of soft pulp beneath the shell and fill your stomach with it. This pulp made a satisfying lunch, but it would not be very long before the hunger pangs returned. The meat from mature coconuts, the kind used for grating and baking, stayed with you much longer, but mature coconuts were scarce.

The food shortage became more widespread in the region. The locals raised barely enough food for their families, they said, and grew more reluctant to sell some to us. Yet, for a fiesta, abundant food seemed to appear like magic. I had many mouths to feed—the number varied depending on who was sent where and who arrived in camp unexpectedly—so I faced a major problem. We needed a "procurement officer," someone to roam far and wide to find food for us.

But who should it be? I couldn't send a native from a nearby village, for natives had a habit of straying from a mission for personal reasons. (I once had a native guide take me on a circuitous three-day hike to reach a destination about a half-day's walk from the starting point. He had decided he wanted to visit some of his relatives on the way.) My Filipino soldiers and radio operators could not be spared from their regular tasks, nor could I do without Sattem's mechanical skills or Konka's cryptographic capability. This left McGowan as the one to go far afield to seek food for us.

George was not reluctant to take on this assignment. In fact, he relished it. He was itching to get out of camp and circulate around the peninsula. More than the rest of us, he was, one might say, socially oriented. He enjoyed being with the Filipinos, especially the women, and was not against drinking all the tuba he could find. With his charm—and a pocket full of money—he might well be able to locate food supplies better than anyone else in our group.

This he did, but it took some time. Meanwhile, our rations in camp got smaller and smaller. I took to sending one of the Americans with a couple of the Filipinos on short but unnecessary missions to the nearby towns and barrios. There they would be fed by the citizens, because it was a matter of pride to feed visitors as well as possible.

Nearly a month went by before small amounts of food started to trickle into camp, sent by George from quite distant places. Meanwhile, I appealed for a shipment of rice from Colonel Smith. Like the gasoline, it was promised but never arrived. I also sent a man to Vera's camp to see if the general had food to spare. The man returned with about twenty pounds of palay and an equal amount of corn. Corn was the lowest item on the food chain, except for unknown roots grubbed from the forest. He told me that Vera had given him every grain of rice he had, and a goodly portion of his corn supply. This from the man I had considered my enemy at one time, the man who had planned to kill my party for its guns.

We took to shooting large birds, then small birds—any wildlife that moved—and roasting them on a spit. We tried to hunt wild cattle—descendants of domesticated herds that were turned loose there years ago after efforts to establish a ranching industry failed. These animals, now scrawny, degenerated runts, had become jungle wise and were quite elusive. We had little success in bagging them. Monkeys were easier to shoot and quite tasty, although, in my mind, this came close to cannibalism.

We were desperate for food during late July, August, and part of September. Then George's efforts started to pay off. He returned in mid-September with a pig in tow, and rice to go with it! And, George had also hired a procurer who continued to send a minimal, but certainly appreciated, supply of food to us. By this time I probably weighed less than a hundred pounds. I had weighed 155 pounds when I got off the submarine on Mindanao.

We had just finished stuffing ourselves with roast pig and rice. I wanted to hear George tell of his travels during the last two months.

"Bob, there ain't much food out there. I covered the whole damned peninsula all the way to the Point, and the little bit I sent you was all I could find.

"But I shoulda' gone to Aurora first." Aurora was a small town on the west coast of the peninsula, about forty miles south of our camp. "The Puyal family there fixed me up with most of the food I sent you. They're nice folks—especially the daughter, Loring." Half facetiously, half seriously, he added, "I wanta' marry that gal."

The Puyals had lived in the Luneta section of Manila, one of the most exclusive areas, before they "buckwheated" to Aurora. Months later, after I got to Manila, I looked for their home. It had been destroyed, as had been all of the area of the city lying south of the Pasig River.

"I stayed there with them for a couple of weeks. That's where I got this." He pointed to a scar below his left ear.

He continued, anticipating the question I was about to pose. "Nah. I didn't get this at the Puyal house. I was settin' there drinkin' tuba in a coconut grove along the shore, and a Jap launch pulled into the bay. It dropped anchor about a half kilometer out."

He paused, and it was easy to see that he was rerunning the events of that day through his mind, even to the extent of changing his facial expressions as he did so. Then he continued.

"Soon as the Japs dropped anchor, the guerrillas brought a machine gun—one they'd captured from some Japs in a skirmish—down to the shore and aimed it at the launch.

"Well, they weren't doing nothin' on the boat, just anchored there, so I sent some guys to get a big baroto.

"Now it was almost dark, so we got in the baroto with the machine gun and a couple other guns—two guys paddling, two with the machine gun, and four of us with carbines. I figured in the dark we could get close enough to throw a hand grenade or two at 'em."

Again he paused, grinned, then said, "I guess I had too much tuba."

He went on: "I guess I figured that if they saw us comin' we could open up on 'em with the machine gun to keep 'em from firing back at us. We were about in pitchin' range with a grenade when they started shootin' at us. We opened up with the machine gun, but it jammed. Everybody in our boat panicked and went overboard but me. I stood up with my rifle and started shootin' at the Japs. Some lucky son of a bitch hit me in the neck."

He laughed. It was a funny event now that it was over.

"Knocked me outta the boat, and I hadda swim to shore. Never did throw the hand grenade. But we sure scared the bastards away."

The slug had entered his neck under his ear and exited about two inches behind. It was just a deep flesh wound, but it was worth a Purple Heart. He treated it with sulfanilamide powder and had no trouble from it.

They say an army travels on its stomach. I disagree. An army travels on its feet, and those feet need shoes. The men who journeyed from Samar to Bondoc Peninsula with me each had two pairs of GI shoes and one pair of jungle boots. I had the same. In addition, I had brought along a small assortment of boots of both kinds in several sizes, and these were stashed away as future replacements. That assortment disappeared in a hurry. I supplied a pair to Robles, who had been on Bondoc since January and was practically shoeless when we arrived. Several pairs went to the three POWs, who had been shod with worn-out Japanese army sandals when we met. Some went to local Filipinos who were barefoot when they joined our group, although many could not find a pair small enough to fit and decided to continue to go without.

In a short time the many miles of hiking and the sloshing around in the mud began to take its toll on the footwear. The leather in the GI boots rotted because we were never able to completely dry them; the canvas tops of the jungle boots wore out quickly, as did the sneakerlike soles. We took to saving our shoes and boots by wearing hand-fashioned wooden clogs around the campsite. And socks were soon only a memory.

Worn-out khaki trousers became cutoffs, to go with a tattered GI undershirt. The only time we were attired in a chino uniform was when we dressed formally to go to town. Shoes were only worn when we were on the trails or in fancy dress.

While the lack of clothing was an inconvenience, and we griped and bitched about the shortage, it was not a deterrent to our operations. We could have done our job in loincloths if necessary. Fortunately, we did receive some supplies before we were reduced to that kind of attire. Nevertheless, we presented a ragtag appearance in our fatigues and combat gear. There could be no doubt that we were irregulars, and not all the sort you would want to invite home to meet Mother or chance upon in a dark alley.

A Different Kind of War

PART 4

The Leyte Landing

CHAPTER 13

When I think of the period from June to October 1944, I consider it to be analogous to a three-ring circus. All of us in that circus had a common purpose—the defeat of the Japanese forces in the Philippine Islands. But, like circus performers, we each had a distinct "act" leading toward that end, and that is what we did, ignoring for the most part the other acts going on around us.

For example, I would send a message to Charlie Smith saying that a courier was on his way to him with some important papers. Once that courier departed my station, he was on his own. I was not with him, could not help him, could not rescue him if the need arose. I had to put him out of my mind for the time being. I had other priorities. The main priority was survival—mine, that of my men, and that of S3L. Our part of the show had one prime objective: to keep the information flowing to GHQ in Australia, assuming that GHQ was still where I left it.

A month later I would send Smith another message asking if the courier had arrived yet. My message would usually end, "I am worried." Not infrequently Smith would respond, "Courier arrived a week ago." Smith had been busy with *his* priorities. Informing me of the arrival of the courier and the materials was not important to him.

Sometimes the priorities of one of us stepped on the toes of another of us. For example, when Lieutenant Labrador departed Samar the day after our rendezvous with the *Narwhal* in May, Smith ordered him to sail up the east coast of Luzon to carry supplies to Bob Ball, who was located in the guerrilla sector controlled by Bernard Anderson. On completion of that mission Smith would have another important job for him. Four months passed before Labrador arrived at my camp on Bondoc Peninsula. I advised Smith of his arrival, and received the following message in response:

LABRADOR ARRIVED TOO LATE, AS JOB DONE SINCE YANKS LANDED. HAVE HAD NOTHING BUT TROUBLE FROM ANDY. TRIED TO GET LABRADOR FOR THREE MONTHS TO DO SPE-CIAL JOB FOR GHQ FOR WHICH HE IS SUITED. ANDY PROMISED TO SEND HIM TO YOU SEPTEMBER 20. NO USE FOR HIM NOW. PLEASE HAVE HIM MAKE REPORT OF ACTIVITIES SINCE JUNE 20.

Labrador's report:

> We landed at the rendezvous point on June 2. We were attacked by hostile guerrillas there, but pacified them and they contacted Major Anderson for me.
>
> Anderson came, took over all the supplies and equipment and told me Ball was in the Bicol region. Ball's agents arrived five days later and took Lieutenant Ancheta, two operators and one radio to Ball.
>
> I was put in charge of communications at Anderson's headquarters.
>
> During the last week in July I was sent to Ball with one radio and my spare parts. Ball did not need me and sent me back to Anderson four days later, where I stayed until September 11 when I left for Bondoc Peninsula.
>
> I was delayed south of Infanta because there was no banca available for me, and because of a Japanese raid on the camp. I left there September 20 for Tayabas, a five day trip by trail and banca.
>
> I departed Tayabas September 30 for Pagbilao, arriving October 10, thence by banca to Robles four days later and arrived at S3L October 17.

Smith and GHQ had had far different plans for using Labrador's talents, but once he was out of Smith's sight he was a pawn to be used by others. As it was, Labrador's skills as an undercover agent went unused as he ran from place to place serving as a courier and a radio operator. I have no idea what Labrador's special talents might have been. An individual's safety and security dictated that such information was only available on a need-to-know basis, and I didn't need to know.

It would be safe to say that each of us operated on a day-to-day basis inside imaginary plastic domes, ignoring the others. Just like circus performers, each did his job—or tried to.

Despite our problems —primarily, failing equipment and lack of food and supplies—our workload increased by leaps and bounds during the summer of 1944. My network of watcher stations reported more shipping movements; agents' stations were sending in more information and collecting more documents to be sent to the south; the guerrillas to the north had more information traffic to be relayed; and Vera's station was overwhelming us with reports of troop movements and Japanese defenses. Many of the last I took with a grain of salt, but my orders were to send *all* information, be it seen, heard, or rumored. I was not to try to assess and evaluate it—just send it along.

Sergeants Herreria and Cardenas, my "Men in Manila," brought extremely useful information out of the city. Not only did they report on the activities there, but they had also established rapport with some Filipinos working for the Japanese—Puppet Government officials who were secretly loyal to the Americans. From them they obtained information of activities on the Japanese homeland gathered while the officials were on goodwill trips to Tokyo.

On one of their early trips into Manila, Herreria and Cardenas had taken with them one of several radios we had that were designed, supposedly, for espionage use in close quarters. We called them "suitcase sets." Packed inside a container a bit larger than a briefcase, these units consisted of a transmitter that emitted a one- or two-watt signal (sufficient to broadcast across town, perhaps, but only under perfect atmospheric conditions), a receiver, and a clear-glass, acid-filled, wet-cell battery with a woefully weak 110-volt converter to charge it. They bore no resemblance to the suitcases and briefcases toted by businessmen in Manila—or any other city, I would guess. Heavy and clumsy, like a suitcase full of bricks would be, they could have drawn more attention only if they had borne a sign: "Nab me! I'm a spy!"

Before they reached the populated suburbs, Herreria and Cardenas put the radio to a test. As a communications tool, it failed miserably. After considering what it might do to their security, they dropped it into Manila Bay.

We distributed the rest of these sets to several of our watcher stations, there to be used as decoys, purposely left behind (although they had been rendered inoperable) if the station was located and overrun by the Japanese, in hopes that the enemy would think they had successfully eliminated the station and would abandon the chase.

Sergeant Nery and two operators spent day after endless day sending and receiving message traffic, sometimes operating two radios side by side to clear the backlog of messages. Often I spelled them to ease the pressure. When we thought we were caught up on the work, a piece of equipment would break down and cause another logjam. To say it was hectic would be a gross understatement.

By September, Japanese air traffic was plentiful. It was obvious that MacArthur, Nimitz, and party were approaching the islands. Large flights of Japanese planes were ranging out in search of the U.S. Navy ships. Now we were given the additional chore of reporting these flights, a high-priority assignment. The reports were sent in a brevity code, which needed no enciphering, but they had to be passed to GHQ within ten minutes of the sighting or they were useless.

Early in October we were told that all messages to and from Anderson, Lapham, and Volckmann were "extremely urgent." This could only mean one thing—submarine rendezvous. Around 16 October, the submarine *Sero* missed contact with Volckmann, and his thirty-five tons of gear was taken, instead, to Anderson. Within a day or so the *Nautilus* successfully met Lapham and put ashore a demolition team to destroy roads, railroads, and bridges leading to Manila from the northeast. The same submarine dropped off a similar team at Anderson's location to destroy like facilities east of the city. The time had come for the guerrillas to go into action in force against the enemy.

Suddenly all was quiet. What is more noticeable than the sudden cessation of din? Aside from the dits and dahs of far-distant stations, there wasn't a sound on the air. The silence was broken on the afternoon of 19 October with this message from GHQ:

DESIRE THAT YOU ALERT ALL RADIO STATIONS AND COAST
WATCHER STATIONS TO MAXIMUM VIGILANCE FOR DETECTION

AND IMMEDIATE REPORT ANY NAVAL OR AIR MOVEMENT DUR-
ING PRESENT OPERATIONS.

I tuned in the Voice of Freedom (VOF) station. Nothing there, but I decided to just sit on that frequency for a while.

I awoke before dawn on Friday, 20 October, the radio still tuned to America's propaganda frequency. Still nothing. I stepped outside, stretched, urinated, and got a drink of water. I thought I heard the drone of many airplanes. No. It's too early. The Japanese don't start flying until daylight. But the sound grew louder. Soon, though still concealed by the darkness, formation after formation of Japanese planes was passing overhead, the noise saying they were coming from the northwest—Manila— heading toward the southeast. We could distinguish between the sounds of American and Japanese planes. We had also developed the ability to guess with accuracy the number of planes in a flight by the sound if the planes were not visible. I had never guessed numbers of this magnitude.

I ran to George's lean-to, which was next to mine, awakened him, and told him to get everybody up. Then I went back to the radio, switched to the AWAW (air warning) frequency, and started to bang out a message. I couldn't give any details on the makeup of the flights, but at least I could let someone know there were flights of Japanese planes on their way.

We had a busy day. Radio operators Advincula and Ramos took our standby sets and headed to two of our lookout posts. Nery and I stayed by the main set and relayed anything we could. I don't remember having taken time to eat anything that day.

Our efforts were rewarded. Late in the day, far to the south of us, we saw a flight of American planes—Navy Hellcats, I presumed, take on a flight of Japanese bombers with Zeros in escort. We whooped it up when we saw two bombers and three Zeros go down in flames. Sadly, two of our planes were also shot down.

In the evening we all sat around the radio listening to the VOF station. Its silence was now broken. It told of the American beachhead being established—not on northeastern Mindanao, as I would have guessed, but on Leyte Island. We cheered, drank any alcohol we could find, toasted everybody we could think of, and got gloriously drunk. Soon we would be going home!

The Filipinos were not about to let a little thing like the Leyte landing interfere with their plans for a fiesta. On 23 October 1944, men, women, and children, about fifty families in all, arrived in the area of station S3L and established temporary campsites in the surrounding woods. For the next three days and nights we enjoyed good food—barbecued pig on a spit, baked and fried chicken, fried and boiled fish, rice, camotes, and many desserts; good drinks—Japanese beer, nipa wine, tuba gathered fresh each day; dancing to live music; and general good family fun. My favorite young man with classical guitar-picking skill entertained us for hours. On the morning of the twenty-sixth, the Roman Catholic priest from San Narciso arrived and invoked a blessing on the festivities and on the one being honored. No matter that the honoree was not a Catholic. The people had gathered to join with me in celebrating my twenty-fourth birthday. I still treasure the memories of that affair, and still have some of the gifts I received that day. It was, without doubt, my most wonderful "surprise" party.

Search and Rescue

CHAPTER 14

Our lives and our operations changed dramatically after GHQ was established on Leyte. The Philippine campaign was far from over, and much was to be done before the Japanese were driven from the islands. Forward echelons of GHQ's communications units were promptly established after Leyte was recaptured. No longer was there a need for us to relay messages from the coastwatcher, weather, and air warning stations to KAZ, since all were within range of direct contact with these advanced units. True, we still had the important job of collecting information from our agents, and of protecting them from detection by the Japanese. This task consumed much of our time and effort.

However, many of our sustenance problems simply ceased to exist. For example, we soon had an adequate food supply—in far less time than would have been required for a new crop of rice or other viands to grow to maturity. As others before me have rationalized one of Jesus' miracles—"The Feeding of the Multitudes"—what might have happened there in Biblical times could have been happening here. One or two families reached into their hidden stashes of food and offered some to their neighbors. Others followed suit. Island citizens suddenly stopped hoarding food, for the fear of starvation was no longer present. Now food was plentiful, and was shared.

The mercenary guerrillas who had ambushed couriers en route to me and stolen whatever it was they were carrying now wanted to get on the bandwagon. They came to me seeking "recognition" so that we would supply them with arms. Most I ignored, secretly hoping they would get their just due from their peers after the war was over.

Since the Japanese were occupied elsewhere, we had little trouble moving supplies and equipment around. Now, instead of being a part of an advance warning system, we became a part of the operations in a war zone.

Our primary task became search-and-rescue missions, hunting for Allied pilots who had to ditch their planes in our area. On 21 November we received the first of many requests for this service from KAZ:

Rescued pilots are taken to a PBY for evacuation. *(National Archives)*

DESIRE YOU TO MAKE EVERY EFFORT TO RESCUE NAVAL FLIER FORCED DOWN 19 NOVEMBER. LAST SEEN ON RAFT NORTH OF MARINDUQUE ISLAND, 13 DEGREES 43 MINUTES NORTH, 121 DEGREES 51 MINUTES EAST.

This was soon followed by another message:

IMMEDIATELY DESIRE INFORMATION AS FOLLOWS: NUMBER OF AMERICAN FLIERS NOW IN YOUR AREA SPECIFYING THOSE WHO SHOULD BE EVACUATED IMMEDIATELY BECAUSE OF PHYSICAL CONDITION. ALSO TWO RENDEZVOUS POINTS WHERE ALL PERSONNEL COULD BE ASSEMBLED FOR SEAPLANE PICKUP ON FIVE DAYS' NOTICE. NOTIFICATION WILL BE SENT YOU OF RENDEZVOUS SITE CHOSEN AND ETA OF RESCUE PLANE. NAME, RANK, SERIAL NUMBER AND PHYSICAL CONDITION AND EXACT WHEREABOUTS OF EVERY RESCUED FLIER IN YOUR AREA AT PRESENT SHOULD BE SENT AS AVAILABLE IN A SEPARATE MESSAGE.

I followed this on 24 November with the following:

SIX NAVY FLIERS SHOT DOWN AT BONDOC POINT ARE IN MY AREA. PHYSICAL CONDITION OK. BEST RENDEZVOUS SITE IS IN RAGAY GULF OFF BARRIO ABUYON, FIVE MILES NORTH-WEST OF SAN NARCISO, TAYABAS. APPROXIMATE POSITION 13 DEGREES 37 MINUTES NORTH 122 DEGREES 43 MINUTES EAST. HAVE THREE YANKS FORMERLY POW ESCAPED FROM JAPS WHO NEED MEDICAL CARE BADLY. REQUEST THEY BE INCLUDED AS PASSENGERS ON RESCUE PLANE.

Then this from GHQ:

PLEASE ADVISE NAME, SERIAL NUMBER AND CARRIER OF FLIERS. CIRCUMSTANCES DO NOT PERMIT EVACUATION IMME-DIATELY. ADVISE IF FLIERS AND FORMER POW COULD SAFELY BE TAKEN TO MARINDUQUE FOR EVACUATION. STAND BY TILL DEFINITE RENDEZVOUS CAN BE ARRANGED.

I did not participate in or witness this, the first of many pickups, for it took place near Bondoc Point and was arranged by the "interloper" radio station I had visited months ago. Sattem, Konka, and McGowan were not on the passenger manifest. It would be several months before they were evacuated.

Probably the most interesting of the rescue operations was the evacuation of Lt. Willard Davis of the Twenty-fifth Photo Reconnaissance Squadron. Davis was a Photo Joe, flying a P-38 made light, fast, long range, and high flying by stripping it of its armament. The plane carried only a pilot, cameras, and lots of gasoline.

Davis and I were sipping nipa wine with Mayor Medenilla on his veranda in San Narciso. It was mid-January 1945. The Americans had conquered Leyte, Mindoro, and lesser islands, had landed at Lingayen Gulf and other strategic points, and were now engaged in an all-out assault on Manila. The Japanese had no troops to assign to seeking out and destroying station S3L. I was small potatoes. I was able to spend practically all of my time in town with little fear of capture, maintaining contact with Nery at S3L by radio. This I appreciated, for I was in sad physical shape. Now weighing less than a hundred pounds, I had constant stomach cramps, full-fledged dysentery, tropical ulcers, scabies, and occasional bouts of malaria—fortunately not of the malignant variety.

Davis described his ordeal: "I had flown out of Mindoro on a photo mission over Formosa. I had no trouble getting the pictures—just went there over the top of everyone else, swooped down and made a couple of low-level runs over the island, then climbed up and out and headed home. But then I encountered bad weather, got lost, began to run out of daylight. I was so low on fuel, I knew I had to ditch."

He paused. We sipped and all lit cigarettes.

"Well," he continued, "I dropped down out of the overcast and saw a small island with an inviting beach that looked like a great landing strip. I went around, cut back to stall speed, prepared to land. But the ground was going by so fast I had visions of me and my plane being scattered from hell to breakfast if the wheels should dig into soft sand.

"I figured jumping might be better, so I went back upstairs to about a thousand feet. I was back in the clouds and couldn't see where my parachute might take me. I chickened and came back down to the island.

"Now I had no choice. I was down to a teaspoon of fuel. I did a wheels-up landing, slid across the beach, and veered into the water. I was bounced around a bit, but I wasn't hurt.

"The plane settled in about three feet of water. I crawled out, grabbed my cameras and survival gear, and went up on the beach. Your guys saw me go in and picked me up the next day."

All this had taken place on Templo Island, 18 January 1945.

At high noon, 28 January, a PBY—a Catalina flying boat—came to Ragay Gulf opposite barrio Abuyon. While it circled afloat on the water a short distance offshore, two natives took Davis, his cameras, and me to its side in a baroto.

We had received an airdrop of supplies about a week previously, which had included several .50-caliber machine guns. Unfortunately, they were useless to us, for there was no oil in their buffers—and no containers of oil in the shipment. Without buffer oil the guns would jam immediately.

I crawled up into the PBY and told the captain of my useless buffers, hoping he would have some spare oil on board to give me. He had none—but he gave me the buffers *out of his own guns!*

"Don't worry about it," he shouted over the noise of the engines. "I've got two escorts up there who'll get me home."

I protested, but not much. I needed those buffers.

Being overgenerous can sometimes get one in trouble, and this was one of those times.

The PBY circled, breaking up the smooth surface of the water to make takeoff easier, then headed out into the slight breeze coming from the northeast. The plane was no more than a hundred feet above the water when three Zeros appeared from over the mountains behind us. The escort planes each took out after one of the Japanese planes, leaving the third Zero to attack the flying boat.

The PBY dropped down until it was barely above the surface of the water. Had there been any chop, it would have been splashing in the waves. The captain reduced speed and maneuvered the plane in a large circle. The Zero climbed, then dove with guns blazing. Missed. Again and again the Zero climbed, dove, blazed, missed. The Japanese pilot couldn't dive low enough to get an accurate shot at the PBY and still pull out of his dive before crashing into the drink.

After what seemed to me to be an interminably long time, but was only a few minutes, the fighters returned. One went after the Zero, and the other went off as escort as the PBY climbed out and disappeared from our view toward Mindoro.

I know they made it back to base safely. I was evacuated to Mindoro in the same manner several weeks later, and I met up with Lieutenant Davis again. To show his appreciation for what we had done, he took

me for a ride, piggyback, in his P-38. He climbed, dove, looped, spun—
"wrung it out," as the pilots used to say. It was a real thrill for me,
although I popped my cookies.

Not all our search missions had pleasant endings. We received the following message from KAZ:

> LT. JOHN WOLF AND LT. EDWIN ROBINSON MARINE PILOTS
> BELIEVED TO HAVE CRASHED VICINITY OF NORTHERN BURIAS
> ISLAND 13 DEGREES 10 MINUTES NORTH 123 DEGREES 00
> MINUTES EAST AFTERNOON JANUARY 6. DESIRE YOUR FORCES
> BE NOTIFIED AND REPORT IMMEDIATELY ANY INFO RECEIVED
> REGARDING ABOVE PERSONNEL.

We located their crash site some sixty miles northwest of Burias
Island, near the town of Catanauan, close to our station. The following
is an eyewitness account:

> The pilot apparently tried to land on the shore but the
> plane was out of control with the right wing burned away.
> At first contact with the ground the body of the pilot was
> thrown clear of the wreckage. Identification could not be
> made as the body was mutilated beyond recognition and no
> identification was found. The plane proceeded into the bay
> and sank to 30 feet. The body of Robinson was recovered
> from there, definitely identified by dog tag. He also was
> wearing a pistol, serial number 909823. Robinson was
> buried in Catanauan cemetery and Wolf was buried at spot
> where his body was found. The plane was numbered 313.

Airdrop—Finally!

CHAPTER 15

Although our food supply problem eased dramatically with the Leyte landing, we still needed military supplies, and we weren't getting them in any effective quantity. I couldn't understand why. No AIB penetration party anywhere in the islands could match our record for consistency of operation. Since our first radio broadcast to Charlie Smith on 31 May 1944, the day we arrived on Bondoc Peninsula, we had not been off the air for one single day. Whenever we were forced to move, we hopped, skipped, and jumped while operating temporary stations in order to maintain radio contact of some sort (admittedly not always the most efficient operations) until the move was completed. Even Fertig's station, KUS, on Mindanao, the most efficient of the guerrilla stations, had closed down for at least one period of twenty-four hours during a Japanese siege. Surely our performance should count for something.

Instead, we were being treated like the poor country cousins, forced to mooch supplies by the handful. It seemed we were being given no choice but to kiss the butts of the Johnny-come-latelies. These relative newcomers to the neighborhood had landed on the Bicol Peninsula on the opposite side of Ragay Gulf less than two weeks before the Leyte invasion. Worse, we were called upon to be the go-betweens to arrange further supply runs for the Bicol bunch, with none coming to us.

We needed supplies—and lots of them. Vera now had a well-trained, well-disciplined guerrilla army. He claimed a force numbering close to a thousand men, and I don't believe that number was much inflated.

Where Bondoc Peninsula joins the mainland in the area around Lopez, the mountains press close to the sea, forcing the only road and railroad connecting the Bicol region to the Manila area to traverse a very narrow coastal plain for some thirty miles. Here, in the Atimonan bottleneck, Vera's army could be extremely useful. Properly armed and equipped, they could effectively cut off the movement of Japanese troops and supplies from the Bicols to the Manila area—troops now moving through freely to reinforce the besieged Japanese defenders of the capital city. In return for his cooperation in gathering intelligence information for the past several months, I had promised Vera plenty of arms when the time came for his army to fight. He had kept his side of the bargain extremely well, and now I couldn't fulfill my part of the deal. He and his men were itching for action, and the U.S. Army was letting them, and me, down.

It became increasingly obvious that GHQ's intelligence-gathering unit was not talking to the services of supply unit. We kept getting requests for intelligence information and suggestions for sabotage operations from G-2, but received no weaponry to carry through on them.

I received the following message from GHQ:

> CHECK ON RADAR STATION REPORTED AT BOAC MARINDUQUE. UNIT WOULD BE LOCATED ON HIGH GROUND AND PROBABLY CONSISTS OF THREE TRUCKS, ONE WITH ANTENNA BEHIND CAB, SECOND WITH EQUIPMENT, THIRD WITH ELECTRIC PLANT.

My reply:

> EQUIPMENT FITTING DESCRIPTION OF THREE TRUCK RADAR UNIT LOCATED AT TAYABAS, TAYABAS. TWO OF TRUCKS IN COCONUT SHED 100 YARDS NORTH EAST OF CATHOLIC CHURCH AND 300 YARDS NORTH OF MUNICIPAL PARK WITH GENERATOR UNIT 50 YARDS WEST UNDER MANGO TREE.

I figured this information was sufficient to lead a plane loaded with bombs to the site. Perhaps so, but I received the following message in reply:

> DESIRE THAT YOU DESTROY RADAR UNIT IF POSSIBLE. OUR

INTERCEPT INFO INDICATES THERE MAY BE A SECOND RADAR
IN CLOSE PROXIMITY. IF SUCH IS THE CASE NECESSARY TO
ALSO DESTROY SAME. ADVISE.

I was livid! How in the hell were we supposed to do this? Tear it apart with our bare hands? I had pleaded, begged, cajoled—whatever I thought might work—to get supplies. Ranting and raving, too, had come to naught. I turned to sarcasm and sent GHQ the following:

IS TOUGH JOB WITHOUT DEMOLITION EQUIPMENT BUT WILL
TRY. ALSO LOOKING FOR OTHER UNIT MENTIONED.

A week later I followed up:

GENERAL VERA'S TROOPS FOUND BOTH UNITS AND
DESTROYED THEM—WITH NO HELP AND NO THANKS FROM
THE U.S. ARMY.

My chagrin apparently registered with one or more of the fat-butted, easy-chaired men in GHQ. Along came this message:

ATTEMPTING TO ARRANGE AIR DROP FOR YOU IN NEAR
FUTURE. DESIGNATE AREA NEAR COAST IF POSSIBLE WHICH
COULD BE EASILY IDENTIFIED FROM AIR. FOLLOWING SIGNALS
WILL BE DISPLAYED BY YOU ON DATE TO BE SENT LATER. EACH
OF THREE BAROTOS 200 YARDS APART IN FORM OF TRIANGLE
WITH WHITE FLAG AT POINT OFF SHORE IMMEDIATELY OPPO-
SITE DROP POINT. HAVE THREE SMOKE FIRES BURNING IN
FORM OF TRIANGLE AT DROP SITE. ADVISE.

Finally, GHQ set 26 December 1944 as the drop date. The site would be inland from barrio Abuyon in the cogon grass field we traversed so often when hiking between San Narciso and S3L. We set the barotos, the white flag, and the smoke fires. Like the young lady whose suitor chickened out just before the first date, we were stood up. After three more tries—the first drop arrived on 2 January 1945—two C-47 cargo planes dropped about a hundred parachute loads of supplies, which, to us, were manna from heaven. Less than an hour later, another C-47 came along with about thirty more parachute loads. Now we could continue to fight a war.

American airman and Filipinos transfer supplies from a PBY to a baroto. *(National Archives)*

My euphoria was short-lived, however, when I saw how few supplies we actually received. GHQ had recognized a fact I had overlooked. Without mechanized vehicles to handle the materials when the parachutes hit the ground, each bundle would have to be toted or dragged by hand to the assembly and distribution area. Each parachute bore a load weighing less than a hundred pounds, a weight that could be handled, with some difficulty, by one or two men, depending on the bulk of the package. Most of the shipment consisted of rifles and ammunition—certainly the priority items. In addition, we received forty-eight cases of assorted rations, a case of ATR4 radio batteries, two bundles of assorted clothing, and some much-needed medicine. The latter I turned over to Dr. Mariano N. Morales, who had come to us from Manila.

As it turned out, we had more than enough men to handle the supplies. Anticipating many more bundles and crates than we actually received, I had arranged for General Vera to send a hundred of his soldiers to assist us in gathering up the materials. Vera himself had led his "army" to the drop site. I gave him practically all of the rifles and ammunition: I had finally been able to keep my part of the bargain made many months previously.

Four days later, 6 January 1945, I received the following message from GHQ:

> STARTING IMMEDIATELY UPON RECEIPT OF THIS MESSAGE IS THE TIME ALL PATRIOTIC MOVEMENTS OF THE PEOPLE HAVE THUS, UNDER LOCAL LEADERSHIP, THE OPPORTUNITY TO UNLEASH MAXIMUM POSSIBLE VIOLENCE AGAINST THE ENEMY TO ASSIST OUR LIBERATION CAMPAIGN. EMPLOY ALL MEANS AVAILABLE TO RESTRICT THE MOVEMENTS OF ENEMY FORCES ON LUZON.

The Tayabas Guerrilla Vera's Party lost no time in making use of the arms I had just supplied. By 9 January, when the American forces landed at Lingayen Gulf, Vera's army was in position in the Atimonan bottleneck, where they were very effective in preventing the free movement of Japanese troops.

Meanwhile, I sent a new shopping list to GHQ, asking for the things they had forgotten to send in the drop just received. I wanted more—more—more!

The Abuyon Airfield

CHAPTER 16

GHQ never gave anything without extracting the extra ounce of flesh. Even before the first airdrop was accomplished, I received this message:

WILL AIRDROP SITE AT BARRIO ABUYON MAKE A FEASIBLE CRASH LANDING FIELD? IF SO DESIRE APPROACH TOPOGRAPHY, POSSIBLE LENGTH AND WIDTH OF STRIP, SOIL CONDITIONS.

My reply:

ABUYON WOULD MAKE FEASIBLE CRASH LANDING SPOT. TOPOGRAPHY: RANGE OF MOUNTAINS RUNNING PARALLEL TO COAST LINE, FORMING COASTAL PLAIN APPROXIMATELY ONE MILE WIDE. APPROACHING SITE FROM SOUTH EAST FOLLOW GRADING FOR PROPOSED PROVINCIAL ROAD FROM SAN NARCISO RUNNING NORTH WEST. GRADING SHOULD BE VISIBLE RUNNING THRU COCONUT GROVE TWO MILES LONG. IMMEDIATELY FOLLOWING GROVE IS LARGE COGON GRASS FIELD ON RIGHT SIDE OF ROAD AT BASE OF MOUNTAINS. FIELD ONE MILE LONG, 500 YARDS WIDE WITH HEAVY COGON GRASS COVER. SOIL IS HARD AND LEVEL. ADVISE IF NECESSARY TO CLEAR GRASS.

As you can see, I knew very little about airfields. Why cut the grass if the field was to be nothing more than a place to crash an airplane? GHQ responded:

GRASS MUST BE CLEARED TO MAKE SITE SUITABLE FOR CRASH STRIP. ADVISE EXACT GEOGRAPHICAL COORDINATES OF SITE, CLEARED LENGTH AND DIRECTION OF LONG AXIS. PLEASE NOTIFY WHEN READY FOR POSSIBLE USE.

Sattem went to work clearing the field. He sent out a call for laborers, and the fascination of building an airfield drew a large assemblage. We hadn't figured out how we would pay the laborers for their toil, but, since they didn't ask, we didn't worry about it at the time. We provided three meals a day, and for the time being everyone was happy.

We encountered several snags. Our trail between barrio Abuyon and station S3L crossed this field diagonally. About midway through the tall grass we would encounter a small wet area. When we stripped the grass, we found that the trail crossed the only narrow spot in a swamp. Hidden in the tall grass to either side of the trail were areas of deep, gooey muck, a hundred feet or more in diameter. Here, dead center in our contribution to the safety of our airmen comrades, was a hazard.

Chopping and removing the cogon grass had been easily accomplished with bolos. When we cut the grass close to the ground, however, we found the surface to be a series of hummocks that would certainly give a landing plane fits. We had no picks, no shovels, and no grading equipment. Creating a smooth landing strip posed a problem. The natives, however, were skilled in creating the tools they needed. They went into the nearby woods and cut saplings, which they trimmed to a chisel point on one end. With these they chopped away at the clods of earth, spreading the dirt to fill in the low spots. Then they brought in several carabao and paraded them back and forth, back and forth, tamping the loose dirt into a compact surface. Like the sheeps-foot rollers used to compact mounds of fill on highway construction projects, we had carabao-foot compactors.

We had completed clearing and leveling a bit more than two thousand feet of runway in this manner. Draining the swamp and regrading the area would require equipment of a different kind. We stopped the clearing operation and pondered a solution, but we didn't let that deter us from reporting the field ready for use.

I sent more information to GHQ:

CRASH STRIP 2,200 FEET LONG AND 80 FEET WIDE WILL BE READY FOR USE ON OR BEFORE JANUARY 20. LONG AXIS RUNS 50 DEGREES WEST OF NORTH. COORDINATES 13 DEGREES 36 MINUTES 10 SECONDS NORTH LATITUDE, 122 DEGREES 31 MINUTES 02 SECONDS EAST LONGITUDE. PLEASE ADVISE IF SIZE IS SUITABLE FOR PURPOSE. CAN MAKE IT THREE TIMES AS LARGE IF DESIRED, BUT I HAVE NO MORE FUNDS AND ALL FUTURE WORK WOULD BE SLOW DUE TO BEING VOLUNTEER LABOR WITH NO MODERN TOOLS.

Again, GHQ was very demanding:

DESIRE STRIP LENGTHENED TO MINIMUM OF 3500 FEET. PICKS, SHOVELS, SUPPLIES AND FUNDS WILL BE DROPPED IN NEAR FUTURE.

We continued with the lengthening of the field as requested, not waiting for the promised airdrop of tools for the work. But, before the work was completed, an unfortunate event took place. On 20 January, the day I had told GHQ the *short* field would be completed, three American fighter planes, escorting eight bombers, dropped below the formation, swept down the crash strip in the middle of the day, and let go with several strafing bursts. This may have been a salute from pilots who knew that an emergency field for their use was being built—a thank-you in advance—but it was not received in that way. The laborers took this to be the starting gun for a footrace for home.

Two days later we received another airdrop, which convinced the laborers of the importance of the field and brought them back to work. This drop included what GHQ thought was a goodly supply of tools for airfield construction. They sent us forty entrenching shovels!

Oh, yes—the swamp in the middle of the field. Sattem had a narrow drainage ditch dug across the field through the swamp and beyond the edge of the field toward the ocean. Then he had the ditch sides shored with bamboo poles, bridged it with more bamboo poles to form a makeshift culvert, and covered it with dirt carried in from a nearby hillside in buri baskets on the backs of the laborers. Voila! The swamp was drained.

We made a feeble attempt at camouflage, although this could be self-defeating. Certainly, we did not want the Japanese to discover and destroy this oasis for disabled American aircraft. Yet, we wanted it to be highly visible to our pilots, for in an emergency they would not have time to study maps and charts on which the location may or may not have been pinpointed. They needed to be able to recognize the strip and get down on the ground in a hurry. Knowing that the Japanese air arm was busy with other matters and did not have time to reconnoiter for fields such as this, we tended to err on the side of visibility.

Actually, not much camouflage was needed. We did not make neatly trimmed edges when we cut the cogon grass, and the stubble that remained on the landing strip itself blended, more or less, into the serrated edges of taller grass. From the air, I reasoned, the field would not be detected unless the pilot knew about it. I was bugged, however, by the drainage culvert area. Here was a rather large expanse of freshly churned and compacted dirt. Certainly this abrupt change in the appearance of the land would be highly visible to all. We solved this problem by scattering several small and easily moved huts around this area. The squad of soldiers assigned to guarding this field could quickly move the huts out of the way if a plane attempted a landing.

No matter. The Japanese never bothered us, and, to my knowledge, no pilot ever found it necessary to make an emergency landing on the "Abuyon Airstrip."

On 8 February I sent the following message to GHQ:

AIRFIELD COMPLETED 3700 FEET LONG 70 FEET WIDE. BEST APPROACH FROM NORTH WEST DUE TO SLOPE OF FIELD. HAVE A SURGEON, TRAINED NURSE AND HOSPITAL READY FOR EMERGENCY AT ALL TIMES.

The surgeon was Dr. Morales.

Still, we had the problem of paying the natives for the month or so of labor they had contributed. Our counterfeit Japanese money was not acceptable, for it was no longer being used. We didn't have enough real money to cover the bill. We did, however, have something else of value—parachutes.

During the 1930s, a group of enterprising sewing machine salesmen had peddled their wares throughout the islands. Every town and most barrios had a seamstress or two with a treadle-operated Singer sewing machine. Our nylon parachutes were very acceptable barter items. Here was the cloth for sorely needed shirts, shorts, underwear, blouses, skirts, and dresses. The parachute cords could be unwound, stripped, and spooled to provide the needed thread. The parachutes, color coded to indicate the type of cargo they held, were dyed in brilliant, but ugly, harsh colors so that they were easily spotted when they landed. Soon everyone was strutting around in new clothing of red, yellow, blue, and white, although the predominant color could best be described as "atrocious green," the basic cargo chute color.

Many of the native women were dexterous embroiderers, and they added intricate decorations with herb- and vegetable-dyed threads to draw attention away from the ugly green color. One woman, not skilled in needlework art (and apparently not skilled in the English language, either), selected for a design on the front of her skirt the panel of a parachute on which was stenciled in black ink the Army's supply number, nomenclature, and other military information. It carried this admonition: "Capacity: 200 pounds at 125 miles per hour."

Like the sacramental wine and flour I had carried for a specific purpose, I now found out why I was carrying a small packet deep inside my toiletries case. Before leaving Australia, I had been given several packages of sewing machine needles. "They might come in handy for trade," I was told. They were the pièce de résistance in a very successful bartering operation.

The airdrop we received on 22 January, after the planes had strafed the crash strip, was a biggie. Twelve thousand pounds! When GHQ told me to expect a load of this magnitude, I wondered if it might include a bulldozer to speed completion of the airfield. Such was not the case.

Arms and ammo were what GHQ had available, and that is what they sent. Great! But we still needed more than munitions if we were to keep sending intelligence information, which was still my primary mission. Vera's army was fast becoming the best-equipped guerrilla force, for its size, on Luzon. But we continued to have shortages of everything except arms.

I thanked GHQ for their generosity, but complained that the drop had not included a battery charger, battery acid, tools, and funds. I added to this message a long list of medicines, medical supplies, and surgical instruments. With these Dr. Morales would be able to set up a dispensary to treat my men and Vera's guerrillas. He planned to treat the native noncombatants as well, for they had been without anything remotely resembling medical care since the Japanese had taken over.

My message concluded with the information that airdrops could be made anytime, since guards were posted at the landing strip day and night. During the next months we received several unscheduled drops of sundry items. Most important, they included my radio station needs and Dr. Morales's supplies.

About this time, Sattem and McGowan were itching for some action—or for evacuation. Konka had already left us to work his way to Leyte and, he hoped, to the United States. He had every reason to do so, for his health was really bad. I'm sure he would have stayed with us until the end, except that he was bothered by a kidney stone—not a pleasant problem in a Luzon jungle. I had sat with him and agonized with him many times when it got lodged in the wrong place.

On one of the airdrops we had received a small supply of plastic explosive, caps, and fuses. Although I had been given a short but thorough course in the use of explosives and had used them to get rid of the launch in the Sibuyan Sea, I liked to separate myself from them as far as possible.

I gained my fear of explosives as a child. At age ten or so I used to buy candy from a sidewalk stand operated by a blind man who had lost his sight by accident when, with some friends, he was firing off homemade firecrackers, short lengths of dynamite fuse attached to fuse caps—a Fourth of July caper. One exploded in his face.

George and Eldred decided to help General Vera disrupt the Japanese railroad operations in the Atimonan area by blowing up some bridges. My fear of explosives told me to decline their invitation to join them. When they returned to camp, Sattem described their adventure.

"We found this small bridge that carried both the railroad and the highway, and rigged some explosives under the ends of two of the beams. We put a good, long fuse on it so we'd have plenty of time to get outta the way. Then we lit it and walked down the tracks a ways and sat down on the rails—waitin' for it to go off.

"While we was settin' there—there was about six of Vera's soldiers with us—some Japs came up the tracks on the other side of the bridge. We ducked down the bank to one side before they could see us.

"George, here, he said, 'Wouldn't it be funny if they got to the bridge just when it let go?' But just about then the bridge blew up. A real loud 'Bang' that sent pieces of it a hundred feet in the air. When the smoke cleared away, there wasn't a Jap within sight. Scared the shit outta them, I guess."

That was the last mission for George and Eldred as a part of my team. A few days later they decided they had had enough jungle life and headed for Mindoro, which was then secured by the American forces. From there they would go to GHQ, wherever it might be at the time, and try to get sent home. Like Konka, they were in horrible physical shape and needed much care and treatment.

My last scheduled airdrop arrived on 24 February. As if they were trying to atone for treating us so shabbily back in October, November, and December, we were becoming overloaded with supplies of all kinds, to the point we couldn't find room to store them. I had Nery move the supplies into the jungle, there to be cached for later use when needed. I ordered each cache rigged with explosives so that it could be blown up in a hurry if necessary, for I had a fear of Bondoc Peninsula being overrun by the Japanese should they decide they wanted to use it as a refuge of last resort. I didn't want them to get these supplies.

Some of my men were puzzled as to why I was giving this duty to Nery, for I had always handled storing and distribution of supplies personally. Nery was the only one who knew that he would be in charge of S3L in two days.

I would be leaving.

Out of the Jungles

PART 5

To Manila

CHAPTER 17

Late in January 1945, I received the following message from Lt. Clinton B. McFarland, chief of the Sixth Army NCS, JD2M:

> DESIRE TO EVACUATE YOU IN NEAR FUTURE. WHO IS YOUR SECOND IN COMMAND AND IS HE CAPABLE OF HANDLING JOB? NOTIFY WHEN YOU ARE READY FOR EVACUATION. DESIGNATE LOCATION WHERE CATALINA CAN LAND.

Leaving Bondoc Peninsula and station S3L brought me face-to-face with a gut-wrenching decision.

Colonel Smith and Lieutenant Royer were no longer in the hills. They had long since left Samar and were safely settled at Sixth Army headquarters. Captain Ball was still with the guerrillas on the east coast of Luzon, with Anderson and many other Americans. U.S. Army troops had joined up with them, and they were on the offensive. Intruding Japanese were not a great threat. Doc Evans was with a massive force of many thousands of American and guerrilla troops on Mindanao who were also on the offensive, so he was not in peril.

My situation was very different. I was the lone American in my area. Units of the Eleventh Airborne Division had landed at Lake Taal, south of Manila but north of Bondoc Peninsula, and were driving the Japanese in my direction. Some *might* move down the peninsula. If they did, the Filipinos could ditch their uniforms and equipment and fade into the civilian population. But where could I go? Even with my dark tan I could not pass for a native, and besides, the Filipinos have very little facial hair. I had a full beard. My assignment was completed. My part of the war was over. I was sick—weary—and I'll admit that I was more than a little homesick.

Why risk getting killed for no good reason? Why try to be a hero? I had nothing else to prove, and decided to accept the offer of evacuation. I procrastinated, but finally sent the following message to JD2M late in February:

> SECOND IN COMMAND IS STAFF SERGEANT GERARDO NERY OF U.S. ARMY. STATION UNDER SERGEANT RAYMUNDO AGCAOILI, ALSO U.S. ARMY. BOTH CAPABLE OF HANDLING WORK COMPLETELY. AM READY FOR EVACUATION IMMEDIATELY IF NOT SOONER. CATALINA CAN LAND AT 13 DEGREES 38 MINUTES NORTH 122 DEGREES 31 MINUTES EAST.

The twenty-sixth of February dawned wet, cold (for the tropics), rainy, windy, and generally miserable. Although the plane was scheduled to arrive between 10 A.M. and 3 P.M., I was on the beach by eight in the morning. I had told Major Barros of my planned departure, and he provided a boat for Ted Suttles, the former mining engineer and former POW I had met at Barros's camp several months previously. The boat would bring him to my side of Ragay Gulf. He wanted out, and I decided to get him on the plane with me.

With me on the beach, awaiting the plane's arrival, were a few of my many loyal companions from S3L, some of the many men who had made my operations possible: Gerardo Nery and Raymundo Agcaoili, radio operators who would now take command; the ever-faithful Ochigue and Madeja, whose courage and marksmanship had kept me out of harm's way; and, especially, Doming, who had been my faithful personal servant for so many months, making the lack of the amenities of civilization bearable. There were others who had sacrificed so much to contribute to my operations but who could not be there because they were still on intelligence-gathering missions. I had purposely kept the local citizens in the dark about my departure, and I felt guilty for sneaking away without saying "Goodbye" and "Thank you." However, security was still a concern, and I wasn't in the mood for a fiesta, which could screw up the pickup.

Also on the beach, waiting to be shoved off the sand, was the pride and joy of the local baroto fleet. Twenty feet long—twice as long as most barotos—and needing four oarsmen to keep it moving, it was loaded with my backpack, a duffel bag of souvenirs, several bags of my personal gear, and a small kit belonging to Mr. Suttles.

I was attired in a sleeveless, collarless khaki shirt, a pair of Australian Army–issue khaki shorts, my last pair of shoes, and a native wide-brimmed hat. And, of course, I was wearing my side arm. I suddenly realized that, except for the souvenirs and the personal trinkets in the backpack, I could replace everything else in those bags once I got back to the AIB office— back to the Army. Everything in those bags was army issue.

"Doming," I said, "I will take only my backpack and that bag with me," indicating the bag of souvenirs. "You keep the rest, and put those things to good use!"

His boyish face lit up. He now owned the things he had taken care of so carefully for me for a year. Meager as these possessions were, they gave him wealth he had never dreamed of having.

"Oh! Thank you, Sair! I will keep them forever!"

I suspect that while he thanked me he was already thinking of which items he could trade away for things he *really* wanted—a wife, perhaps.

When the PBY appeared, the wind was blowing up a storm. The big baroto sat low in the water, and the waves swamped it almost immediately when we tried to move out. Fortunately, there were several smaller canoes nearby—canoes my men planned to use to escort me to the plane. I waded back to shore with my backpack and bag of souvenirs and clambered into one of the smaller boats. Mr. Suttles used another. By now the PBY was on the water, circling as it awaited us. I knew it wouldn't wait long.

Again we set out from shore. But the wind was against us, and we made little progress. Soon the oarsmen jumped overboard, grabbed hold of the outriggers, and, with the strong strokes of natives accustomed to fighting the seas, pushed our two small boats toward the airplane.

Still, we were in danger of having the PBY take off without us. I jumped overboard and swam ahead of the barotos. *That damned airplane is not leaving here without me!* I told myself.

The crew of the PBY fished me out of the water. The baroto carrying my backpack and precious duffel bag of souvenirs arrived in time, as did the one carrying Mr. Suttles.

We had made it.

A crewman on the PBY, Sgt. George J. Buiytendiyk, took a series of photographs of this pickup. He and I made elaborate plans for my getting prints, for we discovered during the flight to Mindoro that people, indeed, do live in a small world. We had a common bond—a connection with the Goodyear Tire and Rubber Company, Inc. Our connections were on slightly different levels in the company, for I had been a lowly tire and appliance salesman in retail stores, while the sergeant was the adopted son of P. W. Litchfield, at that time the corporation's top banana. Apparently, during Litchfield's earlier years he had spent time around the rubber plantations in the Dutch East Indies. He had adopted Buiytendiyk, who lived there.

As the PBY skimmed the surface of the seas toward Mindoro, a maneuver necessary because the mission had no fighter cover, our plans were laid. The sergeant would send prints of the photos to Mr. Litchfield's office in Akron, Ohio, from which I would retrieve them once I returned to the United States. Unfortunately, the plan did not work, and the photos never reached me.

Except for my piggyback ride with Willard Davis in his P-38, I draw an almost complete blank when I try to recall Mindoro. I remember that there was a small office that handled people such as Ted Suttles and me when they came out of the hills. Apparently the guys in this department had seen many guerrillas by now, and the novelty was gone. They didn't seem to give a damn about us. Ted and I split almost immediately, never to meet again.

I managed to hitch a ride on a bomber going to Clark Field, on Luzon. From there I would work my way to Manila, where GHQ, the AIB, and the PRS were now located. When the bomber landed at Clark, it parked along a taxiway across the landing strip, far from the control tower and the operations building. The crew jumped aboard a six-by-six truck to be taken to their quarters, while I was ignored completely. I took the most direct route toward the tower, walking across the active runway. I hadn't walked far until, with sirens wailing, an MP jeep intercepted me and I was placed under arrest. It is not hard to understand why. With my duffel bag of souvenirs—the hilt of a Japanese saber sticking out of the top—and my attire, I was certainly a suspicious-looking character.

After being grilled by an MP lieutenant for an intolerably long time, I was released. When I asked about transportation to Manila, still seventy miles away, I was told, "Tough shit, guy. Walk."

They didn't make me walk to the main gate, however. The MPs were anxious to get me out of the way, and escorted me that far. Then afoot, I tried to hitch a ride toward the city. A steady stream of military vehicles moved in my direction. All the drivers gave me a shout or a wave, but few put a foot on the brake pedal. I did get a couple of short rides from GIs in Jeeps, and some longer rides with Filipinos in oxcarts, but I walked about half of the seventy miles, arriving in Manila three days later.

I rapidly developed a hatred for all U.S. servicemen. Life with the Filipinos was so, so much better.

When, back in 1942, it became evident that America could not hold off the Japanese invaders, we declared Manila an "open city" to protect the civilians there from the carnage of war. When the Japanese moved in, the city and all its buildings were intact and ready for the invader's use.

Not so when we returned. The Japanese barricaded themselves throughout the city, setting up defensive positions in the midst of the populated areas in hope that we, out of concern for the civilians, would use aerial bombs and artillery firepower sparingly. This would force the battle into the only strength remaining for the Japanese—hand-to-hand, building-to-building, infantry-style combat.

Reluctantly, but necessarily, America blasted, bombed, and strafed the Japanese positions, devastating the city. Only one major structure in the downtown area remained upright—heavily damaged, but still habitable. Erasing the Japanese defenses in the residential areas resulted in the leveling of square miles of homes.

Soon after I arrived in Manila, I went to an area south of the Pasig River—the Luneta residential area, where many of the holders of Manila's wealth had lived in splendor. Now it was rubble. Few streets were passable, and getting through required maneuvering around decaying bodies. The stench was unbelievable.

I stopped my "borrowed" (i.e., stolen) Jeep beside a pile of lumber that had once been a home. A man was carefully picking through the debris, raising, then casting aside, charred board after charred board. I was about to climb over the ruins to speak to him when he screamed and fell sobbing onto the object of his search. He had found the body of one of his children.

I had no trouble finding the AIB office in Manila. It and MacArthur's headquarters were in that one building still standing in the Manila business district. The building was one of several belonging to Sam Wilson,

The shambles that was Manila, 12 February 1945. *(U.S. Army Military History Institute)*

an American who had lived in the Philippines for many years and had made a fortune through real estate and other investments. When the war began, he and his Filipina wife went separate ways, she fading into the native population while he went to the hills. He eventually reached Mindanao, where he became finance officer for Fertig's guerrillas. From the time they separated until they met again after the Americans returned to Manila, neither knew if the other was alive or dead.

At the AIB I was greeted cordially—albeit not enthusiastically—by the men I had worked with in the code room in Brisbane fifteen months previously. Our common bond had broken.

I sought out a supply room to get some clothing. Everything I needed was there. The problem was that the supply sergeant would not issue equipment to me since my records as an enlisted man were somewhere else—God knows where. If my guerrilla commission was valid, I was now an officer, and he couldn't furnish me with anything unless I paid with cash, and I had no money. Captain Ferguson, who had been my commander in Brisbane and who still was in charge of the AIB message center, came to my rescue. He bankrolled me so that I could buy something decent to wear. I'm sure the supply sergeant pocketed the money.

Although Ferguson helped me out with money to buy clothing, that didn't put money in my pockets. Had I known the financial straits I was to encounter in Manila, I would have kept some of the funds I left with Nery to pay S3L's expenses. As it was, I was broke, and the prospects of altering that situation lay somewhere between doubtful and impossible.

I was "A Man Without an Army." I didn't exist. No one was interested in what I was doing or where I was doing it, so long as I didn't get in the way. Everyone I knew at AIB headquarters was engaged in his own little part of the war, and since I didn't figure in their present operations they didn't want to talk to me. Somewhere to the south, in Australia or New Guinea, my outfit, the 978th Signal Service Company, First Reconnaissance Battalion (Special), was headquartered. No one seemed to know exactly where. There seemed to be no way for me to get reconnected to the U.S. Army. And without that connection, and proof that I really was in the Army, I was unable to get even a small advance on my pay. As for rations and quarters, I ate and slept wherever I happened to be, bluffing my way as I went along, all the while mooching cigarettes and cadging drinks. I decided to try to find Colonel Smith to see if he could help me.

Locating him was not easy. Charlie had friends in high places, and when he decided he needed a rest from his labors (the most recent being with the First Cavalry Division to free the American internees at Santo Tomas University) he was placed on "special assignment," and information as to his whereabouts was not available to any but a select few. This group did not include me.

I remembered our usual evening chats in one of our huts on Palapag Mesa a year previously. The radio would be quiet for the night, and we would be enjoying a nightcap of Mount Vernon whiskey and water. He frequently related some of the details of life in prewar Manila. During his reminiscing he often mentioned his good friend Pete Grimm, an American who made it big by creating the Luzon Stevedoring Company long before the war began. Perhaps if I found Pete Grimm I would also find Charlie Smith.

I located Charlie living in Pete's hacienda on the Pasig River, east of the city. Here, with cooks, maids, houseboys, and limitless food and beverages, they were enjoying complete relaxation—well deserved, to be sure. Frankly, I had hoped that my close relationship with Charlie would warrant an invitation from him and Pete to move in and enjoy some of these pleasures. When I look back on that period, I shake my head at my own naivete. Within an hour of our meeting, it was evident that our common bond was gone. No longer were we dependent on each other for the success of a mission, or for our very survival. We were already reverting to our own, vastly different worlds.

However, Charlie was gracious enough to offer me a drink on the afternoon we met. And when I explained my problem—being completely ignored and not being able to reestablish myself with the AIB and the Army—he solved it with one telephone call, I know not to whom. The next day I was officially confirmed as a first lieutenant, Signal Corps, Army of the United States, with official orders to prove it for the edification of the Army Finance Office, where I collected my back pay.

But Smith, too, had a problem about money. We had taken thousands and thousands of pesos with us from Australia, all neatly packed in tin cans full of sand and water, cans like those I had buried on Palapag Mesa. When the *Narwhal* brought men and more supplies to us on Samar, there were more cans of money included in the cargo. And when airdrops were made to me on Luzon, even more money arrived.

Clandestine operations survive on money. One doesn't dicker with a recruited agent who is going to risk his life on a mission. Espionage is expensive, and one has to pay the piper.

"Bob," Charlie said to me, "Do you have any records of the money you spent? Did you get any receipts?"

"Charlie, you've got to be kidding."

"Kidding or not, the Army wants me to account for all the money they gave us."

"Shit, Colonel. I got a few receipts for things I bought for the station so that the Chinese merchants couldn't try to collect a second time. But the money I gave to Herreria, Cardenas, Sanchez, and others who were going into Manila? Forget it. Hell! That was just 'Take a handful.' Ain't no way I can tell what that cost. Fifty thousand—a hundred thousand pesos. Who knows?"

"Well, the Army wants me to tell them where it went. If you can come up with some numbers, I can use them."

Thus started a bit of Army training that would serve me well later in civilian life—the creative writing of expense accounts.

A few weeks later I met with Smith again, to give him whatever information I could about the money I had spent. This, however, was not my main purpose in seeking him out once more. He had "hung me out on a line" a long time ago, and I wanted to let him know that he had not done me a favor.

"Colonel," I said, showing my respect, "soon after the Leyte invasion you were transferred from MACA on Samar to GHQ. Have you any idea of why, after you got back there, I was left high and dry and not given any supplies for more than two months?"

"Sure, Bob. I thought you were having trouble with Vera. I thought he was a loose cannon beyond control. At least beyond *your* control. I told them to hold off on equipment for you."

"Whatever gave you that idea? Sure, we started off with a problem, but that got straightened out in a hurry. He was a big help to me."

"Hoff told me you were in trouble with Vera."

I didn't then, nor do I now, recognize the name "Hoff." He must have been some guy who happened to pass through my camp. Many strangers did. He was certainly not an authority on my relationship with Vera.

"But," I persisted, "I kept telling you I had a good thing going with Vera. I sent his man to you asking for arms for him. Why didn't you believe me? I thought you and I were on the same side."

Charlie had nothing to say.

"Perhaps that explains this," I said, withdrawing from my pocket a folded, beat-up piece of paper.

Near the southern tip of Luzon is the town of Sorsogon. Here the land narrows, and anyone crossing the San Bernardino Strait from Samar and heading north must pass through this town. Maj. Licerio Lapus was the local politician, and he had developed a guerrilla unit of sorts that was, more or less, a constabulary devoted to keeping peace during the chaotic times of occupation and resistance. Lapus was not a mercenary. He, like Mayor Medenilla of San Narciso, was an intelligent and forthright person, interested only in maintaining calm in the midst of turmoil until this mess was over. No one entered or passed through this town unless cleared by Major Lapus.

Lapus intercepted and read a letter Smith had sent to me by courier. He deleted one paragraph that he thought might cause trouble for me if it fell into the wrong hands, and sent the rest of the letter on its way with the courier. Lapus then traveled some 150 miles over land and bay to deliver a "True Copy" of that paragraph to me personally. It read:

> I am afraid your Lt. Gen. may become a problem in the future. Handle him the best that you can. GHQ cannot

consider such an outfit so just spread on the soft soap until such a time that it is possible for us to all get together in Manila or some other place. Next month I will send sufficient guns for you to cope with any emergency that might arise.

Had this letter fallen into Vera's hands, who knows how tragic the results would have been for me? What in the hell good would guns have done me without someone to carry and shoot them?

Charlie looked at the "True Copy," recognized his words, I'm sure, but said nothing. No denial. Nothing.

If he had responded—any response at all—I would have been satisfied, I suppose. But his silence made me very angry.

"For Christ's sake, Charlie," I said. "What in the *hell* ever made you do such a stupid thing? What in the *hell* were you drinking when you wrote that?"

During our entire relationship, beginning at Heindorf House in Brisbane, I had never raised my voice to him in anger. I couldn't believe I was doing it now.

He folded the paper and handed it back to me.

"I don't know, Bob. I don't know why—I have nothing to say. All I can say is, 'Yes, it was stupid, but—.'"

I returned to my quarters in Manila, stopping in the Officers Club en route for more than one drink. My respect for someone I had glorified—perhaps even deified—had been shattered. He was just another guy.

Would You Like Another Mission?

CHAPTER 18

Although I had no assignments, no duties, nothing at all to do, I hung around AIB headquarters much of each day. At night, however, I found plenty to do. Carousing and drinking with whoever was interested in carousing and drinking became my routine. I boozed it up with dog faces, swabbies, marines, natives—I wasn't very selective. How I kept from being blinded by the wood alcohol–based "Scotch whiskey" the Filipinos were mixing by day and selling by night I don't know. Just lucky, I guess. It wasn't hard to find someone who was going to a party somewhere, and it seemed there were never any guest lists.

But I wanted to get shipped back to the States, and that seemed to be an impossibility, because I didn't have anyone who would take it upon himself to be my commanding officer. I didn't exist in anyone's table of organization. The only person who might be able to do some good for me was Colonel Smith—witness his getting my commission confirmed with one telephone call—but I had shot that possibility when I told him off the last time we met.

Charlie Ferguson had a message for me one day.

"Major Brown wants to see you," he told me.

Major Brown was a member of the G-2 hierarchy. He was the man who sent people on missions. He was probably the one person I avoided most when I was around AIB headquarters.

I stopped by his office and was given an appointment time: 9 A.M. the following day.

Step into my parlor, said the spider to the fly. These were the words that ran through my mind as I walked into Major Brown's office.

"Lieutenant Stahl, meet Capt. George Davis," said the major, introducing me to an Infantry officer wearing the insignia of a Ranger. "Captain Davis is taking his company ashore at Lucena and moving down to your old peninsula. He wants you to go with him."

Wham! This guy Brown doesn't pull his punches! I said to myself.

"Why me?" I asked. "I'm no Ranger. I'm not even an Infantryman. What good would I be to you?"

"You've been there before," said Davis. "You could be our guide."

"But Vera's guerrillas are already there. They've cleaned up the area—gotten rid of the Japs in the bottleneck."

"Not quite. There are several pockets of Jap troops that must be wiped out. That's our mission," said Davis.

I pictured myself guiding a company of Rangers along the jungle trails in the area. Actually, I was not familiar with the territory around Lucena. My activities had been further to the south. I envisioned myself at the head of a column—the first target for the Japanese—on trails on which I would have to toss a three-headed coin to decide which way to go—right, left, or straight ahead—at each intersection. I did not like what I saw in that vision. I was terrified! MacArthur had told me "You're no good to me dead"—to avoid contact with the enemy—and now these bastards were trying to get me to walk into who knows what? Yet, I couldn't appear to be a coward. My operations had brought me some semblance of respect as being a man of courage, at least in my opinion, and I couldn't toss that away now.

"OK," I said. "I don't know if I'll do you any good, but I'm willing to try."

I received two days of indoctrination into the operations of the Rangers—two days which gave me sleepless nights. Then, on the third day, before the date for our departure was set, Captain Davis and his company were given different orders. The incursion at Lucena was scrubbed. I was home free. Somebody up there liked me.

I decided to try to take advantage of my newfound acquaintance with Major Brown. Perhaps he would "adopt" me and arrange for me to be sent home. I scheduled another meeting with him.

"Major," I said, "could you get someone, somewhere, to send me back to the States? I may not have contributed much to your operations, but I've had enough. I want to go home!"

"Bob. I agree. You deserve a leave."

What's that bullshit—a leave? I asked myself.

"I don't mean a leave. I mean *go home.* Go home to stay."

"I can't fix that for you. But I can make a deal with you."

Now how is he going to try to screw me?

"What kind of a deal?" I asked.

"In a couple of months we are going to want someone like you to air-drop into the Batan Islands to set up a station to report Japanese air flights out of Formosa. Would you do that for a forty-five-day leave to the States?"

This guy never lets go of a pigeon, I thought.

"You mean I can have a 'last supper' with my family if I agree to take this mission?"

"That's it. That's the best I can do for you."

I was desperate. I wanted to get as far as possible from the war. Perhaps, if I was lucky, I would be hit by a car in Shamokin, Pennsylvania. Not killed, but maimed enough that the Army wouldn't want me anymore.

"OK. You've got a deal."

Home Again

CHAPTER 19

The Military Air Transport Service C-87 that brought me home touched down at Fairfield-Suisun Army Air Base, in California, on 12 April 1945. My elation at being back in the United States once more was dampened, however. The nation was mourning the death of President Franklin Delano Roosevelt.

I shared transportation to San Francisco with a lieutenant colonel I met on the plane. We each checked into the Fairmont Hotel and then shared a taxi to the Presidio, where I was outfitted with my first semblance of a true Army officer's uniform. Apparently, so many returning soldiers stopped there to purchase clothing that they had an assembly line of tailors making while-you-wait alterations. We returned to the hotel, then went our separate ways, for the "light colonel" had friends to visit.

That evening I stepped out into the big city with a head full of plans for a stateside meal and a wild night. At the first intersection I encountered, I panicked. I could not force myself to step off the curb and cross the street. All those cars! I had been through too much to get myself struck and killed as a pedestrian. If this were to happen, I, at least, wanted it to occur at home. I retreated to the block in which the Fairmont was located and made the rounds of the bars in that block. And then to bed.

The next day I met the colonel again, and we shared transportation back to the air base.

"Did you find your friends last night?" I asked him.

"Yes. We had a good get-together. What did *you* do?"

"Man! I had a big night on the town!" I lied.

On 19 April I arrived in Shamokin, Pennsylvania, via Fort Dix, New Jersey, due to return to Dix in forty-five days for transportation back to the Philippines. I cast from my mind all thoughts of what would happen then. For the present, I wanted to enjoy my family and friends. To hell with the future!

I was shocked when I saw my father and mother, for the combined stress of my being "lost" and of one of my brothers being in combat in Europe seemed to have aged both of them at least ten years. However, they showed a positive reaction to my being home; at least half of their worries were over. They did not know of my future plans.

Mother was a calm, solid, staid person with very firm convictions, one of which was being anti-alcohol. No alcoholic beverages could cross the threshold of our home, save for the bottle she stored in hiding to spike her mince pies—hidden because my dad was known to enjoy a wee bit of the juice. However, she showed her elation over my return by bringing out her supply and pouring small drinks for all to toast, before dinner, my first day home.

Ruth, my girlfriend, who had also received a letter from the War Department along with my last letter to her from Australia, was there. We found that the ardor between us had not diminished, and we were married five days later, this in spite of my having told her that I would be going overseas again. (That ardor has continued, and we have been married for fifty years as of this writing.)

We had a whirlwind wedding and honeymoon. During the latter we visited a cousin of mine, a psychiatrist, who entertained us royally in New York City. I'm sure he did so only to have the opportunity to delve into the inner workings of my brain—to see if he could locate the short circuit responsible for my choice of military activities.

There have been few events in my life more traumatic than leaving home and returning to Fort Dix for transportation back to the Philippines. I was certain that the past forty-five days had afforded us one of the shortest marriages in history, for I was convinced that I would not survive my next mission. But good news awaited me at Fort Dix. The war in Europe had ended, and all orders to return to overseas assignments had been canceled. I would go on no more missions. I would remain stateside. My war was over.

Confusion reigned at Fort Dix and, I'm sure, at all the rest of the reception and distribution centers throughout the country. With the war in Europe over, the Army and Navy brass in Washington were engaged in a major revision of the master plan for conducting the war against Japan. To clear the decks for this operation, practically everyone's orders were being changed. Most of us who had returned to the States for rest, recuperation, and recovery (RR&R) understood that we would be returned to our overseas stations upon the expiration of the leave. With the transferring of whole divisions and fleets from Europe to the Pacific, individual assignments such as mine were, happily, insignificant. It was 8 June 1945.

I must say that this was the first time I saw the Army do anything efficiently in my nearly three years of service. I sat at some captain's desk at Fort Dix and showed him a copy of my orders. He picked up the phone, called someone at the Fairfield-Suisun Army Air Base in California, and told them I was not coming back. Then he called someone at Camp Butner, in North Carolina, and told them to expect me. Within an hour I was on my way to the Trenton, New Jersey, train station with a ticket to Raleigh, North Carolina.

At Camp Butner they let me play around for several weeks, then sent me to the Signal Corps Replacement Pool at Fort Monmouth, New Jersey. It was 25 June 1945. On the train to New Jersey I met an officer who told me about the Army's Bureau of Public Relations. This sounded like an easy way to make a living, so I applied for a transfer to the Speaker's Bureau the very next day.

This assignment took me to Baltimore, Maryland, where a Capt. Joseph H. McGinty held forth with a one-person staff—a civilian secretary—in a one-room office. I was sent out to factories in the area to give the employees pep talks, urge them to buy more war bonds, tell them what a great job they were doing, and, at the same time, ask them to quit their jobs and go to work for the western railroads. With this mass movement of troops from Europe to the Pacific, the Union Pacific, Santa Fe, and other railroads were hurting for manpower to conduct their operations.

The Bureau of Public Relations put together a road show to demonstrate military arms and equipment, displaying tanks, amphibious vehicles, armored vehicles, artillery pieces, antiaircraft weapons, personnel carriers, and an assortment of command cars, Jeeps, and the like. Mortars fired rockets into the air, while machine guns and cannon fired blanks, adding to the excitement. I emceed this show as it toured fairgrounds and athletic fields in several cities in Pennsylvania and Maryland, seeking recruits for industries in need of manpower.

As part of the festivities, several soldiers who had been awarded medals for bravery appeared onstage. Most told the audience of their exploits. One man who had been awarded the Medal of Honor, a rangy southern farm boy, would appear on the stage but would not talk of his exploits. However, he carried his medal in his pocket and would show it to anyone who asked to see it. The medal was stained and dented, and the light blue ribbon was so dirty it was difficult to tell its color or to find its thirteen white stars.

On 14 August 1945, while putting on our exhibition in Hancock, Maryland, we learned of the Japanese surrender. We blew away every rocket, artillery shell, machine gun cartridge, and anything else we had that would make noise that night, for this would be our last show.

My next assignment was to the Provost Marshal's Office at Fort Monmouth, where I pulled exciting duty apprehending drivers who exceeded the fifteen-mile-per-hour speed limit, investigating thefts, and serving for a while as adjutant for a stockade full of German POWs. Meanwhile, the Army was releasing personnel to civilian life on the basis of points, which were awarded for length of service, length of overseas service, and battle participation. I had enough points to get out with the first wave. The trouble was, I couldn't find my records, and without that proof I was "pointless." I began to fear that I would remain in the service forever.

My status as a member of the armed forces of the United States began to gel in September 1945. The Adjutant General's Office at GHQ in the Pacific Theater discovered that I had never been discharged as an enlisted man when I was commissioned. They also found that somewhere along the line I had been appointed a warrant officer, junior grade, a status I had never known of! I was, in effect, three soldiers, and two of them had to be disposed of. After much correspondence, I received a Certificate of Honorable Discharge as an enlisted man, dated 8 November 1945, effective 15 December 1943. I know not what happened to the warrant officer appointment, but I was never separated from that position.

My problems were not yet over. Although I had not drawn pay as an enlisted man from the date of my commission, the Army had continued to send allotments and bonds to my home, and to pay insurance premiums as well, out of my nonexistent enlisted man's pay. I was finally able to get the Army to accept reimbursement for these items by calling on a chaplain for help. No one else was interested.

On 6 January 1946 I departed from Fort Monmouth, separated from the service except for terminal leave until mid-March. That precious diary of military service, my "201 File," never did catch up with me, and I'd had all that trouble getting out of the service because I couldn't prove that I was ever *in* the service.

Although I was separated from the service, I was not separated from the Army Finance Office. For years I was dunned for reimbursement of the back pay I received in Manila for the time I had spent in the islands. Their complaint: They had no record of my ever having been ordered to active duty! As with other matters military, I ignored the dunning, and eventually the problem disappeared.

About five years ago I sought a copy of my service record from the National Personnel Records Center. I was told that *if* I ever had been in the service, any proof of such service had been destroyed in a giant conflagration at the Records Center in St. Louis, Missouri. Officially, I remain a soldier without an Army.

There exists, however, one item of documentation of my having been on Bondoc Peninsula, Luzon, Philippine Islands, during World War II. It is a personal letter written to me by Dr. Mariano N. Morales immediately prior to my departing the area. To me, it attests to my accomplishments more than any of the citations accompanying any decorations I received or that remain unawarded. It reads:

Mulanay, Tayabas
February 13, 1945

My Dear Lt. Stahl,

When a man enters our back door he is either a burglar or one close to the household. You are one among the few who entered our home country via the back door. Any casual observer, however, can say offhand that you are anything but a burglar. Verily you are a friend and a benefactor of our people.

I am not a military expert to pass judgement on your achievements as a military man. But as one who has been and is still ministering to the health and medical problems of the people of the Peninsula, with easily 100,000 inhabitants who for the last three years have been suffering from acute want of medicine, I can say that what you have done and are still doing to help our people in the way of medicine has elevated you to the highest and most secure pedestal of the people's love and gratitude.

We will surely regret it very deeply if you will leave us through the same door where you entered without giving us a chance to open to you what is in the hearts of our people for the Americano of whom they hear so much and yet know so little. I am speaking not for myself. I am speaking for the people of the whole Peninsula whose people I have known intimately for the few months I have been in the field. I assure you when you leave our shore you will carry back to your dear old home, to your mother and dear one, the loyalty, the love, and the gratitude of no less than 100,000 Filipinos whom you have liberated from fear of disease, from want of medicine, and from actual ravages of malaria and tropical ulcers, not to speak of their liberation from the Nips.

Wishing you continued health and success, I am,
M. N. Morales, M.D.

Epilogue

The First Reconnaissance Battalion (Special) was disbanded 15 August 1945. The battalion had an authorized strength of 85 officers and 445 enlisted men. Although it never reached its authorized strength, some 330 of its members went on secret missions to the Philippines.

Members of the battalion received 304 medals for bravery, as follows: 4 received the Distinguished Service Cross, 6 received the Silver Star Medal, 13 received the Legion of Merit, and 281 received the Bronze Star Medal. In addition, the Combat Infantry Badge was awarded to approximately two hundred men, while the battalion itself received many commendations from both the Army and the Navy. Navy "Well Dones" were numerous. This high number of medals and awards makes the First Reconnaissance Battalion (Special), for its size, one of the most decorated units in U.S. Army history.

Despite the extreme danger of the missions, only nine men were lost in action. This extremely low casualty rate is testimony to the excellent training the men received before embarking on their missions. (In my case it was pure luck, for I had not undergone the training sessions. I moved directly from the jungles of Brisbane, Australia, to those of the Philippines.) Seventeen more died en route to their assigned posts when the submarine *Seawolf* was sunk by the Japanese, and four died of other causes.

Nineteen submarines carried out forty-one missions to the islands.

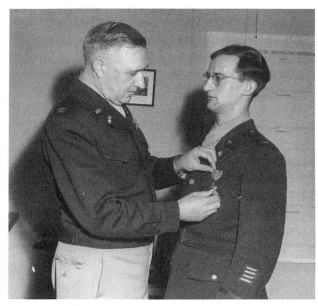

Author receiving Bronze Star Medal from Col. Leon E. Ryder at Fort Monmouth, N.J. *(Signal Corps photo)*

The *Seawolf* was the only submarine lost. The submarines carried approximately 1,325 tons of supplies to us. No estimate is available for the tonnage air-dropped by the Air Force.

These statistics, however, are misleading. The cost in human lives was infinitely greater, for no consideration has yet been given to the hundreds of   Filipinos and Filipinas who undertook espionage missions for us, never to return. Nor have we counted the number of brave men and women who lost their lives as fighting guerrillas protecting our operations. There were also the civilian Filipino martyrs, who suffered torture and death rather than reveal information that would have led to our capture. Heroes all, they will never be known and recognized for their bravery.

The U.S. and Philippine governments treated the guerrillas badly. For many years after the war I was besieged by requests from many of them for statements attesting to the help they had given me. I responded, but to no avail, sadly. Most got no recognition—and no compensation.

I was able to follow the lives of only a few of my Filipino comrades. Gerardo Nery reenlisted in the Army. He married Nacling Medenilla, one of the daughters of the mayor of San Narciso. Madeja, Ochigue, and Doming also married girls from San Narciso and settled there. Madeja made a point of writing to tell me that his firstborn had been named Roberto. Crispolo Robles died soon after the war, in Manila. Of the rest, I have no knowledge.

The three Americans who had escaped from the Japanese and were so instrumental in the success of my mission made safe returns to America. Chester Konka made a career of service in the U.S. Air Force. George McGowan took up civilian life in his native Reno, Nevada, area, where, due to physical problems resulting from military service, he spent much time in Veterans Administration hospitals. Eldred Sattem returned to civilian life in his hometown of Escanaba, Michigan.

Gerald S. Chapman continued his career in the U.S. Air Force, and followed this honorable service with many years as a mover/shaker with the Air Force Association. Charles M. Smith joined his family in Nacogdoches, Texas, where he became a gentleman farmer. James L. Evans Jr., M.D., established a psychiatry practice in Englewood, New Jersey.

And I went off to college.

Annotated
Bibliography

Disette, Edward, and H. C. Adamson. *Guerrilla Submarines.* New York: Ballantine Books, 1972. Good account of the submarine activities in supplying recognized guerrilla groups throughout the islands.

Earle, Dixon. *Bahála Na...Come What May.* Berkeley, Calif.: Howell North, 1961. Relates the story of the ill-fated penetration of Mindoro by the Phillips party.

McCoy, Melvyn H., and S. M. Mellnik. *Ten Escape from Tojo.* New York: Farrar and Rinehart, 1944. Account of the first escape from Davao Penal Colony.

Rola, Ceferino R., 1st Lt., Inf., AUS. "Unit History of the First Reconnaissance Battalion Special." National Archives. Unit history prepared in accordance with Army Regulations 345-105.

Schmidt, Larry S., Major, USMC. "American Involvement in the Filipino Resistance Movement on Mindanao During the Japanese Occupation, 1942–1945." Student thesis, U.S. Army War College, Fort Leavenworth, Kans., 1982. Good annotated bibliography covering much of the activity of the guerrillas beyond the subject island.

Torio, Isaias T., Cpl., and T/5 Albert Halla. "978th Signal Service Company." National Archives. Unit history prepared in accordance with Army Regulations 345-105.

Travis, Ingram. *Rendezvous by Submarine. The Story of Charles Parsons and the Guerrilla-Soldiers of the Philippines.* Garden City, N.J.: Doubleday, Doran and Co., 1945. The story of Parsons's activities in operations with Mindanao guerrillas.

Volckmann, R. W. *We Remained: Three Years Behind the Enemy Lines in the Philippines.* New York: W. W. Norton, 1954. Relates author's adventures in organizing one of the better guerrilla units on Luzon.

Willoughby, Charles Andrew. *The Guerrilla Resistance Movement in the Philippines: 1941–1945.* New York: Vantage Press, 1972. A collection of papers, documents, and reports from the files of GHQ, U.S. Army Forces, Pacific. A good source of documentation, but unorganized and difficult to use.

Wise, William. *Secret Mission to the Philippines: The Story of "Spyron" and the American-Filipino Guerrillas in World War II.* New York: E. P. Dutton, 1968. Relates Parsons's activities in establishing the connection between the AIB and the guerrillas.

Index

About the Author

Born 26 October 1920 in Shamokin, Pennsylvania, Bob Stahl lived in the foothills of the Appalachian Mountains through the boom of the 1920s and the depression of the 1930s. After his military service he enrolled at Lehigh University, in Bethlehem, Pennsylvania, and graduated in 1949 with a bachelor of science degree in civil engineering. He spent the next thirty-five years engaged in the project-development, design, and construction of major highways and bridges throughout the United States and abroad. Now retired, he lives with his wife, Ruth, in Baltimore, Maryland. They have two grown children.